Practitioner-Based Enquiry

How do you carry out small-scale research into your own institutional practices? How can you produce a useful and accessible report?

Learning organizations such as schools and colleges, teaching hospitals, police staff colleges and training agencies often require their students to contribute to the process of formulating curriculum policy, evaluating the outcomes of planned learning, unravelling 'knotty' teaching problems, and so on. This involvement often carries with it some notion of 'research', 'enquiry' or 'review'. To enquire into one's own institutional practices may, on first encounter, appear simple. However, research is a complex activity involving question setting, theorizing, data gathering and analysis and report writing. This book helps students understand these elements so that they carry out useful research and produce accessible research reports.

This book has been written specifically for postgraduate students carrying out small-scale research projects in and around their work environments and for those undertaking research projects as part of their higher education courses. The book will also be useful to teachers, tutors, lecturers and trainers who want to use the concept of practitioner-based enquiry to enquire into their own institutional practices, and produce reports which can be submitted for academic credits leading to the award of certificates and degrees from universities and other professional bodies.

Readership: postgraduate students in employment, in education and training-related professions such as teaching in schools, tutoring in further education, social work practice and healthcare staff development work, technical training in the police service and the armed forces.

Louis Murray is Principal Lecturer in Education at the University of Portsmouth. A professional educator for over 20 years, Dr Murray is author of numerous publications on applied educational research and the social foundations of education. **Brenda Lawrence** is Senior Lecturer in Education at the University of Portsmouth and a practising educational psychologist. Dr Lawrence has an extensive research background and publications record, and has been involved with postgraduate course teaching for a number of years.

Social Research and Educational Studies Series
Series Editor: Professor Robert G. Burgess,
Vice Chancellor, University of Leicester

Practitioner-Based Enquiry

Principles for Postgraduate
Research

Louis Murray and Brenda Lawrence

London and New York

First published 2000
by Falmer Press
11 New Fetter Lane, London EC4P 4EE

Simultaneously published in the USA and Canada
by Falmer Press
29 West 35th Street, New York, NY 10001

Falmer Press is an imprint of the Taylor & Francis Group

© 2000 Louis Murray and Brenda Lawrence

Typeset in Times by Taylor & Francis Books Ltd
Printed and bound in Great Britain by Biddles Ltd, Guildford and
King's Lynn

British Library Cataloguing in Publication Data
A catalogue record for this book is available from the British Library

Library of Congress Cataloging in Publication Data
Murray, Louis
Practitioner-based enquiry: principles for postgraduate research/Louis
Murray and Brenda Lawrence.
(Social research and educational studies series)
Includes bibliographical references and index.
1. Action research in education – Great Britain. 2. Education –
Research – Great Britain – Methodology. I. Lawrence, Brenda. II.
Title. III. Series.
LB1028.24.M87   1999
370'.7'2–dc21   99-28142
                                                                  CIP

ISBN 0–750–70772–0 (hbk)
ISBN 0–750–70771–2 (pbk)

Contents

Contents

Illustrations

Tables

Figures

Illustrations

Diagrams

Series Editor's Preface

The purpose of the Social Research and Educational Studies Series is to provide authoritative guides on key issues in educational research. The series includes overviews of fields, guidance on good practice and discussions of the practical implications of social and educational research. In particular, the series deals with a variety of approaches to conducting Social and Educational Research. Contributors to this series review recent work, raise critical concerns that are particular to the field of education, and reflect on the implications of research for educational policy and practice.

Each volume in the series draws on material that will be relevant for an international audience. The contributors to this series all have wide experience of teaching, conducting and using educational research. The volumes are written so that they will appeal to a wide audience of students, teachers and researchers. All together, the volumes in the Social Research and Educational Studies series provide a comprehensive guide for anyone concerned with contemporary educational research.

The series will include individually authored books and edited volumes on a range of themes in education including: qualitative research, survey research, the interpretation of data, self evaluation, research and social policy, analysing data, action research, the politics and ethics of research.

In recent years, there has been considerable discussion and debate about the role of practitioners in conducting educational research. Among the issues raised have been the role of teacher-researchers, and use of action research in schools and classrooms. In this volume, Louis Murray and Brenda Lawrence have brought together a range of methodological issues which will be of use to all those who engage in practitioner-based enquiry. It is a book designed to be used by practitioners interested in conducting education research.

Robert G. Burgess
University of Leicester

Acknowledgments

The authors are pleased to acknowledge the contribution of the following people to the production of this text. Similarly, we are grateful to the publishers and education authorities who have extended permission for the reproduction of materials from published sources.

Some of the ideas and principles in Chapter 1 were originally published in the *British Journal of Inservice Education* (Vol. 18, No 3, 1992, pp. 191–6). We thank the editor of that journal and its parent company, Triangle Books, for permission to reuse that material in amended form.

In Chapter 2, Figure 2.2 was developed from ideas in M. Fishbein/I. Ajzen *Belief, Attitude, Intention, Behavior* (Figure 1.2, page 16, © 1975 Addison Wesley Longman Inc.), and is reprinted by permission of Addison Wesley Longman.

The ethnographic report that appears in Chapter 4 is a composite based on research reports submitted by students enrolled in Unit 86208, Sociological Systems within Schools, in the Upgrade/BEd programme of the School of Education, University of Southern Queensland. We duly acknowledge the contribution of the students to this work. Supporting material to the ethnography is reproduced by kind permission of the Distance Education Centre, University of Southern Queensland.

The sample practitioner-based enquiry, 'Information Technology and Geographical Education', that appears in Chapter 5 was originally published under the joint authorship of Raymond Felton and Louis Murray in the *Journal of Teacher Development* (Vol. 4, No. 2, 1995, pp. 28–36). We are grateful to the editor and publisher of the Financial Times Management Ltd for permission to reproduce the relevant parts of the PBE.

The extracts from Education Resources Information Centre (ERIC) are used with the permission of ERIC Central/US Department of Education in Washington, USA.

Certain of the ideas on research design and the concept of 'reliability' in Chapter 5 owe much to our reading and use of the seminal volume by F.N. Kerlinger, *Foundations of Behavioural Research*, published by Holt, Rinehart and Winston (3rd edition, 1986).

Acknowledgments

The figures for proportional representation of data used in Chapter 6 were drawn as SPSS output from the data disk supplied with the volume by D. Rose and O. Sullivan, *Introducing Data Analysis for Social Scientists*, published by the Open University (2nd edition, 1996).

The purpose statements for PBEs identified in Chapter 7 derive from MA and Certificate in Education (CIE) research reports submitted by University of Portsmouth students. We are pleased to acknowledge the contribution of the following students in helping us to refine our thoughts about purposes of PBEs: Claire Ralls, Thelma Cahoon, Mark Collier, Moznu Khandaker and Barbara Piddington.

Finally, we would like to thank our colleagues in the School of Education and Continuing Studies at the University of Portsmouth, and also those many students registered on award-bearing courses, who have contributed so many ideas to an emerging concept of practitioner-based enquiry, thereby helping to improve teaching and learning arrangements in schools, colleges, workplaces, training centres and institutions of higher education.

Introduction

The readership for this book is wide and varied. Primarily, the book is intended for the part-time postgraduate student, in employment, in education and training-related professions such as teaching in schools, tutoring in further education, technical training in the armed forces and the police service, and social work practice and health care staff development work. However, other users of this book will include those interested in carrying out small scale research projects in and around their work environments. For such readers especially, the text is an enabling tool. It will help in the process of research-skill acquisition. It will help to energise a process of lifelong learning. It will provide a means to channel an eagerness to enquire into and learn more about practitioners own organizational practices.

The book is 'postgraduate' in the sense that it offers rather more than the conventional undergraduate 'nuts and bolts' books on how to do small scale research projects. It ought to be particularly useful to registered postgraduate students in universities undertaking research projects as part of higher education courses. A central theme in the book is how teachers, tutors, lecturers and trainers might mobilize the concept of Practitioner-Based Enquiry (PBE) to systematically enquire into their own institutional practices, especially as these pertain to arrangements for teaching and learning. Such enquiries may well be used to produce assessable reports and artifacts which can be submitted for academic credits leading to the award of certificates and degrees from universities and other professional bodies.

Learning organizations such as schools and colleges, teaching hospitals, police staff colleges, training agencies and so forth often require their incumbents to contribute to the process of formulating curriculum policy, evaluation of the outcomes of planned learning experiences, unravelling 'knotty' teaching problems and so on. This involvement often carries with it some notion of 'research', 'enquiry' or 'review'. To enquire into one's own institutional practices may, on first encounter, appear simple. However, research is a complex activity involving question setting, theorizing, data gathering and report writing. This book is designed not to oversimplify, but to help in the facilitation of understanding these elements, with a view to producing valid and comprehensible research reports.

The book begins with considered definitions of what we understand by Practitioner-Based Enquiry. The background is explained and some central principles are articulated. Similarly, the emergence of PBE from a loose 'teacher as researcher' movement is outlined. Fragmentation and diversity in social and behavioural science is identified also as contributing to the emergence of this form of enquiry. Manifest forms of PBE are described and the potential contribution of PBE to educational policy and practice is considered.

The next function of the book is the identification of a basis of critique of PBE as a necessary prerequisite for any adherence to the currently popular notion of 'reflection on practice'. The ethical and intellectual character of PBE is examined in this context. The danger of oversimplification in small scale research is illustrated by an examination of the 'props' upon which PBE is founded. The constraints within which PBE necessarily functions are theorized and commented upon.

The idea of a 'toolbag' is used to explore the planning process for PBE. This includes amplification of the conventional features of research proposals. It also includes delineation of planning considerations unique to PBE. An exemplar model of the planning process is illustrated via an actual template or design brief for an enquiry into an aspect of nurse education.

Some further intellectual obligations in PBE and their practical concomitants are explained. Explanation is regarded as a key feature of the design process. A full report of a PBE, designed and written within the rules of ethnographic semantics, is provided to illustrate the research design process. Following this, the idea of perspectives or 'different ways of seeing' is explored. It is suggested that established modes of data gathering such as historical and documentary analysis, survey approaches, experiments, case studies and interview approaches represent 'different ways of seeing and explaining'. Selected examples of data gathering instrumentation associated with these ways of seeing are included in the account.

The distinction between 'methods' and 'methodology' is then re-examined in the light of critique elements discussed earlier. An intellectual framework of criteria by which PBE might be judged is devised to reconcile the 'divided mentality' in educational research. This is followed by a series of essential considerations in the research enterprise. A further full report of a PBE, a case study on the integration of geographical learning with information technology in an Isle of Wight Middle School, is used to show how one practitioner-researcher confronted the obligations in methodology.

Data gathering and analysis techniques are illustrated partly metaphorically through the idea of 'analysing and writing – writing and analysing', and pragmatically with exhibits of interview material, graphical representations and statistical formats. The process of variable transformation as the crucial feature of data analysis is considered. Advice is also provided on the special treatment of interview data. An outline of the technical requirements for the conventional research report is presented.

The final part of the book considers wider policy implications of PBE as a relatively unique form of educational research. This is first achieved by reference to five sets of purpose-statements from actual practitioner-researchers undertaking work in different subject fields. Secondly, further observations of the applicability of PBE are made by reference to social and educational change in the UK. Recent influential reports including Dearing and Harris are summarized as indicators of the professionalization of teaching and learning as required for the twenty-first century. It is against such a backdrop that research enquiries referred to as 'PBE', especially those enquiries arising out of the academic requirements for award-bearing courses in higher education, are to be understood and predicated.

1   What is Practitioner-Based Enquiry?

Introductory Remarks

The essential purpose of this book is to provide conceptual and methodological insights into the small-scale, applied educational research activity that has come to be known in recent years in the UK as 'practitioner-based enquiry'.

It is perhaps ironic that as the publicly funded schools sector of the education system has been subject to increasingly centralized political controls, manifested in six major pieces of legislation under the Conservative governments of 1979–97 and emergent Labour Party legislation post-May 1997 (Unwin and Brown, 1998), and all that is implied for curricula and organization, the higher education sector has expanded, changed and diversified to an unprecedented extent in the same period. Since the incorporation of the former polytechnics into 'new' universities in 1992, the enlarged university sector and remaining institutes of higher education have become much more market-oriented and consumer-led in respect of courses offered and students enrolled. An indicative feature of this trend has been the provision of both award-bearing and short courses for the 'practitioner' in such fields as schoolteaching, nurse education and social work, and technical training for the police, armed forces and similar groups.

Departments of education and health studies, responding to imperatives as diverse as 'Project 2000' in nurse education, and the drive for 'competences' in the initial training of secondary school teachers (DfE, 1992), have been at the forefront of course developments which have established the professional concerns of practitioners as the raw material to be reconstituted in a teaching–learning process that contrasts markedly with content-oriented and direct instruction-based models that characterize much of the conventional higher education environment.

Strands Impelling the Emergence of Practitioner-Based Enquiry

There are several strands to the emergence of PBE approaches to teaching

4

and learning in higher education. They form a complex mosaic that is itself an indicator of: *cultural shift in institutional provisions for the delivery of education and training; the growth of a loose but discernible 'teacher-as-researcher movement' in and around teacher training especially; and paradigm or canon fragmentation within social science leading to competing methodologies and explanatory theories.*

Cultural shift

In recent years the established culture of higher education organizations has come under pressure from the educational agenda of something crudely labelled 'Thatcherism', from the globalization of capital and industrial resources, from the 'Knowledge Explosion' generated by developments in IT, and from the internationalization of the market. Perhaps the most noticeable consequence of these pressures has been the trend towards a mass participation higher education system. The assumption here is that countries with elite higher education systems based on strict selection principles, are 'wrongly geared' to the socio-economic imperatives of the twenty-first century. The 'new truth' is that proportionately more of a given population must not only be educated to a standard higher than previous generations, but that they should also be educated to educate themselves. Without an educated and educationally flexible workforce, so the argument goes, traditional manufacturing countries in the West will be unable to compete with the economic powerhouses of the Pacific Rim (economic downturns notwithstanding) and the other industrialized nations.

The organizational logic that flows from this is that higher education must be less preoccupied with direct teaching of the young undergraduate. It must also concern itself with the 'operating capacity' of mature students already in work, with married women returning to work, young adults without A-levels and minority group members. The concerns of these potential users of higher education have historically been underestimated by the architects of the established system. In emergent market models, 'deficits' in operating capacity can be made good through the incentive that client purchasing of services through fees brings. Allied to this is the notion that abilities to cope will be enhanced by access and credit transfer schemes, by reconstituting curricula to focus on both the personal and occupational concerns of learners, and by generally making the experience of study in higher education institutions flexible through systems of course unitization and semesterization.

The discernible national trend described above makes concrete appearance in the course portfolios of university and college departments of education, schools of nursing and health studies, departments of social administration, and similar formalized agencies. These portfolios include the long-established PGCE now 'revised' under school–university 'partnership' rules for ITE, the Certificate in Education (Further Education) directed towards tutors and technical trainers in the post-16 further education sector, first degrees such as BEd and BA (Ed) which contain educational and pedagogical matter, a large variety of specialist certificates and post-graduate diplomas, and higher degrees such as MA and MEd which usually include a significant research requirement.

In disciplines rooted in natural rather than social science, cultural shift has taken slightly different form. The emergence of Teaching Company schemes around degree courses in physics, chemistry and biology is paralleled by 'franchised' course arrangements between industry and academia in civil engineering, information science and electronics. The 'partnership degree', in which educational institutions enter into joint teaching and research activities with major industrial companies, extends and develops the concept of 'research and consultancy' that is increasingly regarded as a necessary function of universities in their continuing adjustment to the demands of high technology, industry and the information-based society.

Teachers as researchers

In the previous 20 years, educational research, particularly in the UK, has broadened to accommodate a variety of developments. These have included a dissatisfaction with the detached and frequently abstract analyses of educational arrangement by psychology and sociology, and to a lesser extent, philosophy; and an increasingly strident call from schools and policy makers and the users of educational services for research to become relevant to the daily concerns of the educational practitioner.

Prominent amongst these developments has been the emergence of focused groups such as the Classroom Action Research Network (CARN), influential university departments such as the School of Education at the Open University and the Centre for Applied Educational Research (CARE) at the University of East Anglia, and the increased popularity of 'action research' as a method of enquiry appropriate in settings as diverse as factories, psychiatric nurses' training schools and kindergartens. A central theme in these newer definitions of educational research is that of 'continuous professional development'. That is, it is postulated that by engaging in systematic enquiries into one's own practices the possibilities for improvements in practice are made real. Through a process of accumulation of research skill, wisdom, experience, and so on, the educational service is improved. We detail the hidden assumptions in this generalized idea later. At this point it is sufficient to indicate that the 'new' educational research has produced, and is producing, its own orthodox justifications (Elliott, 1991; McGill and Beatty, 1992; McKernan, 1991; Schon, 1983, 1987), its own journals (see, for example, *Education Action Research* and the *Journal of Teacher Development*) and its own thematic agenda for study and research (see, for example, the *Open University 1993 Specification for Professional Development in Education*).

The emergent notion that teachers can be, and should be, both teachers and researchers is an interesting one. Plausibly, there is the claim to common sense: that any professional should continually think about what he or she is doing, and that presumably what one then does subsequently is done better. This fits quite comfortably with the strident demand from society in general for educators, especially schoolteachers, to be increasingly more technically competent at what they do and to be more publicly accountable for what they do.

At a more opaque level is the elusive theme that researching into one's own practices is democratizing and empowering. This is a recurrent motif in British writing on practitioner research (Carr and Kemmis, 1986; Lomax, 1986) and its ideological outlines are resonant of much 1970s to 1980s work that centred upon humanistic themes of learning, alternative pedagogies and sociologically informed critiques of educational arrangements in post-capitalist industrial societies. In essence this theme is anti-statist. Political control and direction of the education system, the de-skilling of teachers by a process of bureaucratizing regulation of the conditions of employment, etc., may be mediated, filtered and possibly subverted by a process of self-enlightenment through research. The extent to which this appeal is desirable, practical, fanciful or plain bogus is examined in Chapter 2.

There is a further, very practical implication of the notion of teachers as researchers. In an organizational sense, the expansion of higher education, especially in the new universities, has required new or different forms of course delivery. 'Student-centred learning' is one form of an organizational coping strategy. Making students seemingly responsible for their own learning partially removes the responsibility over institutions to provide the staff, lecture rooms, equipment and paraphernalia normally associated with teacher-centred forms of instruction. Thus the rhetoric of adult learning is such that it can emphasize home study packs, flexible tutorial arrangements, independently crafted assignments and, especially, the remote accessing of resources through computers. In a sense, the technology of the times in which we live acts to produce inexorable organizational imperatives – that far less time can be spent (or is needed) by the learner in expensively provided lecture halls. Where very large numbers of students are involved, as in Project-2000 for student nurses, the model of student-centred learning involving a significant component of structured research is an attractive one.

Finally, in this section it is important not to discount the pressure that external agencies are imposing upon university departments. Partly through its 'Thematic Priorities' approach and partly through financial stringency exercised via the Research Grants Scheme, the Economic and Social Research Council (ESRC) has been able to influence greatly the emergence of a research culture in those universities that aspire especially to be research-led in character. In practice, national competitions for funding, such as the 1996 Research Assessment Exercise (RAE), have forced universities to become not only more research active but more research adept in the ways they configure strategic planning. HEFCE (Higher Education Funding Council for England) policy requirements, such as the registration (for funding purposes) of higher degree students in education departments with a 3b rating (or above) in RAE terms from April 1998, are an indication of how the research agenda has been shaped by external agencies. Similarly, the expropriation of funding by the Teacher Training Agency (TTA) for continuous professional development purposes in education undoubtedly has consequences for the content and orientation of research-based courses in education. The 'teacher as researcher' may be welcome at the institutional gate, but the gate contains a list of criteria necessary for entry.

Canon and paradigm fragmentation in social science

Several contemporary textbooks devoted to educational research methodology (Cohen and Manion, 1994; Hammersley and Atkinson, 1983; and others) seem to find it necessary to 'discuss' an apparent disjunction between something called 'positivism' and something variously referred to as often as not as the 'qualitative research paradigm'. The reader of such texts may be confronted with a dichotomy between the natural and social sciences that on first encounter, may seem incapable of reconciliation. That is, he must choose a method of enquiry and a form of explanation that is either rooted in the traditions of the physical sciences of chemistry, physics and biology, or draw upon 'people-oriented' methods that seem to derive from anthropology and sociology. In Chapter 2 we say more about the epistemological character of the dichotomy, what it suggests in respect of certain differences between the social and physical sciences, and why (in our view) it has assumed an exaggerated significance in and around sites for applied educational research.

Such a review necessarily incurs a consideration of paradigms, or how knowledge is patterned. In physics, for example, knowledge has been patterned in terms of Newtonian 'analytical mechanics' and, much more recently in terms of 'chaos theory'. In the social and behavioural sciences, alternative and usually competing explanations for human behaviour may be illustrated in the 'positivism' of Augusté Comte – that rules and regularities could be discovered to explain social order – and the response to this position in the symbolic interactionism of G.H. Mead (1934) and his followers – that social order is no more than the million interactions produced by purposeful individuals.

There *are* tensions between the social and physical sciences. Equally, there are tensions *within* the disciplines of physical science, just as there are theoretical and substantive problems within say, sociology, psychology and anthropology. Whilst the history of science suggests that these tensions have always been present, the publication of Kuhn's *Structure of Scientific Revolutions* (1962) provoked a dialogue about the philosophy and character of scientific enquiry that has raged ever since. Sometimes the debate polarizes around absurdist notions of who or what was right. In psychology the humanistic theories of Dewey, Maslow and Rogers have met a determined counter argument from Skinnerian behaviourism and the cognitive processing theories of Gagné and Bruner. Similarly, in sociology the consensus-structuralism theories of social order (Parsons, Merton, see Rex, 1968) have been challenged by various conflict theories, social phenomenology, and 'post-modernist' theorizing. Knowledge has increased in volume and diversified in character, partly as a function of historical accretion, partly as the result of genuine scientific discovery aided by powerful new technologies, and partly as the result of new patternings or paradigms. Fixed bodies of knowledge based on a presumed truth have tended to subside in the last few years of the twentieth century. In consequence, disciplinary boundaries have become permeable and modes of scientific enquiry have become multi-faceted and less paradigm-fixated.

The challenge for those involved in practitioner research is not to seek the superiority of one method over another (a peculiar quest of justification that characterizes certain texts claiming to be about action research), but to understand intellectual lineage of methods selected and/or their relevance to applied problems. That is why, presumably, the textbooks to which we earlier referred take the reader on a 'Grand Tour' of theoretical positions in their early chapters.

We would not wish to treat lightly the complexities of the epistemologies that underpin the practitioner approach to research in education. Nor would we wish to mystify the reader with a lengthy exegesis of the lore and language of the numerous paradigms and 'schools of thought' in social science. What we would wish to do is to enunciate a set of principles for practitioner-based enquiry that are capable of verification and validation via different conceptual and methodological treatments.

The Principles of Practitioner-Based Enquiry

Practitioner-based enquiry (PBE), in which academic credits are awarded for systematic studies into the processes of teaching and learning, is identified as having four primary characteristics. First, the educational focus or research problem of practitioner-based enquiry derives from and informs the professional concerns of educators. Second, such enquiries are conducted as part of a networked and developmental discourse between tutors, practitioners and significant others. Third, practitioners are confirmed in a range of theoretical approaches to the study of education and research methodology. Fourth, through the process of enquiry, educators are directed towards the acquisition of intellectual autonomy, improved judgment-making and enhanced technical competence in the classroom.

In practical terms PBE is a process in which teachers, tutors, lecturers and other education professionals systematically enquire into their own institutional practices in order to produce assessable reports and artefacts which are submitted for academic credits leading to the awarding of degrees, certificates and diplomas of universities, colleges and professional associations.

In such manner, PBE contrasts with essays, assignments and examination work conventionally derived and used by higher education institutions as assessment mechanisms for academic courses under their ownership and control.

In shifting the emphasis from predetermined institutional contexts to the corpus of concerns that confront the educational practitioner in his daily educational life, the principle of professional experience as a resource towards which research activities originating within different epistemological and empirical traditions may be directed is established.

It is important at this juncture to note that practitioner-based enquiry is *not* the awarding of credits for what education practitioners routinely do in classrooms. Practitioners are paid to teach; they are remunerated as a function of their contract of service with an employing authority. A central element in that contract is a 'duty of care' towards a pupil, a student, a patient or other institutional client. We would seek to avoid the misconception, arising in some university quarters, that PBE 'rewards' people for what they are already paid to do.

Rather, the key notion is systematic study of educational practices, usually involving the deliberate and arranged focusing of a research technique on a recurrent instructional or administrative problem. This implies the learning of a range of appropriate research techniques and their theoretical counterparts, plus the acquisition of a capacity to step in and out of two roles: teacher as teacher, teacher as researcher.

'Reflection' in this process is understood as an enhanced perceptual and cognitive ability – one in which reconsideration, reviews of work done and information gained, consultation with self and significant others, recapitulation and self-criticism blend with insights largely stimulated through confrontation with the obligations immanent in the research methodologies adopted.

In this conception 'reflection' is not invested with existential and phenomenological properties. Indeed, in Chapter 2 we take issue with some of the conceptions of the term that Schon (1987) and others have proposed. In this conception of PBE, the idea of 'reflection' is indicative of a process that properly construes continuous professional development. Historically, 'in-service' education for practitioners has meant either formal, award-bearing courses offered by university departments and colleges, or the provision of short courses by LEA advisers on fashionable or imperative 'nuts and bolts' issues. The working assumptions underlying much of this activity are twofold. Either that the award of a higher degree signifies the acquisition of 'cultural capital', which society endorses on the basis of a generalized belief in the proposition that 'advanced study equals advanced skills', or that teachers and practitioners are deficient in contemporary knowledge and instrumental skills and need modest but regular adjustments to their instructional technique.

In PBE, teachers and practitioners are asked to recurrently hold as problematic, the routine conditions of their occupational lives. This is not an easy thing to do under most conditions. It is an increasingly difficult thing to do in an era of externally enforced accountability, organizational change and limits on autonomy. However, if continuous professional development is to mean more than the acquisition of advanced paper qualifications, then PBE should offer the opportunity for teachers and practitioners to gain a coherent understanding of their own professional practices. Similarly, it should offer a means by which practitioners may aspire to transform, remodel and recast such practices to achieve personal goals that are known and expressed.

It is of course, a legitimate expectation of university management, school governors, local education authorities, and the like, to expect the process of practitioner-based enquiry to produce 'pay-offs' that are measurable in institutional terms. This is especially so in the case of sponsored candidates, say in nurse education, where specialized configurations of skill development are expected to form part of an academically codified programme. More directly, the expectations held by sponsoring authorities for the candidates they sponsor might include the following improved capacities:

- The identification of significant problems within teaching/learning delivery systems and appropriate means for theorizing and analysing such problems.
- Where appropriate, to permit experienced education practitioners to gain additional technical skills relevant to their current occupational contexts.
- The emancipation of practitioners' academic, judgmental and administrative capacities so that they may develop a more effective interventionist stance in the conduct of professional practice.
- The acquisition of research-based techniques for the analysis of management and information systems.
- An improved categorical knowledge of curriculum developments in the context of policy-making process and political interventions in education.
- A stable predisposition of teacher, tutor or educational administrator as enquirer thus enhancing individual capacity to conduct required investigations in the workplace.

The above are not irreconcilable with private goals or personal ambitions.

PBE is a process in which individual orientations may be embedded in organizational contexts but not enslaved by them. It is probably true that the days of the intensely privatized, long duration Ph.D student working away in a remote closet on his or her *magnum opus* are long gone. Certainly the research training requirements of the ESRC, commentaries on the research degree process (ABRC, 1993) and universities' requirements for throughput would indicate that the institutional culture for research degree work has dramatically changed. However, when a candidate, even a sponsored one, enrols on a degree or diploma programme predicated upon PBE, he does not surrender his civil or intellectual property rights. PBE is wedded to the concept of academic freedom. There are potential problems though when a sponsoring employer attempts to 'call the tune' in respect of the nature and direction of studies undertaken. Where a project yields findings critical in some way of the authority that sponsored it, as sometimes occurs in the PBE experience, important ethical questions are raised about how such information should be treated. The purpose(s) of the project ought therefore to be kept constantly in view. Ultimately, the aim of PBE is to improve arrangements for teaching and learning in a variety of classrooms. If this simple, but elusive purpose can be kept in view, then variations in the agendas of people, organizations and sectional interests can be managed without sacrificing the integrity of PBE.

Assumptions Underpinning the Principles of Practitioner-Based Enquiry

The principles of PBE are underpinned by a set of assumptions about teaching and learning, and the characteristics of the professionally qualified and experienced learner. The artefacts that the process of PBE produces are the chief means by which these assumptions are tested, made visible and examined for admissibility.

First, adult learners have accumulated significant professional experience that is rooted in a wide and contrasting variety of occupational cultures. This can be drawn upon as a resource in their continuing education. Experiences good and bad, task-oriented and personal, teaching and administrative, shape the view that learners have about what they want to learn and a propensity for particular modes of teaching, knowing and learning.

Second, adult learners are intellectually curious about contemporary patterns of knowledge and how they are transmitted (teaching). The curiosity may be accompanied by an anxiety impelled by the pace and uncertainty of educational change, and the vague feeling that personal skills and competences are, somehow, no longer adequate to the task. This may induce the motivation to seek to acquire, as far as is reasonable, new patterns of knowledge. Later, the knowledge may be used in the solution of problems faced most typically in an organizational context.

This assumption is in contrast to the received wisdom for adult education in many institutions of higher education. The knowledge context of many adult education courses is frequently predetermined in substantive detail, disciplinary bases such as psychology and sociology, scope and degree of abstraction. Lurking in this is the notion of the adult as a deficient or empty receptacle in need of refilling, and a presumption that institutes of higher education shall define, own and transmit what is to count as valid knowledge. Under PBE the possibility for negotiating the constituent elements of knowledge, especially as these are vested in practitioners' claims of relevance, are kept open.

Third, adult learners are sensitive to, and knowledgeable about, the policy initiatives and educational imperatives of their current or most recent educational employer. Indeed, certain sponsoring authorities and educational employers may insist that their institutional concerns be taken as the raw material for any in-service work that they are prepared to finance. There is the potential for a triangular dilemma here: i.e. academic freedom safeguarded by higher education institutions – in conflict with service-oriented objectives of fee-paying local authorities – in conflict with personal and individual career goals of citizens freely choosing to enrol in award-bearing courses offered by competing educational institutions in a democratic, pluralist society. At the higher degree level in particular, PBE is particularly well equipped to mediate these concerns. Certainly, long-established criticisms of higher education by the professions in respect of the so-called 'theory-practice' problem (for an extended account of this in the perspective of educational research, see Chapter 3 in Elliott, 1991) begin to be addressed via the connotation of 'relevance' in PBE work.

Fourth, adult learners typically benefit from strong support networks and a motivational framework which effectively responds to their interests. This may be highly visible in, say, franchise arrangements where a group of further education colleges operate in association with a university. In the case of on-campus, full-time learners, networking usually includes a personal tutor responsible for both the pastoral care of the student and academic guidance of PBE. The proximity of the tutor to the candidates means that he or she usually plays a key role in assessment functions in the process of academic judgment of PBE. In a not dissimilar way, adult or graduate seminar groups have the delegated responsibility to organize meetings to construe the taught elements of the programme in the perspective of PBE.

In the case of off-campus, part-time learners, tutors are assigned in the role of 'critical friend'. Such tutors supervise the academic project, encourage systematic journal-keeping, maintain a watchful eye on the ethical context of the enquiry and liaise formally with institutions acting as research sites for PBE investigations. Ideally, such tutors are best paired with students from a similar subject in a professional background.

Finally, it is assumed that adult learners typically respond positively to a structured, enactive learning environment where direct participation is encouraged and expected and where enquiries are predicated as 'steps to action' in bringing about change in the real world. Internal arrangements for pedagogy do, of course, vary with the providing institution. Typically, however task-oriented workshops (for a further account of this see Murray and Lawrence, 1995) will feature strongly in any taught/course elements designed to support PBE. The individual tutorial, the group presentation, the discussion forum and IT laboratory sessions will all have their place in the range of structured learning activity. Most learning activity though, will take place in the actual conduct of a small-scale enquiry. The candidate will have to develop a proposal, identify a research site, gain necessary ethical and organizational clearances, conduct the enquiry, analyse the data, write and present a report which will have implication for policy and practice. In engaging in such activity there will be opportunities to learn from mistakes as well as from the wisdom contained in books, and modelling behaviour exemplified by tutors and significant others. Similarly, there will be socio-political as well as intellectual 'risks' to be taken. Negotiating these obstacles gives credence to the candidate's claims to 'ownership' of his PBE work. Equally, the dynamics of the process mean that something less inert than textbook knowledge is understood and internalized.

The problem with principles and assumptions is that they are principles and assumptions. They may constitute fairly well-worked-out ideas in the philosophical sense. They may well appear as part of the established canon of secular and liberal education theory. They may also ring a bell with common-sense understandings of how adults perceive and learn. However, if PBE is to gain legitimacy as a particular variant of applied educational research, then it must, through the artefacts and technical reports it produces, put its claims to knowledge in the public domain. In this way the assumptions and principles underpinning the process are tested, made visible and examined for admissibility.

The Manifest Forms of PBE

Practitioner-based enquiry as a process expresses itself through artefacts, some of which are liable for assessment under the academic regulations of the host university or institute of higher education. Other artefacts are formative in character, designed to act as a means of communication between the candidate and the various participants in the PBE process. A journal is a conventional example of the latter. The personal journal includes amongst its functions evidence that accountable study has taken place. Similarly, the journal records the details of the process of problem formulation, derivation of a research methodology or enquiry strategy, and orderly reflection on the practice(s) selected to be at the centre of PBE. It should be noted that the journal is not conceived of as a descriptive, chronological diary of events.

Rather, it is a literary device through which the problematic nature of educational enquiry is rendered intelligible, first to self, and subsequently to significant others, most notably a personal tutor.

As a personal working document and as a more formal record of work undertaken, and which is periodically attested by a tutor, the journal is expected to be fundamentally recursive. Frequent returning to, and reworking of, the substantive theoretical concerns of PBE are an expectation for the journal, as are issues of appropriate methodology that are the logical correlates of theory. In such a way, the journal proposes to offer the practitioner's account as primary source material that may later be included in the data analysis section of more formal reports. These latter are directly assessed in the purview of published criteria (see Chapter 5) that are nominated to be congruent with orthodox approaches to educational research as well as to measurement criteria that attempt to exemplify subjective experience as evidence.

Conceptually, a journal or similar device, is antecedent to a report. Most PBEs are presented in conventional, written academic format. Such reports are regarded as summative, assessment artefacts. Worth is judged according to published assessment criteria, essentially an academic judgment, and by the rather more elusive indications of claims to knowledge that will be admissible, if open to further conjecture, in the public domain. PBE reports present in considered and succinct form, usually a maximum of 7000 words, an account of the research project, its scope, methodology, findings and other outcomes.

As a special case of academic writing (particularly so in the case of higher degree PBEs) a report is invariably critically analytical rather than descriptive. This does not necessarily exclude the usual academic practices such as the formal definition of abstract concepts. However, in keeping with the spirit of PBE it is more appropriate if these are contextually explained as part of a mutually informative technical discourse between the writer and the reader, who is also a potential critic. Such reports have to be particularly sensitive to the dangers presented by impressionism and simple intuition. In part, this is why such reports are consequent to journal-keeping. Evaluative judgments should be accompanied by evidence, by the use of research findings which avoid lengthy reportage, and by plausible abstract reasoning.

Other qualities that PBE reports are expected to demonstrate include delimitations on scope. Examples of PBEs received for assessment reveal a striking commonality: many practitioners have enormous difficulty in specifying the problem they claim to be investigating. It seems difficult for practitioner-writers to superimpose meaningful limits on the scope of their enquiries. Yet this is a fundamental implication of the concept of research design. The issues of focus and conceptual congruence need to be embedded in a report structure that reflects the identification and specification of a problem to be investigated, an exploration of the dimensions of this problem and the 'intellectual *territory*' surrounding it, and conclusions (possibly for self) about the consequences of the problem. Also, given that many PBEs manipulate ideas located in social and behavioural science, reports are required to acknowledge complexity and relationships. The facts and categorical information that PBEs tend to produce, often in large quantities, are important, but if they are to be more than inert they require grounding in a meaningful, usually theoretical, framework. This helps to deal with both explanation and closure. The facts of a specific PBE case embedded in a *theoretical framework* permit the emergence of limited generalizations that inform practical purposes.

Whilst it is true that the written report is the most common form of artefact to be submitted for assessment leading to the allocation of marks, grades and academic credits, other possibilities exist. Depending upon the 'house style' or assessment dispensations within the parent academic institution, PBE research may also be reported in non-print format. Edited videos, scripted audio tapes, computerized data sets, and exhibited materials may also be produced in place of the conventional and time-honoured written assignment.

The Potential Contribution of PBE to Educational Policy and Practices

In recent years, in the UK in particular, numerous claims have been made for the superiority of practitioner-based research when compared with more traditional forms of data gathering long advocated by social science purists in and around educational institutions. These claims have led in places to the celebration of an '*action-research*' posture which, whilst extolling the virtues of its own methods, has remained remarkably quiet about its own potential vices. This is indeed an odd attitude in a stance that purportedly values 'reflection' above all things. It is even odder when one examines the current research project lists of the national agencies such as NFER and ESRC. Many of the projects listed employ sophisticated research designs, are often measurement-based and objective-driven and, in short, pay much adherence to the 'scientific method' rather than to the subjective experience of individuals.

PBE is a process that ultimately involves competing theoretical and epistemological paradigms. This problem is examined in some detail in Chapter 2 for it is at the heart of tensions in social and educational research, and the very powerful criticisms that have been levelled in general terms at educational research. We would not wish to make exaggerated claims of worth for PBE. Rather, we would wish to convey its utility as part, albeit a circumscribed part, of a range of approaches to educational research. It is small-scale and its implications for practice are, in the first instance, implications for professional conduct of the practitioner in his or her institutional workplace. We have previously spelt out the principles or educational justifications for PBE. It remains here to indicate a range of practical correlates of those principles as 'signposts' to the type of enquiries that practitioners might pursue. PBEs may usefully be conducted in the following areas:

- Projects relating attainment and participation to social factors.
- Explorations of teaching styles and interpersonal conditions in classrooms and learning.
- Investigations into the relationships between educational provision, the world of work and formal qualifications.
- Enquiries into the needs, properties and obligations of the adult learner.
- Evaluations of the adequacy of formalized syllabus and curriculum.
- Projects identifying professional development and in-service training needs of particular practitioners.
- Analyses of institutional norms and the magnitude of influence they exert on ways of working.
- Projects attempting to detect or construe, client, parent and 'customer' opinion about the provision of educational goods and services.

It may well be that PBEs conducted in the above and related areas lead to 'emancipation' of the mind. Equally, the results of such enquiries may have implications for macro-educational policy. However, we would not confuse the *stable predisposition of teacher or tutor as enquirer*, referred to earlier in this chapter, with that of radical critic of current educational arrangements. Rather, we would emphasize again the ultimate purpose of PBE, to improve the arrangements for teaching and learning in educational institutions both for those with a responsibility to impart knowledge, and those hoping to benefit by, or in receipt of, such knowledge.

2 The Basis of Critique of Practitioner-Based Enquiry

Basic Objections to PBE as a Form of Educational Research

In order for PBE to legitimately enact the principles described earlier, it must maintain logical integrity. To do this it has to confront and respond to a series of practical and theoretical criticisms that can easily be overlooked or dismissed by researchers of particular ideological persuasions. Practitioner-based enquiry is a process that involves competition between different kinds of theories. Consequently, criticisms of PBE have a 'deep structure' that is rooted in nature/nurture and macro/micro debates in social and behavioural science and in arguments about the nature of knowledge.

Some of the arguments will be analysed later in this chapter. At this point though, it is necessary to present the 'surface structure' of objections to PBE. Such objections are the counter to claims that PBE is a necessary and sufficient alternative to formalized, objectivistic research in educational settings. These objections are both substantive and procedural. They may be listed as generalized assertions, but it should be remembered that such objections assume weight when they are used to test the claims to knowledge of exemplar PBEs.

1 Practitioner-Based Enquiries are epistemologically rooted in complex and controversial theoretical perspectives and philosophical outlooks. These include humanistic psychology, existentialism, social phenomenology, grounded theory, personal constructs and post-modernism. Such perspectives are themselves highly contested on validity grounds within social and behavioural science.

2 Work producing PBE reports may fundamentally misconceive the nature of educational practice allocating a dimension of personal ownership to it that is unjustifiable on legal–rational grounds and which also misrecognizes the normative and institutional character of such practice.

3 The practitioner can be misled into assuming that anecdote, intuition, spontaneous classroom behaviour, habit and subjective preference are the stuff of scientific revelation and which, in pursuit of the goal of science as predictive theory, are to be offered as evidence of prevailing conditions in classrooms.

4   The practitioner cannot hope to match the skills or habits of mind routinely displayed by physical scientists. Indeed, whatever research training is offered to practitioners, it is frequently delivered as a partial, fragmentary, co-requisite to the practitioner's professed interests. This may lead to undue individualization of the research enterprise, inadequate specification of the research purpose, flawed data-gathering techniques and, in consequence, spurious conclusions. The latter may actually retard or impede practice rather than improve it.

5   'Teacher as teacher' and 'teacher as researcher' may be roles that are irreconcilable. Enquiry into practice may fundamentally distort and disrupt learning processes in the classroom, changing the environment from one of routine predictability to experimental uncertainty. In the case of teachers in primary and secondary schools this may well act to destabilize the *in loco parentis* responsibilities that teachers have for safeguarding the learning process. In the case of adult learners in such settings as nurse training schools, police colleges, and technical training institutes, the fundamental duty of care to clients that is at the core of public service may be distorted by the process of research.

6   Conventional ethics governing access to the research venue, confidentiality of information and the privacy of research subjects may all be compromised by the privileged role/status position of the practitioner and the presumption of autonomy that accompanies this position. Indeed, the interpersonal conditions in classrooms and of tutor work may be a primary source for the bias and contamination of data.

PBE as Ethically-Driven Activity

Given the serious criticisms outlined in the previous section and the fact that the fieldwork aspects of PBE take place in venues constituted for other purposes, the ethical framework within which PBE operates is critically significant for the legitimacy of the enterprise. Ethical concerns however, are not to be thought of purely as a charter of informants' rights. Certainly practitioners and tutors need to be particularly careful when conducting educational research. This is especially the case when children and their learning activities in schools are the subject of investigation. An ethical posture though is more than strict adherence to a set of rules. It is also a mental template that translates the intellectual and moral obligations of PBE into steps for action in the enquiry setting. We shall elaborate this for the categories of general ethics, ethical concerns in respect of research subjects and ethical considerations pertaining to research personnel.

In respect of general ethics it is clear that, as a moral priority, the interests and welfare of pupils, students and research subjects take precedence over the self-interest of the researcher. Similarly, practitioners should pursue a topic with honesty and objectivity, bearing in mind the limitations set by methodology. This also requires practitioners as volitional individuals and as students enrolled in award-bearing courses at particular institutions of higher education to represent and encourage a corporate spirit of open enquiry and discussion about educational research. In respect of social and professional responsibility, practitioners should conduct and disseminate their research with due regard to the rights and reputations of people and institutions.

Research subjects require a good deal of thinking about under the rubrics of PBE. For example, where research is conducted in schools and other institutions which act *in loco parentis*, practitioners must conduct their activities within the legal and authority requirements of the institution. It therefore behoves practitioner-researchers to know these. Similarly, where minors are used as research subjects, parental and school acquiescence should always be obtained, typically in writing, prior to the commencement of the research.

Where there is reasonable doubt about the effects of research on subjects, especially those in vulnerable situations, all efforts should be made to protect those subjects, and to proceed after fully informing the parties concerned of the potential consequences. This can be particularly critical in medical and healthcare training environments. Later in this book, we list some titles of actual PBEs in this subject area. It will be seen immediately that they are sensitive in character, requiring explicit clearances from ethics committees in a teaching hospital or acting on behalf of a district health authority. In these environments especially, no research should be conducted upon or with subjects who have explicitly refused to participate.

The important matter of privacy is central here. Practitioner-researchers are usually dependent upon the goodwill of subjects in providing access to personal biographies, working conditions and institutional preferments. There is no absolute right of access to these things. The privacy of research subjects must be respected at all times. Test results, experimental data or other findings should not be disclosed in a manner leading to the identity of individuals being revealed, unless their prior permission has been obtained. Also, practitioners should not abuse positions of authority to exert undue pressure on research subjects to participate as, for instance, in the case of a nurse tutor and a subordinate student nurse.

Rarely, in this day and age, is it desirable or possible to conduct enquiries without informing subjects as to their true purposes. Covert research, as it is sometimes called, has a dubious history and pedigree. However, when circumstances require, unobtrusive measures such as direct observation, event sampling and anecdotal data-gathering may be necessary and justified. If so, it is incumbent upon the practitioner to ensure that subjects are not harmed by such processes. Equally, it is important for the practitioner-researcher not to place himself in a position where damaging litigation may occur. Anticipating worst case scenarios is an important part of the ethical predisposition in practitioner research.

With regard to the people who actively conduct research, the practitioners, ethics takes on an intellectual dimension, a heightened consciousness of knowing and doing. Practitioners should, for example, be knowledgeable about and competent with the methodology selected for use. Experience suggests this is not always the case, particularly in respect of certain qualitative methods. Interviewing may, for example, be directed, informal, semi-structured, reciprocal in question and answer, or interrogative. How many practitioner-researchers know and understand the implications of these variations in the interview technique? Where a practitioner is only partially trained in a research technique, the supervisory relationship between tutor and student becomes critically important. The supervisor has to ensure that the candidate's investigative qualities actually improve as a function of direct experience. Direct teaching or modelling of specific research techniques is important here, but so is the student's use of these in context. Similarly, advice which is offered needs to be energized by the student if he or she is to become methodologically adroit.

'Methodology' here assures a wider frame of reference than data-gathering technique. It includes the capacity to keep all responsible authorities informed as to the purpose and nature of the research and, where necessary, involved as enquiries proceed. Towards the end of a project, where dissemination of findings is being contemplated, due regard has to be given to the educational needs of the constituencies concerned.

Also, there are confidentiality rules implied by methodology that are rather more complex than the anonymity accorded to subjects and guaranteed in conventional research. Where practitioners would like to cross-reference their project to other practitioners working on the same award-bearing courses, confidentiality of communication may be protected either by permission from research subjects, or under guarantees provided by the context in which the communication is made. For example, illustrative examples of informant responses to a project may be usefully shared in a seminar discussion. The seminar may itself be protected by the academic regulations of the institution in which it is conducted. The educational dynamic here is considered important. Seminar participants learn from and about each other's work without a sense of trespass on the intellectual property of others.

The public dimension of PBE requires proper acknowledgement of the contribution of other people. 'Method' here extends to embrace mentorship provided by tutors, access to research sites provided by intermediaries, and published work that has substantively informed the enquiry. The latter refers to rather more than a conventional review of literature. It may take in public documents offered as evidence, content analyses of such documents, and counter opinion. Practitioners should not try to prevent critical reviews of their work or commentary which might offer alternative ways of using their research findings to shape policy or facilitate teaching and learning. Similarly, any PBE which could be published for personal or financial gain should not be favourably endorsed if it is known to be inadequate.

The Intellectual Character of PBE

We have dwelt at length on the ethical character of PBE because such a consideration constitutes first redress to the criticisms of the approach outlined at the beginning of this chapter. The ethical posture so described ought to confer an honesty and a legitimacy on any project purporting to be PBE. This of itself though is not sufficient. It is necessary to understand something of the intellectual tradition from whence PBE derives, its afore-mentioned deep roots in social and behavioural science and the reasons for the scepticism that physical science and physical scientists in some quarters still direct towards certain kinds of social and educational research, even after 100 years or so of psychological and sociological enquiry.

Educational research is not a unique creature. It is a hybrid form of enquiry that draws on the tools and concepts of three behavioural sciences (anthropology, sociology, and psychology) and four social sciences (politics, economics, history and geography). For reference purposes we have modelled this relation in Figure 2.1.

It is difficult to identify boundaries in social and behavioural science. Many of the problems that educational research investigates are interdisci-plinary in character. Behavioural sciences are those that focus on people, patterns of personal behaviour, motives, attitudes, perceptions, and so on. Social sciences tend to focus more on the political and economic structures that have evolved over time and into which we are all inducted from birth. It will be noticed that we have not included philosophy as a separate, bounded branch of study. There are two main reasons for this. First, philosophy stands in reciprocal relationship to social and behavioural science. It has, through the ages, influenced and provoked a desire to know human things that has caused the categories of 'social' and 'behavioural' science to occur and formalize as disciplines. In turn, it has been shaped and shaken – indeed reconstituted – by developments in social and behavioural science. In terms of practical applications, it has been found wanting. Second, it was, and to an extent still is, the starting point for questioning the purpose and institu-tional character of education. In the late twentieth century this cannot be an abstract, value-analytical, context-free activity. We know that sources of aims and purposes in education derive from one or more of the following:

* What reason suggests.
* What natural justice demands.
* What faith dictates as incontestable.
* What established bodies of knowledge provide.
* What culture deems imperative to be transmitted.

Figure 2.1 Educational research as hybrid enquiry process

Behavioural sciences

Anthropology – the study of preliterate, preindustrial tribal societies and the evolution of culture

Sociology – the study of social processes and group arrangements in contemporary society

Psychology – the study of the mental and personality characteristics of human beings

Social sciences

Politics – the study of decision-making behaviour, government and the institutions given power to formulate public policy

Economics – the study of how limited resources are produced and distributed via markets and exchange mechanisms to satisfy human wants

History – the study of past events and human affairs assembled into continuous, explanatory records

Geography – the study of the Earth's physical features and how these have helped to pattern spatial arrangements between peoples

Produce

Methods of enquiry

Concepts/ideas

Theories

Tests for 'truth'

Perspectives

Schools of thought

Paradigms

Propositions

Research findings

'Lawlike' statements

Philosophies

Used by educationalists to

Shape

Interpret

Organize

Order

Analyse

Classify

Reconstitute

Social organization

In its many faceted educational form

- What philosophers claim as 'truth'.
- What the state says is educative.
- What the economy requires for a society to be competitive.

The tools of social and behavioural science are brought to focus upon the institutional form that expressions of educational purposes take. We use the term 'institutional form' quite deliberately. Practitioner-based enquiry, by definition, means education in a social and institutional context. We do not deny that teaching and learning can be relatively privatized. Neither do we deny the importance of the subjective element in the educational process. Nor do we exaggerate the significance of the subjective element. We cannot ignore thousands of years thinking about the human condition. Nor can we ignore the evolution of culture and the existent socio-political milieu into which we are all born. It should be remembered that in most advanced societies, educational and social arrangements have been worked out at an earlier time. In some countries, such as Australia and the USA, these arrangements are politically codified into written constitutions. Educational research is not antecedent to these arrangements. Neither are the individuals claiming to do 'action-research' – although you might think so on reading their books.

PBE is 'system'-based enquiry. That is, research is conducted in and around educational 'systems'. Notice the use of the plural. In Britain, much educational debate, especially about schools and their functions, is conducted as if educational institutions were unidimensional phenomena. Educational institutions come to be seen as undifferentiated, visibly bounded organizations, maintaining unequivocal relationships with social and political structure. Such a conception of education borders on the facile. In Britain alone, quite apart from the distinct educational arrangements in Scotland, there are (in reference to the schools sector) at least five educational 'systems', namely:

- the system of maintained or 'state' schools;
- the system of independent and private schools;
- the system of denominational schools largely controlled by diocesan authorities;
- the system of city technology colleges and counterparts;
- the system of unaggregated 'free' and often emergent community schools.

In practice, most educational debate and research takes place around the first of these systems – the maintained schools' sector. That is because it is the largest system, the system most politically contested and, being taxpayer-funded, the system in which there are the majority of stakeholders. The practitioner, therefore, has two 'recognitions' to make in respect of PBE. First, he needs to perceive and construe the intellectual lineage of social and behavioural science. Second, he needs to know the history and educational claims that institutional forms of educational practice represent.

The Divided Mentality in Scientific Enquiry

Earlier, we drew attention to an established practice in the writing of conventional textbooks on social and educational research. That is, the tendency to 'set-up' a division between social and behavioural science on the one hand, and natural and physical science on the other hand. The division is then interrogated apropos the particularized purposes of writers (who are also, presumably, active researchers, although this is not always clear) on the subject.

Thus, the 'Eight General Traditions in the Study of Education' reported by Carr and Kemmis (1986) are required to be first identified if these authors' advocacy of three conditions for teaching to 'become a more genuinely professional activity' (p. 9) are to be met. The 'conditions' are not without ideological and value content. Namely, the grounding of teachers attitudes and practices in research and theory built on research; the extension of teacher autonomy to participate in educational decision-making; and the extension of responsibilities to include service obligations to a wider community. The recent history of teacher–state relations, especially in the UK can be interpreted to suggest that the Carr and Kemmis criteria for advocacy have been ignored or rejected. Does this mean that their perspective is invalid? It might be on values grounds. It might be on grounds of public service. What is plausible though in the Carr and Kemmis specification is the requirement to 'know' the 'eight' (or is it eighty-eight?) general traditions in education.

The same problem is approached differently by Cohen and Manion (1994). Always alert to the limitations of educational research, these authors prefer to introduce the 14 substantive techniques chapters in the fourth edition of their book, with an examination of 'positivism', 'the assumptions and nature of science', and 'alternatives to positivistic social science'. Featuring strongly as a subsection of the latter is a discussion of 'Phenomenology, Ethnomethodology and Symbolic Interactionism'. These complex words are said to represent three schools of thought that are considered to be united in their opposition to positivism. With an abiding interest in such things as subjective consciousness and the 'essences' of social relations that 'reflection' is believed to reveal, these schools of thought have distinct philosophical and sociological orientation. Indeed, these are all sub-perspectives within the discipline of sociology where their character, connections and location within a parent discipline (sociology) has been satisfactorily explained by forensic analysts of that discipline (Cuff et al., 1990).

It might appear that these authors are attracted to, or are experienced in, sociologically driven educational research. The closing pages of their introductory chapter propose 'normative' and 'interpretive' paradigms or bipolar socio-technical approaches to educational matters which suggest this to be so. Their elucidation of the purpose of educational research is thus somewhat different from that of Carr and Kemmis. It is to 'enable educators to develop the kind of sound knowledge base that characterizes other professions and disciplines; and one that will ensure education a maturity and sense of progression it at present lacks' (ibid., p. 40).

In a compendium reader on practitioner-research, Webb (1990), in Chapter 1, finds it necessary to explain: 'practitioner-research and the psycho-statistical paradigm' followed by a succinct section on 'the origin of action research'. This, in turn, is bracketed by a sub-section on 'practitioner-research within the sociology of education' and a description of the 'Teacher as Researcher movement'. The chapter is interesting because it attempts to serve as a unifying prescript to nine subsequent chapters that report indicative practitioner-research projects, albeit from eclectic methodological standpoints. The presumption is that these practical enquiries only make sense to the reader if their intellectual parentage is understood. That 'parentage' is complex and multidimensional. Its roots may be traced to the abiding concerns of classical psychology and its established methods of enquiry. Alternatively, they may lie in the preferment of HE institutions for a model of practitioner-research largely sociological or socio-political in character. Accounts of action-research, case studies and school ethnographies in British texts rarely venture far from something once labelled the 'new' sociology of education. This academic trend, largely forged from cultural changes in the late 1960s, sought to emphasize group processes, social interaction, inequality and ideology in education. It took strong root in departments and colleges of education after 1966, especially in those aspects of teacher training concerned with the social foundations of education. This now old 'new' sociology of education, at least the post-1971 British version of it, has a lot to answer for. Its demise as a form of explanation in initial teacher training (see Reid and Parker, 1995) has left some university departments of education 'stranded' in the epistemological sense. The national political project for education, driven relentlessly onwards in instrumental fashion since the 1988 Education Reform Act (ERA), has bypassed such preferments by forging new imperatives and technical requirements. Consequently, the most relevant and telling phase in Webb's chapter may be the one that appears in her concluding paragraph: 'teachers have to work within the system and many of them are concerned to find ways of doing so more effectively for the benefit of their pupils. Therefore a major aim of practical action research is to enable practitioners to inhabit the system creatively in order to work towards change through action at the micro-level.'

Action and structure

In our view the concepts of 'action and structure' are central to the analysis of the intellectual obligations of PBE. They are also useful tools of meta-criticism. That is, they help to explain why so much writing on and about practitioner research is recursively sociological, sometimes socio-evangelical in character, and why established wisdoms in natural and behavioural science are treated to lip service or with scepticism by some proponents of practitioner research.

Prior to a detailed consideration of *action* and *structure*, we shall table here a selection of claims to knowledge made by practitioner approaches to educational research. Our purpose in making this selection from the dozen or more textbooks on our desks concerned with practitioner research is to show how divisions in scientific enquiry are identified and ultimately appropriated by the authors. We will then move the analysis forward by summarizing the character of 'normal' science with its roots in physics, chemistry, etc., and 'interpretive' science with its roots in the humanistic aspects of social psychology, while attempting to emphasize that it is really the research purpose that intellectually 'anchors' a practitioner's choice of explanatory theory, a method of data gathering, and a preference for certain kinds of conclusions.

> A reflective practitioner must be attentive to patterns of phenomena, skilled at describing what he observes, inclined to put forward bold and radically simplified models of experience, and ingenious in devising tests of them compatible with the constraints of an action setting.
>
> (Schön, 1987, p. 322)

> Reflective practice seems to be a positive direction for nursing practice and education to take. It offers the chance of developing knowledge which avoids the problems of academic science and also those of technical rationality, since reflective practice depends upon the critical and creative development of knowledge which is linked to practice.
>
> (Reed and Proctor, 1993, p. 30)

> Critical social science involves the formation of groups committed to their own enlightenment. While some social research is evaluated solely in terms of the theoretical adequacy of its formulations, and other social research is evaluated solely by its practical or technical achievements, critical social science requires that both of these criteria for evaluation be employed and that an additional criterion be added: the success of critical social science requires that the community of social participants-researchers achieve enlightenment in their own understandings and for themselves about the nature of the relationship between

their own knowledge and about the nature of the relationship between their own social process and those of the social order in general (ideology).

(Kemmis in Boud et al., 1989, p. 155)

We are making the assumptions behind the action research tasks, framework, and methods adopted by our teachers, explicit to them in order to show we are prepared to test and modify them in the light of their efforts. If we did not do this, we would hinder their capacity to reflect and encourage an uncritical dependence. Any educational support agency which claims to value the teachers power for autonomy in the classroom can be accused of proceeding irrationally if it fails to make its assumptions explicit and to invite teachers consciously to participate in the task of critically testing them.

(Elliott and Adelman in O'Hanlon, 1996, p. 17)

These citations, from papers and books by authors versed in and committed to practitioner enquiry, are illuminating because of their justificatory content. Practitioner research must be a good thing, so the line of argument goes, because it involves the individual in making meaning of his experience. Similarly, practitioner research holds out the possibility for 'creative' development of knowledge, 'skilled' observation, 'critical' understanding of the social order, and the option to change 'assumptions' if these are found to be wanting in some way.

We should make it clear that we have not arbitrarily selected these citations to illustrate our viewpoint. We believe them to be broadly indicative of the writers' general educational and research posture that they have developed over a number of years and made public through influential books and papers. Indeed, so influential have some of these writers become that their ideas now almost constitute an orthodoxy in particular fields such as nurse education and teacher training. Our concern is to balance the tacit and explicit messages in these hortatory claims to knowledge by identifying what they tend to ignore and discount.

First, the recognition that 'experience' is not independent of educational history and that, for hundreds of years, educational purposes have been fought for is relatively absent from these claims. As we indicated earlier, PBE is 'system based' enquiry. To do PBE effectively then one must perceive and comprehend 'system experience'. Second, the notion that 'creative' knowledge can avoid the 'problems of academic science' is false. Academic science, whatever that is, has problems, because it challenges and builds upon accumulated wisdom. Nowhere is that more evident than in medical and nursing practice. Indeed it is exemplified in the words of one of our colleagues, an experienced nurse educator, who, when assessing PBEs submitted for academic credit, routinely checks them to 'see if there is anything present that will kill the patient'. Third, 'skill' in observation, and by inference perception and interpretation, is easy to talk about – but much harder to acquire in actual reality. Perceptual error is common in human interaction. Visual acuity and its development has a neo-physiological and ophthalmic context that is usually quite absent from any routine course in observation methods offered as part of a research training programme. Fourth, and finally, it is not fully clear how practitioner research can add to the 'success criteria' of 'critical social science'. We suggest that the obvious regression in modern writing on action research, especially to the 'Frankfurt School' of critical theory, and to the ideas of fashionable theorists such as Polyani, Habermas and Foucault, is weak in general justificatory terms and especially so in respect of client-oriented PBEs contributing to practice. Why then do these writers sense a requirement to justify their claims to knowledge?

Author Justifications in the Perspective of 'Normal' and 'Interpretive' Science: what the neophyte practitioner-researcher needs to know

The authors cited in the previous section are, in the first instance, reacting to a perceived hegemony on matters of educational concern by the methods and orientation of the natural and physical sciences. What does this hegemony, perceived or real, actually constitute?

A simplification of the natural science position is that events have causes which can be discovered and explained, a principle of causation or determinism. Observations of such events in the natural and physical world suggest an order, a pattern, which can be ascertained and described in lawlike ways. The formulation of lawlike statements gives natural and physical science a defining characteristic, a principle of prediction and regularity.

The formulation of lawlike statements is indeed possible though the device of the 'testable hypothesis', which is dependent upon the factual evidence gathered or observed to support it, a principle of empiricism. When a number of lawlike statements of like character are collated, a formal theory or basis of explanation for events is produced. The evidence used to verify or disapprove a hypothesis is considered scientific if the personal attributes of the researcher (his 'subjectivity' so to speak) are rigorously separated from the objects of the enquiry. This is part of a desired condition of 'objectivity'. Similarly, techniques of data gathering which can be shown to measure what they claim to measure, and which, if repeated produce the same or similar results, are said to satisfy a principle of reliability and validity.

The methods and orientation of natural and physical science have come to be described by sections of the academic community as 'normal science' because the features described above have evolved and proved productive in scientific discovery over several hundred years. A better descriptor might be 'normative' science. That is, a pattern of expectations for conducting enquiries according to a 'scientific tradition' has long been established. As an ultimate aim of science is the production of knowledge by controlling extraneous variables and the analysis of complex data sets, the above features are considered necessary and sufficient if meaningful generalizations about events are to be constructed. As we have indicated, much research in education this century has been conducted within the canon of 'normal science'. This continues to be generally true in the case of large-scale, expensively funded projects such as the Third International Mathematics and Science Study (TIMMS). However, as scientific methods have developed, so has the science of the study of their weaknesses.

Writers and researchers committed to practitioner enquiry are said to belong to an emerging tradition of 'interpretive science'. It is not that the canon of normal science is rejected outright. Rather, the view is taken that events, particularly social events, may not be orderly or predetermined. Causation is always likely to be multidimensional. Therefore the search for measurement control over random and unknown variables is always likely to be problematic. Also, mechanistic models of events and human beings, suggested by words such as 'positivism', are indicative of a belief in the constraining power of environments, external to individuals. 'Interpretive science' is in significant measure 'interpretive' because it tends to assume that human beings constantly recreate the conditions of social life. That events are part of a 'dynamic' state not a 'static' state waiting to be uncovered. Indeed, it has long been the view of critics of 'normal science' that technical procedures borrowed from mathematics and physics, especially statistical procedures capable of inferring relations between data sets, do not of themselves prove causation nor facilitate the interpretation of such relationships.

Unlike the ardent devotee of 'normal science', the interpretive researcher tends to be relatively unconcerned about 'subjectivity'. Indeed, the advocacy of qualitative data gathering techniques by the interpretive researcher may be read as the placing of value on the daily experiences of individuals in defined social and organizational contexts. The term 'qualitative' suggests sampling and noting such things as organizational minutiae, the subtlety of social interaction, perceptual variation and what phenomenologists are fond of describing as the condition of 'multiple reality' in organized social life. Discussions, direct observations, interviews, case study, ethnographic descriptions, content analysis of documents and anecdotal data gathering are all processes deemed scientifically respectable and favoured by the interpretive researcher.

Other rather more sophisticated claims and preferences are made by interpretive science. According to Glaser and Strauss (1980) and their colleagues (Strauss and Corbin, 1990), qualitative data gathering has the potential to generate organization-situated explanatory theory. As a major goal of the scientific approach is the production of theory, tacit knowledge accumulated from informants under qualitative rules may be transformed into coherent principles. In some circles this process of transformation has become known as 'grounding'. It is an inductive form of theory development.

In taking the inductive stance, that is the preference for 'bottom-up' explanations from discrete case examples, interpretive researchers tend to reverse the procedures of normal science. In normal science, theory is often produced a priori, from informed speculation or accumulated wisdom within a discipline, and in advance of facts gathered or techniques used to verify or disprove a testable hypothesis.

The interpretive stance is not just a reaction to perceived hegemony of normal science, it is also a reaction to forces within social and behavioural science that do not offer unequivocal support to the domain of subjective experience as evidence of stable, recurrently measurable social phenomena. Given that qualitative techniques are particularly susceptible to intuitive and reactive biases, to impressionism, to 'halo' effects where researcher proximity can induce a desired response from an informant, it is not surprising that the claims of interpretive science contain a strong element of self-justification.

'Reliability', the much sought after measurement condition in normal science, in which instruments used consistently produce similar or the same results over time with standardized survey populations, is an elusive and problematic condition under most qualitative forms of enquiry. It is a condition particularly susceptible to oversimplification. Later in this text we offer six explanations of the term 'reliability'. These contrast with attempts to construe 'reliability' in qualitative studies which often fall back to a loose use of 'triangulation' – the application of two or more data-gathering devices to check comparatively the stability of the phenomenon under study. This technique, which is derived in part from the fieldwork protocols of classical anthropology to produce rich descriptions of subcultures, has its own obligations under the qualitative method generically referred to as 'ethnography'. (For an account of the ethnographic tradition, see Hammersley and Atkinson, 1983; Spradley and McCurdy, 1972). The extent to which these obligations are known and capable of refashioning to address matters of reliability is a recurrent problem for interpretive science.

The search for, and the established rules of, reliability indices in research in some branches of economics and experimental psychology, sit somewhat uncomfortably alongside the cosy assumptions of human relations theory and the active model of man purveyed by, say, the 'andragogy' of Knowles (1970) and Cross (1981), or the Symbolic Interactionist perspective of sociology.

There is no doubt that much British 'interpretive', 'action' and 'practitioner' research in the past 20 years has been heavily influenced by certain classical ideas in social psychology and social philosophy. Sometimes the intellectual debt is acknowledged. The work of Woods (1979) and Delamont (1976, 1984) is an obvious expression of the Chicago school of thought of Symbolic Interactionism founded by George Herbert Mead. Elsewhere in action research circles links to such founding fathers as Lewin, Rousseau, Husserl and Dewey are elusive. Indeed, it seems likely that in some works the links are not known or recognized in any meaningful perceptual sense. A very worrying matter indeed for 'action researchers' who claim to value 'reflection'. Sometimes, in British educational research, an awkward provenance of ideas is avoided, especially in arguments about 'personal knowledge', first person or 'I' reportage in social science, and the validity of the claims of interpretive science in general.

We said earlier that sociological preferments were never very far from accounts of justification in certain British educational research circles. This leads us to our third point in respect of justifications for 'normal' and 'interpretive' science. It is that justifications for interpretive forms of explanation represent an attempt to deal with the 'action–structure' dilemma; the most fundamental source of tension for person-centred research in social science in general, and the disciplines of psychology and sociology in particular. We now turn to an analysis of the 'action–structure' dilemma.

The Action–Structure Dilemma, Persistent Dichotomies and the Possibilities for Theoretical Frameworks

A fundamental theoretical problem in social and behavioural science is identified as follows. The analysis of social behaviour, particularly as it occurs within the institutions of society such as schools, teaching hospitals, training colleges and the like, is never able to be completely explicated in either cultural, structural or individual terms. This is clearly illustrated in the plethora and diversity of theoretical orientations of many research studies conducted over recent and not so recent years (Shilling, 1992).

Turner (1996) uses the notion of 'dichotomies', that is, either/or divisions within explanation, to illustrate the confounding problem of social theory.

> It is also obvious that social theory has yet to come to terms with the classic dichotomies which have characterized the arena of theory, namely the tensions and contradictions between action and praxis, agency and structure, micro and macro approaches, and the basic dichotomy between individual and society.
>
> (Turner, 1996, p. 11)

Individual and society! In a nutshell it is this conundrum which encapsulates the issue of what might influence an educational researcher's choice of explanatory theory. Following Robertson (1974, 1992) it is possible for the researcher to choose a cultural frame of reference in which the beliefs, values and symbols shared by members of a social system are focused upon. Alternatively, the frame of reference may be a structural one in which the relations between individuals, roles and collectivities in particular institutional combinations take precedence. Third, the researcher may establish his or her own conceptual categories based on objectively derived information. Such categories may then be applied analytically to the institution under investigation. A further alternative frame of reference is the 'subjectivist' posture in which the predilections and orientations of particular individuals, dyads, triads and other groups are taken as the point of analytic departure.

Subjective–objective dichotomies characterize much of the activity of contemporary social theorists and educational researchers. Indeed, the five sections into which the *Blackwell Companion to Social Theory* is divided (see Turner, 1996) are indicative of the underlying problem: At what level might an analysis of institutional or individual behaviour be located? The sections are: (i) Foundations; (ii) Actions, Actors, Systems; (iii) Micro–Macro Problem; (iv) Historical and Comparative Sociology; (v) The Nature of the 'Social'. Turner, as a major commentator on developments in social theory as well as the editor of this standard reference work, offers a justification for the way the book is organized.

> One basic criticism of social theory is that it has failed in any significant or genuine fashion to resolve some of the fundamental problems, dichotomies and puzzles which have been the perennial issues within Twentieth Century theoretical activity.
>
> (Turner, 1996, p. 11)

He goes on to argue that among the community of social theorists, educational researchers, policy analysts, etc., there is little agreement about what 'theory' actually is, or what might be taken to be genuine advancement in explanation – 'theoretical progress' as he calls it. Accordingly, a researcher's basis of explanation (theory) may be a broad framework of ideas for organizing and ordering research. Alternatively, it may be a discrete set of concepts useful in directing research attention. Attainment, achievement orientation, performance indicators, accountability, professionalism, etc. are concepts of this sort of order. 'Theory' may even be the appellation given to unformalized ideas that lead the researcher towards sweeping accounts of late twentieth-century society. Ideas of this type – lifelong learning, globalization, deconstructionism, modernity, postmodernism. etc. – may retain a considerable degree of abstraction. Equally, they may have a Messianic, evangelical, nihilistic or ideological flavour. Turner is of the view that 'recent developments in feminism and postmodernism have only confounded much of the existing confusion and uncertainty' (ibid.).

A digression on postmodernism

It is difficult to characterize 'postmodernism'. It is not a paradigm in the sense that there is a relatively bounded set of ideas which can be labelled the substantive core and to which adherents subscribe. It is not susceptible to easy definition. Postmodernism is variously described as: a 'cultural condition' produced by decline and change in industrial capitalism; an anarchic mental state among social observers produced by an approaching new millennium; a challenge to the rational principles of twentieth-century science; a much delayed reappraisal of the Enlightenment; a terminology for construing the social functions of language; a rejection of 'grand' or 'totalizing' theories of the human condition; and numerous other complex exegeses.

Insofar as it is possible to adduce postmodernist assumptions and recurrent themes for study and metaphysical appraisal, the following constitute a by-no-means exhausted list. There is an abiding 'poststructuralist' orientation – literally, beyond 'structures, towards people and social organization'. There is an interest in the meaning of symbols and social practices and the 'crisis of representation' occasioned by limits placed upon understanding by language. Indeed, language, discourse, textual material of all sorts, are viewed as mediators of social life and its explanation by postmodernists. The place of the electronic media in shaping mindsets is less clearly an object of interest. However, formal scientific explanations for things, and the artefacts produced by science, are susceptible to questioning and scepticism by postmodernism. Knowledge is viewed as having 'insecure' rather than 'absolute' foundations, though this does not stop some postmodernists from regressing to Marxist explanations when it suits them. Similarly, the Enlightenment period is said to have caused an 'inappropriate' assumption of the individual as a rational and autonomous subject. Rather, it is through the ways in which individuals are constituted as subjects (presumptive of a concept of 'society'?) that postmodernist contrasts and comparisons are able to be made.

Postmodernism has certainly produced an extensive literature (Woodiwiss, 1990; Turner, 1990; Seidman, 1995; Ritzer, 1997) and is, in our judgment, accurately portrayed by Skeggs (1991) as a 'hegemonic war of position within academia'. It has also produced a wave of 'criticism' in fields as diverse as film appreciation, literature and sociolinguistics, art and architecture, contemporary politics and economic theories of social change. It has made celebrities out of four Frenchmen (Foucault, Derrida, Lyotard and Baudrillard). Indeed, Derrida's now notorious claim that 'there is nothing beyond the text' has sparked a deluge of enquiries, essays, counterpoints and meta enquiries into something called the 'postmodern condition'.

Smart (1996) has attempted to construe and synthesize postmodernism as a form of explanation that is somehow an intellectual product of the times in which we live. The loss of 'grand narratives', the decline of formalized and inclusive 'totalizing' theories such as Marxism or consensus structuralism, the emergence of widely divergent standpoints in 'critical theory', may be indicative of an erosion of faith and an absence of confidence in established canons and maxims previously held to explain the workings of society. Whether this is a good or a bad thing is not clear. What is clear though is the basis of choice upon which fabrics of explanatory frameworks may be predicated. Turner (1996, p. 8) puts it this way:

There are two contradictory and opposed trends in social theory. On the one hand there is postmodernism, which has embraced what we might call the weak paradigm of social theory. On the other hand, rational choice theory, which is an influential theoretical movement in social sciences, has adhered to a strong position of social theory construction.

Weak paradigms or strong paradigms? Objective emphases or subjective emphases? Micro or macro? Such distinctions are interesting and 'emergent' in the sense that they have to do with what the social scientist or researcher says is 'true' on the basis of his or her categories of analysis, regardless of the actual meaning that behaviour might have for members of a particular social system. Given our underlying claim that practitioner researchers have a singular responsibility to recognize the differentiated nature of social motives as they are related to professed or ascribed intentions, it is worth extending somewhat our view on rational choice theory.

A further digression on rational choice theory

Max Weber's sociology of action (Cuff et al., 1990) has influenced contemporary conceptions of rational choice theory. The classical Weberian view is that the most comprehensible type of motivated action was that form of action which seemed to be the product of rational judgment and expedient choice. This form of action could be seen in the economic functions of governments and the repetitive practices of legal and judicial administrators. More abstract forms of motivated action are those which derive from affective sentiments and lead the individual in pursuit of idealized or non-rational ends. A third category of action is that of traditional conduct, characterized by unreflective habits, and approaching an automatic form of response to situations in which the behavioural expectation has been publicly codified. In this sense, 'action' is what has always been seen and done as action.

Rational choice theorists are particularly interested in extending the Weberian concerns for rational activity to a contemporary concept of 'expectations for behaviour'. If these can be posited to exist, then the social sources from which they spring may be identified and explored through processes such as practitioner research. These sources include: the pervasive influence of culture; formal norms patterned by a system of sanctions and broadly understood and endorsed; and emotion-based and subjectivized response to symbols, rituals and the contingent practices of everyday life.

Such 'sources' of expectations for behaviour are interpreted by rational choice theorists via three major assumptions. These are summarized by Abell (1996, p. 260) as follows:

1   Individualism. It is individuals alone who take action. When such actions are 'social' in character, i.e. involving other people and eventually evolving to shape collective activity or institutional patterning, the macro social outcomes or events we wish to explain are caused.
2   Optimality. The actions that people choose to engage in are optimal in the sense that they are the best that can be achieved given 'transitive' or passing preferences generated by the opportunities and limitations individuals face in daily life.
3   Self-regard. Even in the face of clear 'expectations for behaviour', individuals' actions and social actions are concerned with their own individual welfare.

Returning to 'action' and 'structure'

It is useful at this point to define our terms: 'action' refers to the nature of social behaviour; 'structure' refers to the nature of external influence on that behaviour.

Thus, returning to our earlier characterization of normative and interpretive science, we can offer an epistemological starting point to the practitioner researcher. Research into educational institutions and practices within the normative paradigm takes expectations and dispositions of people as being in a predictable relationship with the physical situation of such people. In the case of expectations in physical situations such as schools and colleges, the relationship is an imperative one backed up by sanctions. Research into educational institutions and practices within the interpretive paradigm considers the dynamic nature of social interaction, including emotional responses, occurring between people. Here the practitioner imputes a pattern of motives essential for describing situations and actions, whilst at the same time examining the individual content of actions and situations for the source of motives and the nature of their operation.

The dichotomy between 'action' and 'structure' in social science is the major contributor to the dilemmas that we have earlier referred to. Some theorist-researchers are quite conscious of their explanatory frameworks. Others appear ignorant of the dilemma. Still others, such as Anthony Giddens (1990, 1998), have located 'action–structure' at the centre of their theoretical schematas. In 1999 the Reith Lectures of the British Broadcasting Corporation were given over in part to the popularization of 'The Third Way', a Giddens-inspired conception of social democracy for the twenty-first century. This is based in some measure on theoretical reconciliation of 'action' and 'structure', through a series of books published since 1977, and wedded to the politics of 'New Labour' that emerged with the election in the UK of the Blair government in May 1997. We return to Giddens shortly.

Other theorists, actively working within the interpretive paradigm, or within a phenomenological tradition (Becker, 1992; Douglas, 1973; Garfinkel,

1967), though it is not logically possible to have a phenomenological 'tradition', and as we have observed in postmodernism, tend to refute 'structure' altogether. If, as Derrida suggests there is 'nothing beyond the text' (see Smart, 1996) then it is not surprising that structures external to the person are of little account to this form of theorizing. What this body of work does help with though in regard to 'explanation' is that it denotes that idealized conceptions of behaviour and practice in educational institutions are rationally explicable insofar as they are acknowledged and subscribed to by the academic community. Such a proposition sustains practitioner research as system-based enquiry. Indeed, it is a proposition that rational-choice theorists invariably predicate their enquiries upon when seeking to explain macro level outcomes:

> The focus must be on the social system whose behaviour is to be explained. This may be as small as a dyad or as large as a society, or even a world system, but the essential requirement is that the explanatory focus be on the system as a unit, not on the individuals or components which make it up.
>
> (Coleman, 1990, p. 2)

Methodologically, of course, it remains for the practitioner-researcher to discover whether idealized conceptions approximate to the 'rationality' socially described and sanctioned as rational in actual research settings by real people.

The Nature of Normative Constraints

We have been at pains in this chapter to emphasize a conception of practitioner-based enquiry as system-based. Our reasoning is informed by our understanding of the 'action–structure dilemma' and the judgment we make that it exerts a powerful restraining influence upon phenomenological and personal approaches to theorizing educational research. (For an analysis of the nexus between personal, professional and propositional knowledge, see Hoyle and John, 1995). The concept of 'system' suggests constraint. A constraint is a limit on action. It may be self-imposed or it may be externally imposed as in the case of a social norm. A constraint is not only a limit on action, it may also be a sense of restriction on feelings and emotions, and acting in this way sharpens an individual's sensitivity to social circumstances. Constraints produced by and in social structure are said to be 'normative'. That is, they become transformed into rules which not only publicly define expectations in institutional life, but also contribute to the beliefs and knowledge that people hold about institutional life.

The work of Fishbein and Ajzen (1975), contemporary in social psychology, is useful here in reconciling social influences to individual orientations.

These authors suggest that performance or non-performance of behaviour with respect to some target cannot be entirely predicted from knowledge of a person's attitude, i.e. his affective and evaluative orientation towards that object. Instead, a specific behaviour is viewed as determined by the person's intention to perform the behaviour. The postulate is formalized as follows:

> Normative beliefs (beliefs residing in socially structured expectations) and the motivation to comply (in common social situations) lead to normative pressures. The totality of these normative pressures may be termed the 'subjective norm'. Like his attitude towards the behaviour, a person's subjective norm is viewed as a major determinant of his intention to perform the behaviour.
>
> (Fishbein and Ajzen, 1975, p. 16)

The logic of this position is that behaviour in educational and similar institutions is constrained behaviour. It is constrained by normative beliefs – that significant others think self should or should not perform a particular action. It is constrained by beliefs, the cognitive component representing the knowledge and information that an individual has of an object, and differing between individuals in terms of the subjective probability to associate objects with attributes. Institutional behaviour is also in part a function of attitude, the predisposition to respond in a consistently positive or negative manner towards an object and opinion which may be thought of as a verbal or written expression of an attitude. Most importantly, the within-institution behaviour of such 'actors' as tutors, teachers and students is constrained by subjective norms, the totality of normative pressure arising from the perceived expectations of referents plus the motivation to comply. The power of constraints is ultimately expressed through intentions, the subjective probability that a student or teacher will perform a behaviour in question. These relationships are represented in Figure 2.2.

This representation of plausible sources of influence on the in-school behaviour of teachers and students (based on active practitioner research in Australian state high schools) draws together and compiles, the types of social influences and their sources and weds them to the upper half of the model which conceptualizes the nature of 'constraint' at the level of individual people. Additional detail should help the practitioner-researcher to recognize the orienting or directional character of the model.

Following Elboim-Dror (1973) the model establishes an analytical point of origin for each group of influences. The 'Implementation System' is the system of schools and classrooms and it is here where such things as the age–sex cleavage of teachers and students, the different treatments accorded to pupils of varying ability, the social class position of children and the adult authority vested in the teacher can be found. In our research, the term 'social system' eventually replaced 'implementation system'.

Figure 2.2 Orienting theoretical model: Plausible sources of influence on the in-school behaviour of teachers and students

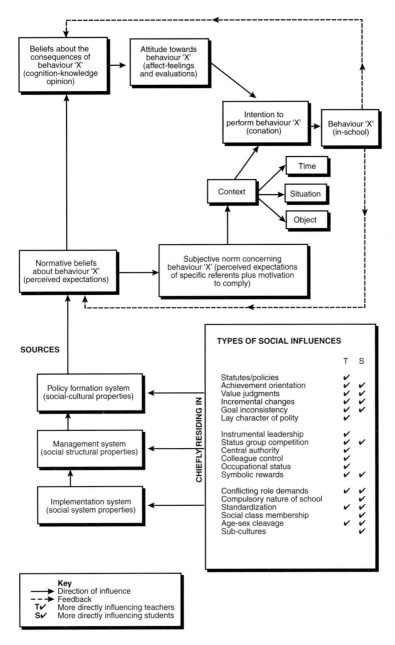

Source: Developed from ideas in (i) Fishbein and Ajzen (1975); (ii) Elboim-Dror (1973)

The 'management system' is the organizational entity (school board, department of education, local education authority, etc.) which controls groups of schools and their populations. The occupational status of teachers, the administration of policy regarding resources, class sizes, staff allocations and the executive control of competition between educational status groups are the typical responsibilities of the 'management system'. In our research the term 'social structural system' eventually replaced 'management system'.

The 'policy formation system' includes the political institutions, organized interest groups, parents, employers and those members of the public who are able to exert influence on educational policy. Direct and tangible influences on education may emerge from the 'policy formation system' in the form of laws, statutes and legal precepts. Less tangible influences may be more abstractly experienced in the form of a pervasive achievement orientation, incremental changes to Acts of Parliament and alterations in the moral or values fabric of society. In our research the term 'social cultural system' eventually replaced 'policy formation system'.

In summary, the model incorporates : information, in shorthand construct form, about the types and sources of social influences on teachers and students in school and a reconciled position on the reciprocity of 'action' and 'structure' on behaviour in schools. Similar models could, of course, be constructed for behaviour in social institutions other than schools.

The theoretical matters we have discussed above have received, over the years, considerable attention in the literature of psychology and sociology. They have received distinctly less attention in sections of the educational research literature concerned with practitioner approaches. This is a matter of concern as practitioner research is likely to be sidelined if it cannot keep up with developments in social science. The work of Anthony Giddens (1976, 1990) is salutary in this regard. The stable benchmarks for explanatory theory that Giddens' work provides, in line of descent from classical sociologists such as Spencer, Marx, Weber and Durkheim, ought to be routinely known and comprehended by practitioner-researchers:

> The social world is differentiated from the world of nature essentially because of its moral character…This is a very radical disjunction because moral imperatives stand in no relation of symmetry to those of nature, and can hence in no way be derived from them; 'action', it is then declared, may be regarded as conduct which is oriented towards norms or conventions. This can then lead in different directions, depending upon whether the analysis concentrates upon actors purposes or motives, or whether the emphasis is placed, as by Durkheim, upon norms themselves as properties of collectivities.
>
> (Giddens, 1976, p. 93)

The 'new rules' of social science method as formulated by Giddens include: the recognition of power as a crucial, inseparable component of action; the acknowledgement of norms as both constraining and enabling; the idea that the enactment of moral obligations does not necessarily imply moral commitment; and the acceptance of the principle that the production of society is always a skilled accomplishment of its members.

Reflecting on Reflection

The theoretical and intellectual tensions we have described should, in our view, be a first constituent of the process of reflection. It is not possible to be a 'reflective practitioner' if the intellectual milieu of the practices being reflected upon is not known or understood either in terms of its own historical antecedents or its theoretical possibilities. Practitioner research ought to be informed about and by established paradigms or bases of explanation in social and behavioural science. It should also be guided by well-established precepts in the literature. It is absurd (and probably dangerous) to try to enter an educational institution free of all assumptions and ideas – a course of action we have frequently heard advocated in otherwise respectable educational arenas. The recognition of normative constraint does not/should not blind practitioner enquiries to the responses and orientations of individual people to those constraints. An expression of this important point is as follows:

> From our theoretical perspective, we cannot imagine any noteworthy observations occurring (in fieldwork settings) without a minimal set of social science categories: social structure, ideology, work, social control and so on. Such concepts do not necessarily predispose the observer to the direct use or test of any given theory, rather they provide some initial order for observing activities that might otherwise seem chaotic. Hopefully, categories will, in time, move into the background as they are supplemented, or preferably supplanted, by grounded concepts more descriptive and analytic of the activities actually observed.
> (Schatzman and Strauss, 1973, p. 56)

Earlier in this book, in the section entitled 'The Principles of Practitioner-Based Enquiry' (p.9), we provided a definition of 'reflection' that incorporated the elements of critique we considered earlier in this chapter. We will now move the account forward to a listing and analysis of data-gathering techniques that are particularly useful to practitioner-researchers. While the analysis will identify the features of these techniques from the conventional standpoint of educational research, we will also show how the reflective predisposition as defined may be injected into the use of these techniques in particular fieldwork settings.

3 Opening the Tool Bag

Proactive Behaviour in Planning an Enquiry

Preparation and Planning

Systematic planning and preparation beforehand, are the essence of 'strategy' for the conduct of practitioner-based enquiries. Some enquiries and information-gathering activities are likely to be straightforward. Others, probably the majority, are likely to be complex and full of hidden, potential pitfalls. Where difficulties are likely to occur, the prior planning task is even more important. Entering into any kind of enquiry involving people and systems is necessarily a complex and sensitive task. To study effectively real-life settings, the researcher has to be a practising sociologist and also an inquisitive citizen. More urgently, the researcher must have or acquire the technical competences that are part of the 'tool bag' of the applied researcher.

The very first move in planning a PBE is an in-depth consideration of the topic area. Ideas tend to be rather general at first. They have to be further scrutinized in respect of such questions as: Why research this topic? What knowledge will be gained? Will the enquiry lead towards improved skills? This in-depth consideration may range from empowering self to practical, professional benefits in the workplace leading to organizational change and improved management. From the outset, the practitioner must not only 'know' his or her purpose and who or what it is for, but must also keep it clearly in view throughout the life of the enquiry. A good sense of audience and an expectation, even at this early stage, of what the results of the enquiry are likely to be is helpful. In taking such a step, the process of focusing the general ideas commences. Sometimes, the way ahead may be self-evident or, on the other hand, confused and opaque. Matters may be shaped by whether you are deciding for yourself or whether outside agencies are influencing the purpose. A brief from a line manager is one such well-known external influence on the selection of research problems. Ideally, the drive towards focus should be impelled by what you as researcher are interested in and care about. If you are not strongly motivated about a topic, the whole exercise tends to become much harder and can slide into drudgery. Similarly, prior enquiry and research experiences can be re-engaged to drive towards focus. Beware though the deceptive perception that 'prior experience' is an index by which topics can be listed and interrogated. Fitting topics to something you are conversant with may be comforting, but it is no guarantee to adequacy in the expression of the research purpose and the imaginative consideration of topics.

It is also worth examining self-beliefs and attitudes at this stage. Are there any beliefs, sincerely held or otherwise, fixations, predispositions, attitudes, prejudices, etc., that are likely to colour the view of the enquiry being undertaken or the outcomes envisaged? There is a need for honesty here; a requirement to avoid a 'closed mind'. Personal background, family, gender, race, religion, socio-economic circumstances, levels of education, and so on, are inevitably part of the attribute 'baggage' that potential researchers bring to enquiries. Including them in the consideration of topics is, in our view, a healthy thing, helpful in minimizing the contamination or 'bias' of data if you like, and an appropriate primary component of 'reflection'.

The word 'bias' is important in social and educational research. It does not refer to the prejudiced attitude as might be first thought. Rather, it is a technical term that suggests influences on an enquiry beyond the control of the researcher. These sources of *extraneous variance*, as they are formally called in the research literature, pose problems for topic definition and measurement control in any enquiry. In quantitative research, extraneous variance is usually controlled mathematically, by rules for computing random samples, by statistical assumptions under the normal curve of probability, and so on. In qualitative research extraneous variance is reduced by adherence to ethical procedures, by declaration of known interests and preferments, and by careful accounting for the subjective features of the enquiry.

Traditional positions on topic specification are rooted in academic disciplines, revealed through the established research literature and pointed-up in standardized methodologies and theories. A thorough and up-to-date understanding of the literature base for a topic or topic area is as fundamentally important to PBE as it is to any research worthy of the name. Similarly, there is no substitute for a good background knowledge of relevant disciplines. A keyword here is 'background'. It is useful to obtain information from people who have done work in a related field, perhaps via unpublished dissertations, or direct via word of mouth. Expert 'witnesses' in social science disciplines and educational theory are also obvious repositories of topics. There will though, be the challenge of *originality* in topic selection. Like other researchers, people who undertake PBE want to try to make an original claim to knowledge. In a knowledge-rich environment this becomes ever harder. The classics of social science were written a long time ago.

The classical Greeks formulated the concept of democracy over 2000 years ago. Karl Marx provided a trenchant critique of industrial capitalism in the late nineteenth century. In the 1930s the theoretical insights of George Herbert

Mead and his colleagues into the processes by which children progress into adulthood (socialization) gave the world an idea that is now in almost common parlance: *self-concept*. There may well be new classics to be written in the future but, in the meantime, the active researcher is obligated to take heed of accumulated wisdom. To ignore or be neglectful of such wisdom is to risk 'reinventing the wheel'.

Access to accumulated wisdom is facilitated not only by printed books on library shelves. It is usual and useful to accompany topic identification and focus by undertaking keyword or author search of established print, CD-ROM and 'on-line' databases such as the British Education Index (BEI) and Educational Resources Information Centre (ERIC). Most universities and large public institutions have access to these databases. It is important to know which databases serve which subject areas. As well as the aforementioned, Medline serves the health and medical subject areas, Anbar serves business and management subject areas, and Psychlit is the CD-ROM equivalent of the printed Psychological Abstracts, a long-established database serving psychology and behavioural science. Most libraries have detailed guides and printed leaflets on the procedure for both accessing and using such databases. It is now almost axiomatic for the practitioner-researcher to be competent in information retrieval using electronic sources. We have included in Appendix 4 sample output from the Educational Resources Information Centre popularly identified by its acronym ERIC. This very extensive computerized information service has its headquarters in Washington DC. ERIC is a database of educational materials collected by the US Department of Education. It is organized in two sections: Resources in Education (RIE) covering documents, and the Current Index to Journals in Education (CIJE) covering over 700 periodicals and journals. A detailed keywords thesaurus that helps in the clarification of topic and research purpose as well as acting (along with author surname and other identifiers) as a device to interrogate the database, is available. Access to ERIC is achieved either by direct on-line computer link or by using regularly updated CD-ROM versions normally held in the libraries of most academic institutions. In some libraries, ERIC is still available in its earlier microfiche form. In the appendices to this text you will find two self-instructional exercises, one for the BEI and one for ERIC. Completion of these exercises should facilitate the tasks of information retrieval and topic specification. Practice via the exercises should also help to develop skill and acuity in the essentially technical task of database interrogation.

As well as thinking strategically about topics, purposes and foci, it is important to consider from the outset practical realities. Many a well-conceptualized research study, especially at Ph.D level, often founders on the rocks of reality. Considerations of time, resources, access and the messiness of real situations all need to figure in the assessment of topic viability. In dealing with people, especially busy professional people, the choice of topic and its focus should include a judgment about the likelihood of cooperative behaviours. It is also imperative to understand that social and educational research is intrusive. The researcher 'invades', so to speak, the private domains of people. Such people are under no obligation to participate and it is always wise to respect the privacy of research subjects from the outset. It is equally wise to regard research subjects as the first destination of the outcome and the results of the research. If you can convey the idea that the people who were kind enough to provide the information in the first place are also the people most likely to be interested in the findings (in the first instance), then practical problems of access to research sites and venues can be controlled.

Having undergone the prior consideration phase in the conduct of PBE, the practitioner-researcher must then move on to what is, in our experience and judgment, the most critical activity in the enquiry process – the careful specification of the research purpose.

The Research Purpose

Expressing a research purpose, whether it be in the form of a question, a testable hypothesis or some formalized declaration of intent is much more difficult than is generally supposed. Having surveyed a topic area, the tried and trodden view is to narrow the topic area down to specific research questions. In practice, things may not quite work out. In the process of reduction, additional considerations crowd in. These include the matter of educational justification, the use of organizing ideas or constructs, variables and their measurable relationships, and so on. Questions may readily spring to mind, but then there is the problem of finding a context for them. Uncertainties and intuitions abound. If a PBE purpose is indicated by the need to solve a practical problem, you may end up with a purpose that is characterized by a problem in search of a technique. You may go into reverse. That is, decide on a method of data collection first and then, later, cobble the specification of the purpose to it.

To minimize the above sorts of problems we suggest our 'trinity utility test'. If the purpose as stated points in the direction of a practically useful enquiry, a positively viewed enquiry (by others that is) and an educationally measurable enquiry, then the purpose is likely to be 'good'. It is then incumbent on the practitioner-researcher to find the form of words, question, hypothesis, issue, problem assertion, or whatever, to express the purpose. More often as not this is a wordsmithing or penmanship exercise. Without labouring the point, the expressed purpose ought to have concern for theoretical understanding, suggest active connection to educational practice and be recognisable in the subject concerns of journals, publications, books and other materials contemporaneously operating in the topic area. Similarly, any methods of data collection suggested by the research purpose ought to be seen as appropriate to the sorts of questions being asked or hypotheses tested. A general principle here is that methods should not govern questions asked.

We have emphasized earlier that practitioner researcher is small scale in character. It follows that the expression of purpose will usually be narrow in scope. The tradition in the experimental methods of natural science is to control scope via the testable hypothesis – a conditional statement in which one variable is said to act on another in a discrete direction. Whether a PBE needs a hypothesis or is best served by a question to be answered is really a function of the kind of study it is. However a tentative statement of what you are likely to find out is always useful. Coupling a hypothesis to a set of research questions may also prove helpful. In thinking about the elements of expressed purposes – questions, issues, problems, hypotheses, and the like – a framework for the complete enquiry becomes clearer. Below we list a selection of research purposes from the field of technical training, primary and secondary education, and nurse training.

These are expressions of purpose presented as PBE report titles. They vary in clarity. They are, though, real PBE projects. Technical trainers, nurse educators, school teachers, etc., undertook these projects in BA (Education), Certificate in Education (post-16) programmes, MA in Education courses and the like. To help in understanding the importance of topic purpose, we invite the reader to apply the 'trinity utility test' to each of these purposes. Similarly, we would ask the reader to make a general assessment of the adequacy of these purposes in terms of the ideas listed above. So important do we consider the expression of purposes to be that we return to it at subsequent points in the text.

Statements of purpose for a selection of practitioner-based enquiries

- The use of learning contracts in pre-registration nurse education courses.
- Learning problems are proportional to text-editing skills in WordPerfect.
- Third-agers and adult education provision in Dorset
- To what extent is 'appraisal' the tool of 'organizational man'?
- Trained staff's perceptions of patient alienation in an Ear, Nose and Throat (ENT) Department of a public hospital.
- What factors influence option choice amongst a Year 9 group of boys in a coeducational comprehensive school?
- Scores on Standard Attainment Tasks intercorrelated with Receptive Vocabulary scores of Year 1 pupils in Portsmouth primary schools.

Later in this chapter we will take one of the above statements of purpose, 'The use of learning contracts in pre-registration nurse education courses', and expand its dimensions to show how it illustrates a complete PBE enquiry. Prior to this, however, we will enumerate some of the other components of PBE planning as a research strategy clarifies and begins to take shape.

Practical Preparation for Practitioner-Based Enquiry

Once the research purpose is clarified, a working title for the enquiry can be established. In some enquiries the title and the dominant statement of purpose are *synonomous*. However, we would generally recommend against using a question as a main title. Titles tend to have more communicative power if they are phrased as declarative statements. Once a working title is formulated the outline template for the enquiry can be written. This may take the form of abbreviated notation. Usually, in PBEs designed to meet academic requirements for formal qualifications offered by universities, the template will have the features and the appearance of the conventional research proposal. The structure of the conventional research proposal is outlined below.

The Structure of the Research Proposal

1 Title

A succinct specification of measurable relationships. Best phrased in declarative sentence form.

2 Purposes of the investigation

A concise account of the objectives and goals of the enquiry.

3 Rationale

This addresses principles of justification. This section implies why the research is important, the contribution to knowledge, policy and practice it will make, and its integration into accumulated wisdom on the topic(s) under investigation.

4 Research questions/hypothesis

Purposes outlined in 2 above are now represented in measurable form, i.e. either as questions to be answered or hypotheses to be tested. These questions and hypotheses should be clearly phrased and both the variables to be manipulated and the relationships between them specified.

5 Limitations

In this section constraints beyond the control of the researcher but known to influence the objects of the enquiry are listed. These may have to do with access to research venues, limits on sample size, ethical constraints, and so forth.

6 Delimitations

In this section the study is 'ring-fenced' or controls on scope are actively established by the researcher. Delimitations usually include considerations of time available for fieldwork, systematic exclusion of extraneous variables, resource-related issues, and so on.

7 Sample/survey population

In this section information is provided about the 'population' that is under investigation (e.g. homeless families). The sample details provided should closely reflect the argument in 3 above. Once the 'population' parameters are accounted for, actual details of the sampling frame can be provided. This should include:

(a) total number of respondents to appear in the sample;
(b) demographic characteristics (age, sex, occupation, etc.) of the sample;
(c) the type of selection principle(s) used for sampling – e.g. random, opportunity, proportionate, stratified, random sample, etc.;
(d) geographical location(s) of the sample.

8 Review of the literature

In a proposal a review may be both substantive and methodological. Ideally it should consist of between 12 and 20 references that 'shadow' the methodology you propose to adopt; *and* analyse or comment on in a contemporary way (the last five years) the conclusions reached by other researchers in aspects of your topic. The review should pick up on 'gaps' in published research underpinning the importance of the claims made in 3 above.

9 Methodology

Here you list the following:

(a) measurement instruments such as questionnaires, observation schedules, standardized tests, etc. to be used;
(b) principles of justification for the selection of these instruments;
(c) a time-frame for the collection of data;
(d) procedural steps through which the investigation (particularly data to be gleaned in fieldwork settings) will proceed;
(e) a preliminary framework for the analysis of data – for example, in correlational studies you might specify subprogram 'Partial Corr' in the menu of Statistical Package for the Social Sciences (SPSS), a well-known set of computer programs for analysing social science data.

10 Conclusion

This should be brief. It should suggest or outline the expected 'direction' of findings and the policy implications that follow from the work.

11 List of references

This should always be provided in complete form (author names, titles, publishers, place of publication, date of publication, etc.) even though the number of books and articles accessed for the purposes of the proposal will be small (e.g. 12–20 discrete references).

12 Lexicon of terms used

Provide a list of all keywords to be used in the research (e.g. occupational status, destitution, participation ratio, etc.) and succinctly explain their meaning either by formal (dictionary) definition or operational (context-dependent) definition.

In our experience, novice researchers like to use and follow this outline structure to the letter. Rehearsing the provisional template for PBE this way is probably very good practice. As experience is gained in research, the steps and features that this outline structure purveys tend to become internalized and part of the habitual mindset of the active researcher. However, we would not want to overemphasize 'structure' in the provisional template for PBE. How templates are actually contrived and written is part of the 'word-smithing' activity to which we referred earlier. The important point is that the features of the conventional research proposal, broadly endorsed by the university community as required and appropriate, should be taken account of in the planning phases of the enquiry. We will now offer some further advice in respect of the features of the template.

We have already flagged up the importance of *purposes*. Once the title has been settled upon, the purposes of the enquiry are then listed in the desired form, either as issues, hypotheses or questions. We have found well-phrased research questions to be the most suitable form of expressed purpose for PBE. Whatever the form of expression of purposes, these will have to be construed and justified in a succinct *rationale*. Whether or not the rationale is placed after the title and prior to the statement of purposes is a matter of judgment. Remember though that the rationale will also inform the *abstract* – the synopsis that tells the complete story of the PBE.

Limitations and *delimitations* are essentially technical devices to inform the readership of constraints on research design. The term 'limitations' is usually taken to mean things beyond the control of the researcher. They often appear in the form of the failure to achieve mathematical probity in survey samples, the denial of access to research sites or sources of information, and strictures imposed by external authorities such as ethics committees. Under certain conditions, 'limitations' may severely strain the potential worth and *justifiability* of an enquiry. Knowledge of limitations must always be balanced with the likely benefits of the outcome of an enquiry. 'Delimitations', on the other hand, are controls on scope imposed by the researcher. They are an illustration of the decision-making that the researcher has consciously undertaken. They set design limits that the reader of the research report, and potential critic, must acknowledge in any judgment or appraisal of the adequacy of the research design of the study, and by implication, worth and validity of the findings. Inevitably, PBEs being small in scale are heavily 'delimited'. If the practitioner-researcher is unable to delimit his study effectively, it is likely that an informed readership will do it for him – and an externally imposed 'delimitation' is invariably a critical one.

Sometimes, PBE work involves constructing and using survey instruments. The instrument, be it a factual questionnaire, some sort of personality inventory or attitude measure, or checklist for learning, is distributed among a *sample* of a survey population. Such *populations*, as statisticians describe them, exhibit the characteristics in which the researcher is interested and towards which research purposes are directed.

In such work it is important for the practitioner-researcher to have a good working knowledge of sampling theory. However, given that sampling theory includes detailed considerations of probability rules that are unlikely to be attained in survey research conforming to PBE, it is rather more important for the practitioner-researcher to know (and construe) the qualitative character of the respondents who are the subject of the enquiry. We shall say more about this later. At this point it is sufficient to say that most samples of respondents in PBE work are *opportunity* samples. That is, they are groups of people often inhabiting the same learning or occupational space as the practitioner-researcher. Indeed, the practitioner-researcher may have responsibility for the sample as in the case of a school teacher and his or her pupils. Alternatively, a senior charge nurse may have under her control a group of student nurses whose learning is the centrepiece of the enquiry. It is not really possible to *generalize* findings from such 'opportunity' samples in the same way that statistically respectable generalizations are made on strictly random samples of large survey populations. In PBE, conclusions and generalizations relate in the first instance to the group of respondents selected for the study. If the qualities of this sample have been decided at the planning stage as of importance, then it follows that they should be listed and described in as much detail as possible. This will certainly help in the cross-classification parts of data analysis in the final report.

A *review of the literature* is both a planning requirement for research work as well as an established feature of a written report. We have already explained how accumulated wisdom on a topic is critical to the specification and development of purpose. We have also provided structured examples of search strategies for CD-ROM and 'on-line' databases (see Appendix 4). We now need to make a few more formal points about reviews of the literature in general and their place in practitioner research and the artefacts produced.

First, a review of the literature is always purpose-directed. It is not simply an uncritical listing of books read. Information derived from the literature review will be of different orders. There will be substantive information that is both basic and advanced in respect of the topics concerned. Most typically, such information will be found in books in academic libraries. However, it may also come from specialist repositories such as the Public Records Office. Similarly, it may be archive material held in museums and specialist collections such as the Naval History Collection of the Portsmouth Central Library. The review will also include methodological literature. That is, book and journal material that is informative of the research design aspects of the enquiry. Thematically, such literature may be allocated to a specific part or section of the review.

Second, the literature review actually constitutes part of the database for the enquiry. This is a point often missed or misunderstood by the first-time researcher. Research builds on what is already known. Established works on a topic may be interrogated further, reinterpreted, used as a starting point or as a central focus around which the current enquiry crystallizes. Indeed, findings from the fieldwork parts of practitioner research are usually interpreted and presented in the perspective of established knowledge.

Third, undertaking a review of the literature is an exercise in methodological brevity and relevance. Simply put, doing a good review requires the researcher to know his study intimately. Practice in information retrieval using CD-ROM and 'on-line' databases is more than practice in the recovery of information: it is also practice in refining and understanding terminology; it is practice in utilizing journal and subject parameters; it is practice in the recording of abstracts, either by taking notes from the on-screen display or by downloading to disk and printing after text-editing via bibliographic packages such as PROCITE. This software is a bibliographic database for use on personal computers. It is designed for, and directed towards, students and academic researchers to enable them to manage their personal collections of book titles, journal articles, documents and other print works that constitute a *bibliography* or *reference list*. PROCITE packages are now standard in many university libraries. This software will do electronically what was previously done by hand. That is, one of the more essential but laborious tasks of research material handling, the construction of detailed bibliographies according to a preferred style such as the *Harvard Format*, an internationally used reference and citation system (Turabian, 1973), can now be done through modern computer techniques that come as part of an integrated 'electronic library' package.

In a subsequent chapter we analyse the distinctions between *data-gathering techniques*, *methods* and *methodology*. It is our contention that these terms are used interchangeably in an often confusing and conceptually questionable manner. Methodology includes data-gathering techniques. It also includes an *epistemological* posture, a reasoned framework for the enquiry that takes a range of theoretical presumptions into account. Suffice to say at this stage that the planning template ought to give some account to 'methodology'. This may well include the listing of useful data-gathering techniques that seem appropriate to the research purposes. A consideration of methodology and data gathering implies also a consideration of data analysis. In the planning phase it is worth identifying data-analytical techniques that will most likely be used in the enquiry. These may be drawn from the qualitative or quantitative inventories or may be permutations. A summary of statistical and qualitative analysis techniques is provided below. Examples from the qualitative side may include the ethnographic semantic technique of Spradley and McCurdy (1972) in which respondent verbatim utterances are taken as the unit of data or the text analysis packages (TAP) described by Tesch (1990) in her wide-ranging analysis of qualitative research analysis tools.

Conventional Statistical Analysis Techniques Useful in Small-scale Research

1 Tabular and graphical displays of data: charts, figures, tables.
2 Frequency distributions: 'least' to 'most' scores on measurable criteria.
3 Measures of central tendency: mean, mode, median.
4 Indicators of relative position in a distribution: rank orders, percentiles, deciles.
5 Measures of variability: standard scores, standard deviations, analysis of variance.
6 Measures of association: t-tests, correlation coefficients, chi-square.

Conventional Qualitative Data Analysis Techniques Useful in Small-scale Research.

7 Behaviour observation checklists: direct, indirect and participant observation.
8 Interview schedules: informal, structured, semi-structured.
9 Case study reports: descriptive profiles, logs, biographies.
10 Ethnographic accounts: text and semantic analysis, narratives, field diaries.
11 Content analyses: text-edited documents, notes, historical records, keyword lexicons.
12 Personal constructs: repertory grids, attitude inventories, matrices, construct models.

A *conclusions* or *recommendations* section will obviously not feature significantly at the planning stage. It is though important to understand that there will need to be *warranted conclusions* – end statements justified by the data gathered and analysed. An early decision as to whether *formal recommendations* will be made also has to be taken. Some thought has to be given to *closure*, or how the project will end, and how the results will be used and information disseminated.

As soon as information is retrieved, whether it be from book, journal or electronic sources, it should be formally recorded and incorporated into a working list of references that may well expand to become a full bibliography on the topic. It is a very good habit to store this information on separate system cards as well as in computer memory banks. The format for presenting the information should be established at the outset and adhered to throughout.

The Harvard system, adopted for this book and fully explained by Turabian (1973), is now very commonplace in academic writing and research in the anglophone world.

A *lexicon of terms* used in the PBE, or to be used, should be early established. This activity may well form part of the delimitations process referred to earlier. Excessive jargon is to be avoided but an appropriate technical vocabulary for a project is highly desirable in order to communicate with audience, to control abstraction and to bring as much potential measurement control on to theoretical and substantive objects and ideas. An indicative lexicon of terms for a study entitled 'An analysis of normative pressures in Queensland state high schools', illustrating these points, is given below. In the interests of helping the reader to come more readily to terms with the lore and language of educational research itself, we have provided an exemplar lexicon of meanings for common research terminology in the appendices.

A Lexicon of Terms/Content Analysis Dictionary for a Project Entitled 'An analysis of normative pressures in Queensland state high schools'

Social norms — rules which guide behaviour and which typically appear at three levels of institutionalization:

(a) folkways, or informal rules that may be governed by minor sanctions and which may be consensually negotiated;
(b) mores or powerful constraints usually widely understood and shared in the culture and which may be governed by strong sanctions;
(c) laws, or legally binding rules involving strongly institutionalized sanctions.

Organizational characteristics — administrative procedures that are of a regulational kind, and which may be defined as procedure required by statute in state education departments in Australia, or the social structure of particular schools.

Teacher attitudes/values — those traits, expressed opinions and dispositions which are reported on

	as being evident in teaching duties in classrooms and which are described as related to the occupational context of teaching.
Teacher expectations/needs	those prerequisites of a personal and professional role-policy kind that are deemed crucial to the attainment of satisfaction in teaching.
Pupil attitudes/values	those traits, expressed opinions and dispositions which are reported on as being evident in the general demeanour of pupils while on school premises and which are regarded as a function of school membership.
Pupil expectations/needs	those features of school life that both foster and impede the development of a positive self-concept and propensity to action in school.
Community expectations/ needs	those perceptions, opinions and aspirations that the community holds for the formal purposes of schooling, especially relating to concepts of sound morality and public service.
Authority in school	those mechanisms of a formal and informal kind that are established to confer legitimacy upon the holders of particular offices such as Deputy Principal and Form Captain.
Classroom controls	those sanctions of a positive and negative kind that are used to induce conformity amongst members of school populations.
School effects	the consequences of prolonged involvement in schooling for individuals especially in terms of achievement for pupils and career mobility for teachers.

Senior school	the policies, practices and demography of Years 10, 11 and 12 pupils and their teachers in Queensland and Australian state high schools.
School decision-making	those formal and informal procedures that generate and activate policy in schools, with special reference to the prefectorial systems of pupils, and the classified position/promotional system of teachers employed by state governments in Australia.

Structure, Sequence, Timetable and Related Matters

From reading the above, you will note that we believe with any piece of recorded research, PBE or otherwise, an *outline structure* both at the planning stage and during the active conduct of the enquiry is highly desirable. That is not to say the planning template will not change. Of course it will, as modifications and forced choices assert themselves. That is the reality of researching in the real world. The rigorous academic template should not, however, be thought of as an intellectual straitjacket. It should be thought of as a resource to be used and energized. A plan may be a variation on the academic theme; equally it may be creatively unique to the particulars of the project. It will be important to keep in view: purposes, rationale, techniques, and to improve your understanding of these as the project develops. The good researcher gets better at telling the story each time it is told. As understanding of both enquiry process and substantive topic develops, so it will become easier to impose order on data and the depiction of the processes producing the data. Ideas will gradually stabilize, information will be grouped and categorized, linkages between data and explanation will become more obvious. By the time it is necessary to write the final report, the overall pattern of the enquiry should be clear.

Crucial to patterning is *time*. The contemporary world is a very busy place. Many people who undertake PBE are working full-time for a living. They also have family commitments and myriad other interests. It is therefore useful, indeed imperative, to break up the research enquiry into projected stages and to plan time segments for the realistic completion of these stages. This is particularly true for fieldwork and for time-intensive activities such as interviewing. As we have defined PBE as *system-based enquiry*, it is important to acknowledge that enquiries in system settings may well require formal permission for access. This is especially true of schools, teaching hospitals and armed forces operational bases. Having a well-structured plan will facilitate access to such venues and will most likely ensure time is well spent once inside. If your design is 'loose', you will probably find that people and venues are less accommodating. Similarly, you will find it difficult to keep to a personal timetable. The time-frame, like the expressed purpose of the project, should reflect the professional commitments of the targeted respondents. When such respondents see that demands on their time have been realistically accounted for, and that the project is meaningful to their activities, then they will be most likely to confer *legitimacy* upon it.

The planned staging of an enquiry ought to remain under the intellectual and procedural control of the practitioner-researcher. When an enquiry is to be conducted wholly or in part at the request of a host institution, it is important for the enquiry not to be seen as a tool of the management of that institution. 'Fitting-in' means adjustment to the demands of the system venue. Planning ought to include time to manage the distinction between what is formally required by way of permission for access, and what is required by way of presentation of self once on the inside of a system venue. People in the venue, potential respondents, may not have been party to the act of permission-giving. Time must be given to an assessment of the nuances in the venue, any sensitivities and, if possible, opportunities for group discussion with individuals likely to be involved. Encounters with sensitive matters and timetabling difficulties should always be met with *adjustments to the plan* and not to the personal work circumstances of the respondents.

As a practitioner conducting research, you have certain advantages over other researchers. Teachers have access to classrooms and other teachers. Technical trainers have access to the automotive workshop and apprentices. Healthcare personnel have access and exposure to patients and ancillary workers. The practitioner already has a lot of cultural knowledge both about the system venue and about its inhabitants. 'Outsiders' would take a long time to acquire such privileged information. All this can be thought through and appropriated in terms of a meaningful *time-frame* and data-collecting period. Other advantages to be taken note of include: short travelling distances to venues; *known formal politics* of the system venue, plus common-sense understandings of institutional 'short-cuts' and ways of getting things done; knowledge of peers and their relationship to you and each other; and the resource and facilities base in the venue. In respect of this latter, it is important, for example, to know of (and to book ahead if required) quiet rooms where interviews may be conducted.

There are also certain disadvantages to the role of practitioner-researcher which may have negative consequences for time and forward planning. The roles of both researcher and colleague may be hard to sustain leading to *credibility* problems. Interviewing people of higher occupational status always invokes questions of power and authority which may get in the way. It is usually important with such people to acknowledge their status but to emphasize the importance of the *vantage point* this status confers on the objects of the enquiry. Similarly, it may be necessary to explain to the status-role incumbent how he or she may profit from the findings of the research.

The collection of sensitive and confidential information may well require elaborate 'fail-safe' security mechanisms for the protection of such data. It may well be difficult to maintain an objective stance in relation to operational matters, particularly where policy has an impact on the practitioner side of your own conduct. Finally, it is quite likely that you will make numerous mistakes during the enquiry. In PBE these are often highly visible and embarrassing and will reverberate in consequential terms long after the research is finished, written about, reported on. It often comes about in 'insider' research that people forget what they have agreed to informally as well as formally. This can lead to damaged expectations and bruised egos. Planning, therefore, is all about minimizing these very human contingencies. Formal agreements help to remind all concerned of the operating conditions of an enquiry. There will be a need, though, for informal negotiation and exchange of trust. Consent forms of various kinds, but especially when working with young people in schools under the age of 16, may well be part of the planning schedule here. In the event of constraints and problems becoming too great while in a system venue, the option of complete withdrawal and termination of the project should always be available.

We cannot emphasize enough the importance of human variation and response in practitioner research. Whether you intend to carry out fieldwork in person, to conduct surveys at a distance by post, employ research assistants to conduct interviews, or to observe practices in system venues unobtrusively, it is important to plan fully and to anticipate contingencies. There is no substitute for politeness and mutuality in active cooperative behaviour. Do not waste people's precious time, do not abuse hospitality, and do not engage in interpersonal negativity or institutional *micropolitics*. Keep people as informed as possible about the enquiry as it progresses through its stages and keep the practical potential of the findings in the view of the respondents. An early commitment should be the promise to make available the final report.

Active and Proactive Behaviour in Planning for PBE

The practical preparations that we have sketched out above are fairly commonplace with regard to planning educational research. There are additional planning considerations that may be thought of as unique to PBE. These particularly evoke the ideas of *cooperation* and *networking*.

1 Avoidance of isolation in research work

It is important not to become too physically isolated or intellectually privatized in PBE research work. Ask the question: Is there anyone in my institution or the wider community likely to have done similar work? If the answer is yes, then it makes sense to try to get in touch with such people and to benefit from their understandings. Similarly, there may be people who can help with technical matters such as the statistical analysis of data. In a university or college environment it is imperative to maintain an active relationship with a designated personal tutor – two (or twenty) heads may be better than one. Ask around, particularly in departments with similar subject leanings. It is worth remembering that research usually ends up being tested in the 'court of public opinion' in some way. Thus, even though study preferences may be towards the individual and the solitary, having a public dimension to the project will most likely be valuable in the medium term.

2 Ethical clearances and negotiating access

We referred to the matter of ethics in terms of first principles in Chapter 2. Professional associations and certain institutions often have formal statements of ethics and sets of non-negotiable procedures that must be followed by all researchers working within a particular field. In health and education especially it is often necessary to negotiate or take a planning proposal through an ethics committee. Contact significant others, therefore, with a view to using their organizational and cultural knowledge to ease access, to circumvent 'gatekeepers' (a term used mainly by social scientists to describe those people, often official role holders in positions of power and authority, whose support must be won before access to a research venue can be gained), and to extend your familiarization with custom and practice in the institution to which the research plan is directed.

3 Group sharing and technical division of labour

Research is a complex process. It often involves careful allocation of resources and a precise division of labour. Where research assistants are to be employed, research functions shared and sums of money distributed for goods and services, the procedures for these should be written down, agreed and efficiently costed in terms of time and overall budget allocations. Everyone involved in a project should know their responsibilities and the resources which they may call upon. In the case of paid interviewers and secretarial support, these matters are particularly valid.

4 Practise the method you preach

Social processes are crucial to the success of most PBE research. The conduct of PBE, its modelling of a set of interactive relations between people, is often thought of as just as important as the formal results of the enquiry. In that sense *process* is as important as *product*. Indeed, the ultimate users of the research may well be more interested in how the project was conducted than what was actually found out. If the research aims to further participation, collaboration and democracy, then these elements ought to be built into the plan. If the research is about experiential learning, then there ought to be experiential gains made by the researcher.

5 Make use of committee structures

Formal institutions usually have committees of governance and for teaching-learning. The published minutes of such committees can be a useful source of information for researchers. In the practical sense, advice and endorsement may also be sought from such committees. Higher degree research projects are often controlled in a university environment by an influential Research Higher Degrees Committee or a Graduate School. If a researcher wishes a project to be endorsed as part of the research portfolio of a university, as well as in part fulfilment of requirements for academic certification, then the support of such committees is vital. Publication matters to do with copyright and intellectual property rights (IPR), and adjudication rules on 'ownership' of materials produced within the 'gift' of a university, are also usually within the remit of such committees. As with ethical clearances, it is sometimes necessary to gain formal endorsement of a plan or proposal, particularly where funding is sought. The Economic and Social Research Council requires institutions to endorse all applications formally under the competitive Research Grants Scheme. This attestation of an application is usually done via the imprint of the university seal or other official declaration mark to Section 26 of the Application Form.

6 Multi-agency approaches

More and more, in this day and age, research is collaborative and multi-agency in character. This reflects the growing recognition of the interdisciplinary character of educational problems. It also reflects the wider collective interest in the solution to such problems. Educational researchers for example, work closely with schools, LEAs, charitable foundations and government departments such as Social Services. Where multi-agency involvement in educational enquiries is present, this will probably involve 'leg-work', phone calls, visits, lobbying council members, writing lots of letters and generally 'putting yourself about'.

7 *Memorandums of agreement*

Memorandums of agreement are formal letters signed by a researcher and any third party or potential partner to a research enquiry. These letters are usually written for situations where the primary researcher asks the partner or third party to conduct some activity on his or her behalf. For example, a set of direct interviews may be contracted out to a market research agency. Alternatively, a university archives unit may be engaged to survey its records and provide a detailed and annotated bibliography on a research topic. Where an institution and its members are subject to an enquiry, for example, teachers in a secondary school or nurses and ancillaries in an Accident & Emergency ward in a hospital, it may be critically important for the researcher to have secured agreement with the responsible officer in that institution concerning the obligations and responsibilities of all parties connected to the enquiry. More formalized and networking partnerships can also be established through memorandums of agreement. These are potentially a source of law rather than having the force of law. They are somewhat stronger than the 'gentleman's agreement' of yesterday, and function as a means to clarify expectations, control unrealistic demands on both the researcher and the target institution or system venue, and also act as an aide-mémoire when 'fuzziness' sets in as the research process develops.

8 *Publication of a technical prospectus*

When a plan or proposal has developed to the point where it contains abundant detail, a concise educational rationale, an explicit statement of data-gathering techniques and a list of likely outcomes, it may be usefully re-presented as a *technical prospectus*. This requires some attention to typeface, the use of colour and graphics, and visual appearance. Technical prospectuses give credibility to research work. They help to professionalize the enquiry process. Such documents can be printed up in user-friendly form and distributed to a wide range of potential users and third parties. The prospectus may not only inform 'sponsors', but also contain invitations to participate in a variety of ways. For example, an open forum or a public launch of a project might well draw in likely participants.

9 *Practitioner contexts*

A further point to those contained in item 8 above is that a prospectus is above all a document of *conviction*. People, especially managers and the aforementioned 'gatekeepers', tend to become interested in practitioner research if they can see and be convinced of its practical merits. They are not attracted to the arbitrary mailed questionnaire that lands on their desk on a Monday morning. To do effective research in what Robson (1995) calls the 'real world', it is necessary to engage in a battle to win hearts and minds. Gaining and sustaining interest and involvement in a research project by third parties is crucial in PBE. It is important, therefore, that the managers of the practitioner contexts in which the research is to be conducted should be able to perceive the potential value of the enquiry. That is, they should be able to judge its worth on the basis of what is required from their standpoint as managers. The managerial perspective is often quite different from that of the researchers. Energy has to be devoted consistently to this aspect of the research enterprise.

10 Influencing policy through cooperation

We have said elsewhere that the first and primary user of practitioner research is the practitioner. *Ambition* though, should be a further quality characterizing PBE. Many research projects provide detailed lists of recommendations for a policy the only function of which is to gather dust on a shelf somewhere. As part of the methodological and planning posture, ideas for cooperation and networking are possibly the best means to influence policy right from the outset. Tacit intervention in policy formulation and decision-making is possible through consciously planned cooperative approaches. In educational research focusing on classroom interaction, for example, participant observers are often welcome in classrooms (by professionally secure teachers and tutors at any rate) for they provide an additional perspective on the processes of teaching and learning that is valuable to the regular classroom teacher.

We have now identified many of the planning steps in the conduct of practitioner-based enquiry. In the example that follows we offer a model or characterization of a planned project that uses many, but not all, of these steps. The model may be thought of as a substantively 'fleshed' version of the template presented. Readers may well wish to base their own PBE plans on this model.

Model of a Planned PBE Project

Title: The Use of Learning Contracts in Pre-Registration Nurse Education Courses

Research questions: Expressing the purposes of the enquiry

What is the character of learning contracts?
What is the purpose of learning contracts?
What evidence exists to show that learning contracts facilitate knowledge and skill acquisition?

In what ways is the nurse education environment conducive to the use of learning contracts?

Introductory remarks and rationale

This research proposal represents the specification of an enquiry into the use of learning contracts in pre-registration nurse education. Learning contracts are signed agreements between tutors and students. They are widely used as both instructional and assessment devices in higher education programmes in the United States. Their application to nurse education is popular but recent. The contracts guarantee a percentage mark or assessed letter grade (A, B, C, D or E) for a fixed amount of study and assignment work completed to a standard indicated by published criteria. The primary justification for learning contracts is that they place responsibility on the learner, routinize grade allocation, ensure minimum throughput of professional and academic work and permit discretion in the selection of topics for assignments. In pre-registration nurse education courses, contracts are particularly useful for non-clinical topics such as patient–nurse relationships, aspects of public health policy, psychological factors in skill acquisition and the legal rights of patients. It is hoped that that this research, when completed, will verify the educational claims made for learning contracts in a specific institutional setting.

Delimitations

The research proposal does not extend to encompass criticisms of the educational validity of learning contracts. Similarly, the proposal refers to an enquiry that is focused exclusively on a group of 16 first-year student nurses allocated to a large teaching hospital in an urban area.

Provisional contents list for the final report

- Introduction: learning contracts in nurse education practice.
- Rationale: the educational justification of learning contracts.
- Purposes: research questions (see above).
- Reviewing the Literature: analysing selected references on learning contract usage in pre-registration nurse education in the UK (1980–99). This historical period is interesting for it has witnessed

major change to initial nurse training in the UK. Established, largely clinical, models of education based in teaching hospitals were augmented (and sometimes replaced) by reflective practitioner models of nurse education relocated to university departments of health and medical studies. Particular emphasis was given to nurse education via a curriculum movement known as 'Project 2000' (see UKCC 1986). Statements to the press and ministerial pronouncements in early 1999 have suggested a growing dissatisfaction with academic models of nurse training.

- Methodological Context of the Enquiry: specifying a sample of nurses using learning contracts. Identifying two forms of data gathering, content analysis of documents and directed interviews.
- Data Collection and Analysis: time-frame for the collection and analysis of data; explanation and conduct of ethical clearance procedures; theoretical framework for data analysis; tabulation and explanation of results; conclusions; recommendations for policy.
- Concluding Remarks: in which the efficacy of learning contracts in the target institution is commented upon; also to include brief but warranted commentary on the general utility of learning contracts in professional practice.
- List of References: see below for an indicative listing.
- Appendices: to include copy of the interview schedule, extracts from completed transcripts, one fully completed interview transcript by way of illustration, the list of documents treated to content analysis.

An abbreviated reference list for the exemplar topic

Boud, D., Keogh, R. and Walker, D. (eds) (1985) *Reflection: Turning Experience into Learning*, London: Kogan Page.

Brophy, J.E. and Good, T. (1986) 'Teacher behaviour and student achievement', in M.C. Wittrock (ed.) *Handbook of Research on Teaching*, New York: Macmillan, 3rd edn.

Entwistle, N. (1985) *New Directions in Educational Psychology: Volume I. Teaching and Learning*, London: Falmer.

Knowles, M.S. (1986) *Using Learning Contracts: Practical Approaches to Individualizing and Structuring Learning*, San Francisco: Jossey Bass.

Lwanga, S.K. and Cho Yook, T. (1990) *Teaching Health Statistics: 20 Lessons and Seminar Outlines*, Geneva: World Health Organization.

Polit, D. and Hungler, R. (1989) *The Essentials of Nursing Research*, Philadelphia: Lippincott, 2nd edn.

Reed, J. and Proctor, S. (eds) (1993) *Nurse Education: A Reflective Approach*, London: Edward Arnold.

An example of an annotation of an item in the reference list

Bennett, J. and Kingham, M. (1993) 'Learning diaries,' in J. Reed and S. Proctor (eds) *Nurse Education: A Reflective Approach*, London: Edward Arnold.

This article is in a book primarily concerned with student-centred approaches to nurse education. As the title implies, the article examines the practical value of diaries kept by student nurses. The possibility of incorporating these diaries into learning contract arrangements and other assessment devices is explored. A template for the organization of a diary is provided. It lists the following seven subsections for recording information in the diary: introduction; diary purposes; overview of clinical or community environment; care in action; analysis of care; technical bibliography; additional clinical and professional notes. The learning principles underpinning the diary are adapted from other published work on experiential learning.

Outline Methodological Orientation

Data-gathering technique (1)

Content analysis of six (6) key documents located through Medline and British Education Index databases. Content analysis is particularly useful to projects defined by, or in some way, dependent upon formal documents. In this case documents such as *Project 2000: A New Preparation for Practice*, act as a crucial repository of data for the enquiry. The functions of the content analysis technique are: it enables orderly classification of documents; it permits terminology and concepts associated with the core construct of 'learning contracts' to be interrogated and understood; it establishes a lexicon of terms that give direction and boundary to the enquiry; it broadens the researcher's categorical knowledge of the topic under study; it defines the epistemological basis of 'learning contracts'.

Content analysis amplification

In a more generic sense *content analysis* is a process which permits documentary evidence to be read, analysed and classified in forms suitable to the purposes of the enquiry. There are several different ways of conducting content analyses. The simplest form of content analysis is to read a document more than once and make notes. A technically more sophisticated means, one inferred in this exemplar proposal, is to apply keyword indicators to documents identified as vital to the literature base of the enquiry. The keywords may arise during general reading for a research project. More likely, they will be pre-known and embedded in the research purposes as in this example. Thus, Research Question 1: What is the character of learning contracts? – sets up some indices for the content analysis. 'Learning contracts' will need to be examined as both a general and a specific idea. The understanding of the term may be encapsulated in a *formal definition*, which is able to be expressed in the rationale for the enquiry. Further examination of documents on learning contracts may point up the need for a more discrete *operational definition* of the term, a definition that takes account of learning contracts *in use* by the sample population. Note though that the content analysis here is a stage point on the way to somewhere else. As meaning and usage of terms and phrases for a context become more explicit, they can be further interrogated by other means. Thus a directed interview may draw the substance of its questions from a content analysis.

Data-gathering technique (2)

Directed interviews with six (6) student nurses are drawn from the enrolment cohort of 16. These will be voluntary participants. The directed interviews will take a maximum of 30 minutes per person. The interview schedule will consist of 12 questions based on information produced in the content analysis phase. The characteristics of this technique are: it permits the investigation of the topic of learning contracts in depth; the direct experience of the respondent is tapped;

the reliability and validity of information drawn from the content analysis is subjected to further rigorous examination; the face-to-face conditions of the interview provide opportunities to contextualize the purposes of the research and to reduce any ambiguities produced by the questions posed. All interviews will be conducted solely by the practitioner-researcher.

The 'sample'

The sample consists of six volunteers drawn from a small research population of 16 enrolled student nurses. It is presumed that they would all have direct experience of 'learning contracts' in their training. The sample may be described as an *opportunity sample* – i.e. fitting the measurement requirements of the research purpose, available in situ and willing to cooperate. The nurses represent larger groups towards whom the research questions are ultimately directed. However, caution must be exercised in any extrapolations to wider populations of student nurses.

Framework for data analysis

In the content analysis, each document selected will be retrieved in full through library stocks or inter-library loan after identification via the databases. Each document will be read, annotated and ten keywords associated with the core construct of 'learning contracts' will be identified. The frequency of appearance of these keywords, either directly or idiomatically, in each document will be noted. A concise but holistic interpretation of 'learning contracts' will be derived from this activity.

In the directed interview phase, each interview (with permission) will be tape recorded and transcribed in full without editing. The information in the interview transcripts will be compared with the key descriptors derived from the content analysis. An analytical report, using selected but verbatim statements from the interview transcripts, will be compiled to illustrate the use of learning contracts in the student experience.

Concluding remarks

In the *concluding remarks* section of the final report the synthesis of the data produced will be undertaken to provide direct answers to the research questions originally posed.

Indicative time-frame (approximately 8–12 weeks or one semester)

- One week on preliminary theorizations. Two days in academic libraries accessing Medline and the British Education Index. A further two weeks to locate and summarize the documents.
- Two weeks deriving and preparing the interview schedules. Limited 'piloting'.
- One week writing letters, seeking permissions, identifying respondents.
- One week allocated to six 30-minute interviews in an appropriate location.
- Two to three weeks analysing the data, writing the final report, and dealing with last minute 'hitches'.

The model above should be useful in envisaging the totality of the PBE planning process. It has to be remembered though that it is a model, a necessarily simplified characterization of the complexities underpinning the research process. The model, however simple, is an illustration of *research design*, a plan to provide answers to research questions, to control variance, to make explicit the features of the research enquiry, to bring an element of reliability and validity into any measures used, and to direct inference making, conclusion reaching, and decision-taking. For one eminent authority:

> research design is the plan and structure of an investigation so conceived as to obtain answers to research questions. The plan is the overall scheme or program of the research. It includes an outline of what the investigator will do from writing the hypotheses and their operational implications to the final analysis of data...A structure is the framework, organization, or configuration of elements of the structure related in specified ways.
>
> (Kerlinger, 1986, p. 279)

In Chapter 4 we will move forward from planning PBE to a more detailed consideration of research design. A subsequent, more detailed 'second stage', if you like, about the conceptual, methodological and substantive features of practitioner research. We will try to illustrate some of the intellectual tensions surrounding even the more simple research designs, and how some of these tensions, especially those in the minds of the practitioner-researcher may be assuaged by attending to the ideas base of the enquiry.

4 'Ologies and Analogies
Tuning the Mind to Research Design

The design of any particular PBE, like research projects in general, is shaped and conditioned by the nature of the research problem and questions and hypotheses that are to be addressed. It is because of this that 'design' is not a foregone conclusion. Taking the 'problem', the 'purposes' and the 'research questions' as the point of departure mitigates against the a priori application of a favoured methodology or design brief that appears to fit the context of the PBE. There will, of course, be situations where PBEs are particularly amenable to treatment through 'off the shelf' and established data-gathering models and research designs. It is always tempting to construe or filter a PBE outwards through the respectable maxims of social science disciplines. This has its advantages. It is possible to utilize the conceptual tools developed as part of disciplinary structures to illuminate the ideas base of the PBE. The sociological concepts of 'norms' and 'statuses' may be activated in the analysis of the organizational structure of hospitals. Similarly, the psychological concepts of 'attitude' and 'personality' may be activated in the analysis of the decision-making behaviour of police trainers. However, there is also the potential immanent in social and behavioural science disciplines to intellectually constrain an enquiry, to limit its conceptual horizons, and (possibly) create somewhat stereotypical operating conditions for the practice of data gathering. In PBE we try to avoid stereotyping research design. We are particularly concerned that PBEs, following a certain television commercial, are not 'ology led. We are not saying here that a particular methodology is taboo. Rather, we are guarding against the presumption that social and behavioural sciences are the necessary and sufficient starting points for enquiries. Under certain conditions they may well be; under other conditions they will not be appropriate. A thoughtful methodology for a PBE ought to be a servant of that enquiry.

Research Design and Analogy

The questions or tentative hypotheses of a particular PBE may be thought of as a 'bee in a bonnet' or an 'itch' that the practitioner researcher needs to scratch. First, we should ask where these itches come from. Are they part of a common rash currently afflicting a certain group of people? Are they part of a wider epidemic? Are they a unique bodily ailment only amenable to self-administered medication? They clearly do not come from heaven. Neither it seems are they innate in the brain. Their defining feature is that they emanate from practice. Further, some 'itches' are given by, for example, managers, colleagues, institutional structures, politicians and professional bodies. Recurrent low examination grades in A-level mathematics courses, absenteeism in the workplace, effects on morale caused by redeployment and 'outsourcing' are all examples of 'given itches'. These things have an obviousness. They are frequently concerned with institutional efficacy and efficiency. They operate on consciousness, shape personal occupational behaviour and are perceived as 'real' by the people experiencing them.

Sometimes, problems may not be 'givens' in the way described above. Rather, they may be 'made' by the practitioner. They are made in the sense that they do not possess the immediate obviousness of the 'given' and are often uncovered through questioning the interpretations of practice, either taken for granted by others (especially official superiors) or, perhaps, written up in rule books and job specifications. Here, the practitioner by virtue of being personally challenged on a daily basis in his or her educational situation or workplace, digs beneath the surface to find the reasons for things. 'Made' problems often have micropolitical, industrial and critical undertones. This is particularly likely to be so where power relationships define the working habits and practices of groups of individuals within the same institution. Where the power is obtrusive and comes to be seen as non-legitimate in the eyes of the practitioners, then a whole range of 'made' problems may begin to crystallize. Our archives suggest this to be so. It is remarkable how many PBEs seem preoccupied with the legitimacy of actions taken by superiors towards subordinates, especially in public sector institutions such as comprehensive schools. Similarly, 'made' problems may arise as a by-product of policies on controversial or sensitive issues upon which there may be no real consensus. The 'isms' of the age fall into this category – racism, sexism, ageism, unionism, and so on. Regardless of whether a PBE problem is 'given' or 'made', attention will have to be given to the alleviation of the 'itch'. That is where 'design' takes over. Some itches will need several medicinal treatments. Some will respond to a single application. Some treatments will be more efficacious than others.

Consider the following example of a simple research design (suggested by and following Kerlinger, 1986, p. 280):

Problem

Private golf clubs apparently discriminate on the basis of gender in enrolling members.

Purpose

To analyse variation in admissions practices of private golf clubs, controlling for 'sex'.

Key construct

Discrimination: (a) Operationally defined as covert selection on the basis of preferred, but not necessarily shared criteria; (b) Formally defined as the practice of acting on the basis of differences between people (Concise Oxford Dictionary).

Sample

Two hundred golf clubs are randomly selected across the UK. These are sent postal applications for membership, half from men, half from women. The applications contain information derived from model cases on a wide range of criteria known to interest golf clubs. These include age, occupation, gender, income, place of education, credit rating, recreational preferences, etc.

Hypothesis

There will be equal numbers of acceptances and rejections for each sex.

Dependent variable

This is 'acceptance', and it may be measured by reference to the number of full acceptances, the number of partial or qualified acceptances and the number of outright rejections.

Treatment matrix

The treatment procedure is as follows:

(a) Each golf club receives a single application for membership, either male or female. Mean acceptance scores (MAS) are then computed for the sub-groups 'male' and 'female'.

(b) The difference between the mean scores for the sub-groups MAS(M) and MAS(F) is tested for statistical significance (i.e. a suitable inferential statistical procedure such as Student's *t*-test is applied to the scores to detect any results patterning that has greater probability of occurrence than by chance alone). The substantive measurement hypothesis is: MAS(M) > MAS(F), or more males than females will be accepted for admission.

(c) If the pattern of results fails to reveal any statistically significant variation based on gender, then MAS(M) = MAS(F) in a statistical sense. The failure of an inferential statistic to reveal a significant difference between the two sub-groups suggests two supplementary research questions: Was the selected statistical test sufficiently robust, and were its probability and arithmetic assumptions met? Can we be sure that there is no discrimination in the selection of applicants for membership? If we cannot be sure, then the research design is not strong enough. If, on the other hand, the statistical test does show that the mean difference is statistically significant, then the previous operational definition of 'discrimination' is verified. That is, in this enquiry 'discrimination' in application for membership of golf clubs occurs on the basis of gender. The 'direction' of the discrimination, in favour of males or females, will of course be suggested by proportionality in the results, where equally qualified female acceptances fail to match male acceptances (or vice versa). In this scenario, the connection between purpose, construct, measurement hypothesis and statistical results suggests that the research design of the study is simple but robust.

A research design such as the one above would also benefit from a theoretical discussion, based on an extensive review of the literature of the meaning and character of 'discrimination' as variously reported in private employment, club and association membership, and in public sector agencies. Similarly, the orientation of the researcher towards the research problem, and the sense of it as 'made' or 'given', might push the enquiry in the direction of more formal theoretical explanation or allocation of the construct of discrimination to a parent perspective or paradigm, such as conflict-structuralism within the discipline of sociology.

In this simple example, an apposite research methodology for a PBE has not been selected off the shelf in a DIY research supermarket in random fashion. Rather the use of established statistical techniques reflects constrained choice. That choice is conditioned by the nature of the research problem, by the context of the research (i.e. the invocation of ideas of equality between the sexes in late twentieth-century affluent societies), by what the literature suggests, and by what the researcher is particularly interested in (i.e. golf club membership).

Research Design and Knowledge Criteria

Perhaps one of the most disturbing trends in educational research in recent years has been the tendency towards the denial of 'itches', particularly those felt by schoolteachers. More formally, the pragmatic concerns of professional educators have not been given sufficient attention by the admittedly 'broad church' of the community of educational researchers, ranging from groups of university experts working on large funded projects to individuals working in isolation. Official criticism of this default tendency grew in stridency in the period 1996–8. It culminated in the commissioning in 1998 by the DFEE of a 'Review of Educational Research' by the Institute of Employment Studies (IES) at the University of Sussex. We are not surprised by increasing disquiet over the character, direction and effectiveness of educational research. It is our contention that the 'divided mentality' to which we earlier referred is implicated in this problem. This is because despite appeals to the contrary, the divided mentality or paradigm argument leads to an either/or position. Research methods textbooks and training courses in educational research increasingly come from the standpoint of, what we called in Chapter 2, interpretive science. Sometimes these books and courses take on an alarming evangelization that causes the discerning reader to question the underlying integrity of what is presented. Arguments and epistemological principles are touted as if they are self-evidently true. Clearly, ideological positions are sold as orthodoxies to which all must conform. Not to do so, the tacit message implies, is to risk a kind of intellectual exclusion from the research club that matters.

Ideological jousts, epistemological conflicts, power plays over words associated with Foucault's 'Regimes of Truth' can prove sterile in the genuine practitioner-researcher's search for adequate research designs. In the case of large-scale funded research, effort may be deflected towards second-guessing the epistemological and ontological predilections of fund holders, proposal committees, and the like. This can act to compromise research design and deflect research directions. Research projects which derive from an epistemological standpoint, be it psychometry, ethnomethodology or structural Marxism, make a number of fundamental assumptions about knowledge and the natural and social worlds. Technically speaking, this is 'blinkered' research, not because of what it includes and its ways of seeing, but because of what it systematically excludes and does not see because it is ruled out of court by epistemological presuppositions.

Consider the following summary which outlines, in sociological speak, the classic *consensus-structuralist* perspective on the character of society. While this theoretical schema was worked out by its advocates a long time ago, its resonance with the Thatcherite revolution of the 1980s, and the economic basis of social organization in the 1990s, is clear for all to see. Its cleverly formulated assumptions, almost *lawlike* in their assertiveness, are undoubtedly plausible. Does that make them right? Does the plausibility provide a necessary and exclusive basis for explanation? We think not.

Summary characteristics of the consensus-structuralist perspective

1 Society strives to attain conditions of order, stability and integration.
2 Every society is faced with the same fundamental survival and adaptation problems.
3 Systems of norms, values and sanctions play a crucial part in the integration of social systems.
4 The institutional arrangements of society, including work organization, reflect the necessity for coordination and also demonstrate the interdependence of parts of the social system.
5 Social stratification and the division of labour is necessary, inevitable and ubiquitous.

Associated names:

Emile Durkheim (1858–1917)
Augusté Comte (1798–1857)
Herbert Spencer (1820–1903)

Consider the second, comparative summary, a classic *conflict*-stucturalist explanation for the organization of social life. While coming from the same parent discipline (sociology) as the consensus perspective, the basis of explanation is different and conceptually irreconcilable with that perspective.

Summary characteristics of the conflict-structuralist perspective

1 Normal conditions in society and its social institutions approximate to change, turmoil, competition, instability and conflict. People have many different value systems.

---

2   Social arrangements, including work arrangements, reflect the competition to obtain society's rewards and resources.

3   Coercion, formal authority and the use of political and legal-rational power are characteristic social controls designed to induce acquiescence and conformity among citizens, institutional members and employees in work organizations. It is through these sanctions that rewards are distributed.

4   Divisions of labour are potentially undemocratic, perpetuate unequal access to society's goods and resources and contribute to the maintenance of a social stratification system that is divisive.

Associated names:

Thomas Hobbes (1588–1679)
Karl Marx (1818–83)
Max Weber (1864–1920)

The obvious question then is: Can the researcher have/should have more than one explanation in the research enquiry? The reality is that there could probably be several adequate theoretical explanations. In our conceptualization of PBE, practical system-based realities will always modify explanations emanating from 'Regimes of Truth'. In establishing a knowledge base to, and an explanatory framework (theory) for, PBE within a research design, limitations set by reality must be understood and incorporated.

Our argument does however beg a few questions, as we readily admit. After the identification of contexts, resource constraints, ethical matters and other working conditions for an enquiry, there is still the question: What knowledge-related criteria should be taken into account in the enquiry? The question might be usefully phrased in another way: What 'ways of seeing' are needed by this enquiry? By 'ways of seeing' we are not referring to the explicit location of a research project within a disciplinary perspective, paradigm or school of thought. Nor are we referring to the studied development of analytical concepts and formal theories. Our position on 'ways of seeing' is somewhat simpler. Occupational contexts and teaching-learning practices are multifaceted. 'Ways of seeing' suggest knowing about facets. The design task, and subsequent conduct in the empirical setting then requires knowledge-facilitating techniques; devices which will allow the researcher to examine facets differentially.

Consider the example, a real one, of a large science department in an 11–18 comprehensive school in the south of England. The department in question is wholly located in a wing of the school building. Six laboratory classrooms cluster starlike around a central staff room. The staff room has large observation windows into each laboratory. The particular department has satisfactory examination results records in GCSE science, but has a reputation in the school of being somewhat 'difficult' in respect of accepting general principles for school organization. This is a recurrent problem for the principal. Anecdotally, he is aware that the science department is said to have a 'mind and a will of its own'. As the principal is chief executive, he is concerned that this orientation should not work against the collective interest of the school. To learn more about the orientation of the science department, information is needed that is stronger than anecdote. The 'facets' involved include: informal meetings of science staff in the shared staff room at break times; the unusually public revelation of teaching activity (sometimes including six teachers at once) afforded by the presence of the windows; the opportunity that the windows present to the head of the science department for routine 'surveillance' of her colleagues' classroom activity; the diversity of science activity taking place by year group, sets and syllabus orientation in each classroom laboratory; the number of free periods enjoyed by individual staff members indicated by presence in the staff room during timetabled periods. No doubt there are additional facets, but the studied analysis of those identified could and should enable the principal (wearing the hat of practitioner-researcher) to understand better and to explain the mindset of the science department. Techniques available in this circumstance include the unusually fertile opportunity for direct observation of teaching activity 'once removed' – i.e. not in the actual classroom and thereby reducing the contamination of data by physical presence. Other possibilities for knowing facets include staff room discussions about commonly shared classroom management problems. The problems may have been directly witnessed and the opportunity to conduct informal interviews with the involved staff member may be occasioned by subsequent free periods.

Explanation as a Feature of the Design Process

The facets of the example provided above show that research design is necessarily dynamic and flexible. 'Ways of seeing' suggests an approach to understanding which is a bit more subtle, and probably messier than the testing or application of formal theories to situations such as the one described above. How might the principal come to 'know' his science department? Robson (1995, p. 42) has provided a useful model for classifying the purposes of enquiries. He suggests that these can be classified according to whether they are exploratory, descriptive or explanatory. Our principal is faced with all three possibilities. Like an explorer he may seek to discover something. He should enter the science department's domain with (ideally) no preconceptions and no predetermined questions other than: What is going on here? There is also the need for self-consciousness about his role and experience as principal. The attributes required for this role suggest an immersion in a certain category of occupational culture that, despite being linked by the commonality of teaching and learning, is somewhat removed from the daily cut and thrust of the science department. The social situation of the science department therefore is such that the principal should try to minimize 'seeing' it through the cultural spectacles that his position infers he wears. Ideally, from an explanatory standpoint, the situation should be explored by reference to the world of the science department, perhaps a small world, as experienced by its inhabitants. This necessarily means entering the realm of description, seeing and describing what the inhabitants do on a daily basis. Exploration and description may well go hand-in-hand with tentative attempts at explanation. This may be particularly the case if the principal wishes to 'know it like it is'. He may wish to respect the relative autonomy of teachers by not probing too deeply beneath the surface. But what if the anecdotal evidence that the department is 'difficult' begins to accumulate? What if this evidence further points in the direction of dysfunctionality in the science department in some way? This cannot be ignored. The principal may therefore need to investigate causes, perhaps in order to predict irregularities in staff behaviour. Here the principal as researcher is beginning to operate in a more direct explanatory mode. Formal explanations for events and social phenomena tend to move beyond, but sometimes via the exploratory and the descriptive to investigate cause and effect. This may be especially so where cause and effect is not necessarily acknowledged by the subjects at the centre of an enquiry, in this case the teachers in a science department. Indeed, a common source of strain in staff relationships in schools is that which arises out of the separate perspectives of subject departments, their competition for resources, and the power relationships they contest with the senior management team (SMT). Once an example of the type outlined here becomes part of a class of similar examples, then 'explanation' too becomes part of a class of explanation which may eventually turn into formal theoretical explanation.

In the more general sense, 'explanation' is the indicator of those processes trying to construe knowledge criteria in research design. The established concepts of social and behavioural science, social class, extraversion, anxiety, self concept, and so on have developed historically out of the requirement for explanation. Such ideas gradually acquire a dual character. They remain as 'variables' to be allocated certain properties which can be recurrently measured in a variety of social and empirical contexts. Social class, for example, can be allocated the measurement criteria of 'breadwinners occupation', 'place of residence' and 'length of education'. Such ideas also retain an explanatory capacity or knowledge-transmission function. Thus, social class connotes the allocation of certain groups of people to certain strata in society on the basis of understood criteria.

In the conduct of PBE, exploration, description and explanation are different ways of seeing and judging complex interactions and patterns in teaching/learning environments. In a variety of ways these three processes take shape and form in established data-gathering techniques. One such technique is ethnographic data gathering. As we have stated, classical anthropologists undertook prolonged observations of cultural, often tribal, groups living in remote locations such as the Trobriand Islands. The geographical separation of such places from industrialized Western countries meant that in the nineteenth century these groups retained a traditional lifestyle largely uncontaminated by influences from the West. Whatever the motives of classical anthropologists in studying such groups, their concern to understand and explain the evolution of culture first required systematic description and documentation of group life. This gave rise to ethnography – which may be defined as the task of describing in detail, a particular culture, subculture, or the subjective social experience of informants. Ethnographic techniques are richly descriptive in character. That is their way of seeing. Later in the chapter we provide an extended example of ethnographic technique: a form of description and explanation based on the ethnographic semantic schemata of Spradley and McCurdy (1972). In this example it will be seen that 'ways of seeing' are not purely confined to the mind. Rather, that the relationship between thought and action is exercised by applying the rules of ethnographic semantics to what Spradley and McCurdy call a 'cultural scene' – cognitively shared information which makes life meaningful for those who share it. Hells Angels, the Antedeluvian Order of Buffaloes and the Women's Institute are all cultural scenes in this sense. Despite our misgivings about action research, it seems probable that that 'way of seeing' is also concerned to achieve some kind of useful conjunction between thought and action. We also suggest here that 'ways of seeing' may in the first instance be largely cerebral. But, an ongoing relationship between research and practice constitutes a 'way of seeing' in itself, a kind of secondary function. To close on this matter, therefore, ways of seeing are not only concerned with action that is informed by research, but also with research that meets the requirements of action.

Consider the following abbreviated example of a PBE entitled 'Stating and Debating: Aspects of the Culture of a Debating Society'. The PBE is actually a composite, drawn from several ethnographically-oriented PBEs conducted on and about debating societies. We want to try and understand the author's conjunction of exploration, description and explanation. We want to know if this PBE is robust enough to support the general claims of ethnography. That it:

- helps facilitate understanding and use of the syntax (concepts) of the social and behavioural sciences;

- develops an enriched appreciation of the nature and significance of culture;
- demands a meaningful basis of communication between the ethnographer and his respondents;
- encourages understanding and tolerance of varied social customs, lifestyles, habits and traditions;
- typically, may result in an increased sensitivity towards, and awareness of, one's own beliefs, values and behavioural orientations.

You be the judge. Read the PBE. Do you now know more about debating? Did the practitioner researcher put his or her thoughts and actions together in useful ways? Are the general claims of ethnography (above) at least in part substantiated by this PBE work?

Example of a Practitioner-Based Enquiry

Ethnography title:

Stating and Debating: Aspects of the Culture of a Debating Society

Author:

A.N. Other: Derived from work submitted in Unit 86208 Sociological Systems Within Schools, School of Education, University of Southern Queensland.

Format

Ethnographic Semantics, see: Spradley, J. P. and McCurdy, D. W. (1972) *The Cultural Experience: Ethnography in Complex Society*, Chicago: SRA.

---

1 Introduction

This practitioner-based enquiry is about aspects of the culture of a debating society. In particular, the debating experience of three members of the society is examined through the technique of ethnographic semantics. Of especial interest is the *evolved and shared culture* of this group. Spradley and McCurdy (1972, p. 7) report that culture is often defined as 'nearly everything that has been learned or produced by a group of people'. However, they object to the generality in this definition. They restrict the meaning of the term *culture* (p. 8) to 'the knowledge people use to generate and interpret social behaviour'. For these authors therefore, an ethnography is the description of a particular culture. The preferred technique of description is *ethnographic semantics* in which informants own utterances, expressions, speech acts and preferred terminology are used to describe their cultural experiences. Where, when and how cultural information is shared by informants is referred to as a *cultural scene*.

2 Fieldwork

The main reason for selecting a debating society as the source of cultural scene(s) is that it is a unique form of *education* for the participants. It is also a fairly mysterious activity, televised parliamentary debates notwithstanding, to most people most of the time. That makes it interesting. Also, I have never witnessed nor participated in debating society activity. For me, as ethnographer, it is therefore virgin territory waiting to be explored.

The informants were two male students (David and Christopher) and a female student (Claire), aged 16 and all in Year 11 at a large state high school in south-eastern Queensland in Australia. The school was *comprehensive* in its curriculum arrangements and catered for the age range 11–18. David is an extroverted character with a particular interest in outdoor pursuits. Christopher is a much more studious and introverted and had been introduced to debating by his father as a means of improving his son's social skills. Claire is tall, dark-haired and quietly spoken. She was described to me by her Year Head as 'scholastically very able' and will 'undoubtedly do very well at university'. David, the youngest of seven children, lives with an older sister as both his parents had divorced and were leading separate lives. I was informed that he was of above average intelligence but inclined to be lazy about schoolwork. Christopher is an only child whose leisure pursuits are almost wholly intellectual in character. Rarely venturing out of the house, he will apparently write page after page of science fiction stories.

I knew Christopher indirectly as his father and I are members of the Rotary service organization. David and Claire I knew only by sight. I arranged to interview the informants at my own home after school. I first obtained parental and guardian permission. The students had previously been *spotlighted* to me by their headmaster when I had expressed an interest in studying a debating group. I should explain that my connections with the school were long-standing. My branch of Rotary frequently sponsors community activities in and around the school. Indeed, the school chapter of the local debating society had come about as a result of Rotary initiatives.

I interviewed each informant individually on two separate occasions. I then conducted a group interview with all three informants. A tape recorder was used for all interviews and the tapes were transcribed. After establishing some rules of confidentiality, the informants seemed quite happy to have their utterances recorded. I had considered taking written notes. After a practice 'dry run' with a friend I abandoned this technique as being impractical and likely to disrupt the spontaneity of the interviews. This decision turned out to be a good one for, when the informants realized how little I knew about debating, their explanations became much more detailed and graphic. The fact that I knew little beforehand of debating procedure meant that I had few *preconceptions* with which to clutter the interviews.

However, the first interview, with Claire, revealed that the group had lost in the first round of the Rotary-sponsored regional youth debating championships. This caused me to consider whether the group had, in Spradley and McCurdy's terms, been together for a sufficiently intensive period to evolve a rich cultural scene. Early remarks from Claire suggested that the group had prepared reasonably well and had come to understand debating culture. Thus encouraged, and in the knowledge that the informants would not/had not been exposed to the more demanding later stages of the debating tournament, I decided to continue.

3 The setting

The essential characteristics for venues for debating tournaments are good acoustics, good lines of sight between debating teams, judging panels and audiences, and good light. Thus much of the practice for the competitive debate was carried out in the school's music room that had these qualities. The school chapter of the regional debating society had 17 members. From this, four teams of three members had self-selected to participate in both practice debating sessions and in a knock- out competition to find a representative team for the regional tournament. Claire, David and Christopher emerged victorious from the practice and in-school knockout competition. The competitive debate for the knock-out finale was organized faithfully to duplicate the practical arrangements for Round 1 of the regional tournament. Tables for the two 'finals' teams were placed on either side of the chairperson's table with *affirmative* being to the right of the chair and *negative* to the left. An official timekeeper sat alongside the chair. In the middle of the room, facing the two debating teams, twenty audience chairs were placed in two lines. The audience for the knockout final consisted of interested teachers, members of Rotary, debaters from the school chapter who had lost in earlier rounds, and interested Year 11 and 12 (6th form) students. The adjudicator sat behind the audience.

Diagram 4.1 The setting: A school music room

AFFIRMATIVE	Chair – Timekeeper	NEGATIVE
xxxxxxxxxx	Audience	xxxxxxxxxx
xxxxxxxxxx		xxxxxxxxxx
	Adjudicator	

Major domains from the culture of student debaters.*

Team selection – preparation before the debate – reasons for joining a team – gathering information – roles of speakers – good debates – bad debates – rules of debates – bending rules – avoiding 'trip ups' – features of the setting – procedure – using palm cards – adjudicator judgments – point allocations – peer group dynamics – member benefits – intra team relations – member disadvantages – assorted other topics.

*Domains: Discrete aspects of debating identified by the informants.

4 The cultural description: based upon informant utterances

I commenced by trying to find out why the informants had joined the debating society. It had briefly occurred to me that it might have had to do with adolescent status and prestige in the school. This perception was early dispelled. Claire was the keenest: 'It's useful for adult life after school. You have to talk your way into things these days.' At first interview Christopher conceded he had, against his own judgment, gone along with his father's wishes: 'Dad thought it would be a good idea. Meet people and stuff. I wasn't so sure.' Both Claire and David told me that they had had to talk Christopher into it. David had volunteered because 'nobody else was, and it's a good way to meet girls'. Once they had joined however, other motives came into play. Christopher had surprised himself by 'being better at it than I thought I would be'. Claire thought the 'school ought to be properly represented in events organized by the community'. David admitted he wanted to 'do something a bit smarter than football to impress my mates'. Peer group reaction to members joining the debating society was lukewarm. As David said, 'When I first joined they thought it was a bit wet but they gradually got used to the idea.' Claire felt that some of the other girls thought she was taking on 'airs and graces'. Other friends thought all three were 'crawling' to the teachers. In conversation a *taxonomy* (set of informant-provided categories related by inclusion) of those involved in debating became apparent.

The Head of Years 11 and 12 is the adult responsible for organizing the school chapter of the debating society. The Rotary service organization is responsible for the youth debating tournament. It organizes the venues, funds the event, provides the prizes and arranges the team draw.

The Head of Years 11 and 12 is important to both affirmative and negative teams in the school. He advises on topics, tactics for argument, and coordinates all procedural activity in the school. Time spent with each team gives special emphasis to debating as extracurricular activity. The basic feature of debating is that two teams compete 'head to head'. As a result of a procedure known as the *draw*, one team is *affirmative* and one team is *negative*. Each team has three members – first, second and third speakers.

Diagram 4.2 Taxonomy of people involved in debating

People/Groups	Duties/Roles
School chapter of debating society	Pick teams, choose topics, arrange competitions
Head of Year 11 and 12	Liaise with Rotary, organize venue, coordinate, encourage, find prizes
Affirmative	
First speaker	Introduce and define topic, present strong case
Second speaker	Rebut, continue and strengthen argument
Third speaker	Rebut and consolidate argument, closure
Negative	
First speaker	Rebut, accept, modify, reject argument
Second speaker	Continue to put case against. Rebut rebuttals
Third speaker	Counter argument. Final rebuttal. Only use new material in defence. Conclude.
Chairperson	Conduct meeting, perform introductions, call on speakers.
Adjudicator	Advise on procedure/rules. Judge debate on the strength of argument, announce winner.
Timekeeper	Warning bells at 4 and 6 minutes.

Under the rules of debate the affirmative team has to 'agree' and speak 'for' the topic. The topic itself is often presented as a formal motion – for example, 'This house supports the prohibition of smoking in public places' (although, privately, affirmative team members may not believe in the motion). It is the responsibility of the negative team to 'disagree' or speak 'against' the motion (although again, privately, negative team members may agree with the motion). Under debate procedure, *first speaker affirmative* is not required to rebut. The informants agreed that this made the speaking task easier. Christopher picked this task because he did not think he 'could rebut effectively or summarize the weak points in an argument'. First speaker affirmative introduces the topic or motion, defines it and puts forward the case. First speaker negative begins with a rebuttal of the argument put by first speaker affirmative; he or she may modify, accept or reject the definition of the topic. Second speaker negative presents an alternative case on the topic. He or she is then followed by *second affirmative* who rebuts first negative and continues and extends the original argument. Second negative then has a turn to speak. The task here is continued rebuttal and presentation of the negative team's counter argument. *Third affirmative* has the responsibility to rebut the complete counter argument and to consolidate and summarize affirmative team's viewpoint. The third negative is the final speaker. He may continue the rebuttal, summarize the counter argument, but, under the rules, may only introduce new material in defence of material already presented. This is because affirmative team no longer has the option of rebuttal. Claire and Christopher thought the third speaker position held by David was the most difficult because 'you can't actually comment on the topic, all you can do is keep rebutting to wear down the other side'. The informants all thought fluency in speaking and tactical choices came with practice and experience. They felt they didn't have too much of the latter.

Other key participants in debating tournaments are the chairperson, the adjudicator, and the timekeeper. Their duties are set out in the *rules* but all informants thought a 'lively audience' could sway the decisions of the adjudicator. The chairperson actively conducts the meeting. He or she begins by introducing the participants and officials. A brief résumé of the rules is read aloud. The chair then calls upon the speakers in turn. On receiving an indication of the winner, he or she may publicly announce the successful team and offer congratulations. A vote of thanks to 'worthy losers' is a part of the ritual. The official timekeeper controls the debate by strict adherence to speaking times. A bell is rung at 4 minutes as a warning and again at 6 minutes to indicate 'time up'. Speaking times may vary slightly with the age and experience of the debaters. The adjudicator, or panel of adjudicators, judges the debate on three known criteria: 'matter, manner and method' and awards set points for each. At the end of the debate the adjudicator may offer feedback and advice for use in future competitions.

Views amongst informants about *good* and *bad* debating varied somewhat by individual. The following taxonomy emerged:

Claire and Christopher, as first and second speakers respectively, had met six times prior to the first round of the competitive debate. Meetings were usually held at Claire's house or in school. David did not attend the first two meetings. Partly because, as third speaker, he did not really need to rehearse his lines as much. Both Claire and Christopher agreed though, that David's 'natural talking talent' and intuitive grasp of the issue during the debate, meant he didn't need to practise quite so frequently. Claire and Christopher devoted much time to preparing *palm cards*, small (7 cm $\times$ 12 cm) note cards which listed key points or *prompts* – on the topic on one side and tactical *do's and don'ts* in red on the other side. Preparing palm cards often involves

Diagram 4.3   Points allocation pro forma for use by adjudicators

Team A or N	Matter: 40	Manner: 40	Method: 20	Total out of 100
	What was said	How it was said	How it was connected	
First speaker				
Second speaker				
Third speaker				
TOTALS				

Diagram 4.4   A taxonomy of good and bad points in debating

Good	Bad
Able to speak in front of people	Overuse of palm cards
Speaking fluently and easily	Speaking too fast or incoherently
Use of gestures and facial expressions	Going over time
Eyeballing the audience	Grunting, hoh-humming and wheezing
Stressing key ideas	Dressing badly
Rebut robustly	Repetition of ideas
Use of wit and sarcasm	Third person bringing in new material
Full knowledge of the topic	Not knowing the topic and being boring

library research when debate topics are published in advance by the organizing committee. Claire explained their use. 'The trick is to secrete it in the palm of your hand. You must glance quickly and unobtrusively. You can't let the audience or the other team know you are dependent upon palm cards.' Claire and Christopher wrote whole sentences on their palm cards. David wrote only keywords.

When I asked each individual whether they had got to know each other socially as a result of debating, Claire and Christopher agreed they had, but David said 'partly'. All three agreed that they now knew 'each other's habits much better' and that they were now 'known around the school'.

Being in the debating team seemed to generate inner conflict for Christopher. When asked if he would continue to debate competitively, he replied: 'I doubt it, all that putting yourself on show, just to please others. And the headwork, for what?' However, he conceded he had made what he thought might be a lasting friendship with Claire. As the practice debate times often coincided with sports and extracurricular activities, David couldn't see his involvement as being anything but passing. While he enjoyed the debates and liked the competitive edge, there were simply too many other interests that made demands on his time. He did not seem to feel the same sort of need as Claire and Christopher to belong to a particular kind of group. However, all three expressed some pride in representing their school.

Competition between the three was muted. This was surprising as the school offered a speech night prize to the debater that had scored most points in competitive debates. In Round 1 of the regional youth tournament they actually achieved similar scores, though they were hazy at remembering. Their teacher, Mr J., said it was Christopher who scored the most points whereas both Claire and Christopher had thought it was David. Claire was the most disappointed in losing in the first round. Christopher seemed privately relieved. David was philosophical. 'You can't win everything.' Their teacher thought they were unlucky and had suffered from a poorly adjudicated debate. 'The chap simply wasn't up to scratch on the rules.'

Diagram 4.5 Taxonomy of steps in preparing for a competitive debate

1 Receive three topics from Rotary.
2 Define and research the topics under teacher direction. Identify keywords.
3 Prioritize topics. Decide on team speaking order. Plan affirmative/negative strategies.
4 Research further. Each team member to scan papers, CD-ROMs, atlases, books, etc.
5 Allocate 'talkpoints'. Partition responsibilities per team member.
6 Construct palm cards.
7 Impromptu debate using palm cards. Practise timing delivery.
8 Anticipate opposition rebuttals. Put planned counterpoints on cards.
9 Structured debate under teacher direction. Audio record and playback. Study.
10 Receive competition topic and results of draw for affirmative and negative.
11 Final full practice or 'dress rehearsal' with other scratch school teams.
12 Competition debate.

5 *Conclusion*

Through the device of the interview, three informants, Claire, Christopher and David, have described a cultural scene and their involvement in it. As competitive debaters they have shared knowledge and understanding, and developed group communication skills. Their experience is relatively unique and most meaningful in terms of group members' perceptions of themselves. Their schoolmates have not participated in this activity to anything like the same level of competitive intensity. Thus, the competitive experience has set the group members apart. They have had to reflect on the consequences of participation for themselves as individuals. Similarly, they have had to reflect on the public character of debating. They have evolved a quiet satisfaction in representing their school, but also perceive that debating is not highly regarded by their peers. If they had progressed beyond the first round of the tournament, the cultural bonds between group members would most likely have strengthened and intensified. The ethnographer has characterized the cultural scene of the debates under the rules of *ethnographic semantics*.

That is, informants' utterances, explanations, verbal cues and descriptions provided in interview have enabled taxonomic categorizations of competitive debating to be constructed and presented intelligibly to a lay audience.

Edited transcript of an interview with Claire

Note: This example transcript shows the kinds of *grand tour* and *attribute* questions that are typical of the interview approach of ethnographic semantics. Claire's responses, and those of her co-debaters, represent the *raw material* from which the cultural description, taxonomies and domains were constructed.

How did you become involved in debating?
I was already a member of the Debating Society. Mr J. announced that the school chapter of the society was to participate in the Rotary tournament. He asked people to put their names on a list on the Year 11/12 noticeboard. Few volunteered. After a while I thought I'd have a go so I put my name down.

Are you an experienced debater?
Not really. I first did it at primary school. I like talking to people about serious things. I believe in supporting the school so I joined the debating society a while ago. But I had to wait until 'Seniors' for competitive debates. They prefer Year 11s.

Was there much competition to be selected for the tournament team?
Yes, but from a fairly small pool of people. About 17 in all. We managed to put together four teams for a 'round robin' knockout. We won.

Were you with David and Chris from the start?
No. I was with Chris and another girl as third speaker. She couldn't rebut and pulled out. One of the blokes in the Canoeing Club thought David would be a good choice. He's an 'in and out' member of the society, but he was keen enough when we explained the Rotary competition.

Who organizes the debating competition?
Do you mean in school? Mr J. He is very keen. Thinks it's very good preparation for adult life. The Rotary Club organizes the regional youth tournament.

They pick the topics and circulate them to schools. They provide funds and prizes. They usually ask schools to provide chairpersons, timekeepers and adjudicators.

How many people in a debating team?
Three. Me, Chris and David for this school. I'm first speaker, Chris is second and David third.

How do you prepare for the debate?
Firstly, we prioritize the topics. We know only one will be the competition topic but we have to research all three. Mr J. helps. He suggests sources of information, TV, video programmes, books and the like. When we've researched the topics we share all our information at a team meeting.

What happens then?
We devise a speaking plan. If we think we will draw 'affirmative' on a topic I'll plan to speak first affirmative. Chris will plan second affirmative and David will try to guess what the opposition will do by way of rebuttal.

Do you have rules to guide your topic research?
Yes. You have to define the topic. All debates do that. Look at keywords and work out what they mean. Sometimes we check with a dictionary. Then you have to look for the things in the topic that will guide an argument. You have to be precise about what you intend to say.

How does each speaker know what to say?
You have to really know the topic and know the rules of debate. For example, if you are the first speaker affirmative you don't have to rebut. You just have to know your argument. If you are third speaker you have to pick up on the opposition's weakness and rebut their argument.

What does rebut mean?
It is a way of showing your team is right and the opposition is wrong. It's tactics.

Can you plan for rebuttals before the debate?
Partly. You can anticipate the weaknesses in an argument. But really it is a skill. Third speaker has to zero in on the opposition's case.

Do you always learn your lines before the debate?
We try to. There is no substitute for knowing the topic.

What if you forget your notes?
We use palm cards.

What are they?
Small note cards with key points written on them. You keep them hidden in the palm of your hand. The trick is not to let the opposition know you're using a palm card. Also, the adjudicator will score you down if he sees you using a palm card.

How long do you speak for?
Six minutes.

Who speaks first?
First speaker of the affirmative team. Then the first speaker negative of the opposition, then second affirmative and lastly third negative.

Who controls the debate?
A chairperson. He or she introduces the debaters, calls upon each speaker, and asks them to reply. A timekeeper times each speech. It is a cardinal sin to go over time. A warning bell is rung at four minutes and a terminating bell at six minutes. An adjudicator scores each speaker out of 40 points on two criteria and 20 points on the third. What was said. How it was said. How it was all connected up. The adjudicator also speaks at the end. And penalizes any breaking of the rules. Sometimes, the adjudicator messes things up. They are supposed to be neutral.

How will the adjudicator know a good debater?
He will give high marks to people who speak well and clearly without stammering. Knowing the topic and getting it across helps. If you can be witty and use sarcastic put-downs it also helps.

How will the adjudicator know a bad debater?
Somebody who stutters and hums and hahs all the time. Going over time is a disaster. Too obvious use of palm cards will count against you. So will a bored audience. The worst thing is to keep repeating the same idea.

How did you go in the tournament?
We lost, but not by much. We thought we had covered the topic: 'Britain's Future is Irrevocably Tied to Europe and Not Australia' pretty well. Mr J. thought the adjudicator was erratic. There seemed little consistency in the allocation of points. It seemed like it was the first time he had done the job.

Are you now firm friends with David and Christopher?
Well we are certainly closer. We share the same bruises. I've gotten to like Christopher and see more of him around the school. David is friendly with just about everybody. It is hard to say if it is a lasting friendship.

Will you all continue to debate?

Hard to say. We will probably continue with debates organized by the school chapter until we leave school. I would like to do more competitive debates. To get more experience of speaking in public. It is a skill useful in later life. I cannot really speak for Christopher. I doubt if his heart is in it. David is too restless even though he is a natural debater. He likes to argue about everything. He'll probably try something else next year.

A Summary of the Interpretation of the Ethnographic Semantics Technique of A.N. Other

The theory and practice of ethnography is characterized by a number of crucial concepts. Particular theorists ascribe restricted meanings to social science concepts but these also have widely shared public meanings – that is, meanings which are identified and used by the body corporate of social science. It is therefore necessary to appropriate some of these concepts and their meanings for PBE work directed by the ethnographic tradition. They include:

Culture   A system of shared symbols, the meanings these have for people, and the ways in which such meanings guide behaviour.

Ethnocentrism   A focus on the immediacy of one's own culture, sometimes allied with the belief that one's own culture is more meaningful or superior than other cultures.

Ethnographic semantics   A technique, using the colloquial vocabulary of informants, for describing the cultural experience of those informants. The technique accepts the impossibility of complete objectivity on the part of the ethnographer. It therefore employs informants own conceptual categories as they describe their experiences.

In using the technique of ethnographic semantics to construe a debating society cultural scene, the practitioner-based enquiry not only relies on the semantic categories of informants for substantive information, it also relies on the constructs provided by Spradley and McCurdy for methodological guidance. The following, therefore, are explanations of constructs to be found in their book.

Informants   The subjects of the research who provide through discourse or observable action culturally significant information

Cultural scene   The cognitively shared information that makes meaningful aspects of the experience of individuals.

Social situations   Physical settings for action in which behaviour and objects are combined to produce or evoke the knowledge that is the cultural scene.

Categories   The conceptual classification of objects usually done on the basis of similarities and differences.

Taxonomy   An inclusive conceptual structure or list of categories that permits classification and allows for reference at various levels of generality.

Grand tour questions   These are interview questions so designed that they will identify the components of conceptual categories.

Attribute questions   These are interview questions so designed that they will indicate differences amongst related categories.

Structural questions   These are interview questions so designed that they will identify the components of conceptual categories.

The importance and use of definitions

Most classes of ethnographic fieldwork typically require the researcher to spend a prolonged period of time in the field working with informants. This contrasts with the transitory form of communication between researcher and respondent engendered by such techniques as the mailed questionnaire. As the key characteristic of ethnography is the systematic description of people, places, events and social experiences, it is crucial for the ethnographer to be able to define what is seen and heard in adequate form in reports such as those constituting PBE.

Spradley and McCurdy place great emphasis on definitions. These are of different kinds and perform different functions. Perceptual definitions use the affective or sensory properties of people and objects to indicate their substance. To say, for example, that 'Miss Jones is warm, sincere and generous' is to define the substantive character of this person. Definitions by naming involve the attachment of a label, usually from common parlance and with publicly recognized connotations. Similarly, these types of definition may employ words devised to identify a physical object or condition. Enquiry about the nature of people, artefacts and actions precedes the naming. The question: 'Who is he? precedes 'He is John Smith, a stipendiary magistrate'.

Dictionary definitions are highly specific, publicly recognized and understood descriptions of people, places and things. Taxonomic definitions explain and define a term by denoting conceptual categories of restricted similarity. For example, 'limbs' may refer to arms, legs or the branches of a tree. The word ' limb' does not have a great deal of meaning out of taxonomic context. Componential definitions include the attributes of objects, people and things that are both necessary and sufficient. That is, they tell us what is distinctive about people, places and things. Human 'limbs' are flesh and blood appendages of human anatomy; the 'limbs' of trees are vegetable, woody projections more often referred to as branches, in that they are covered with leaves at the end furthest from the central, woody trunk of the tree. A taxonomic definition is a device for restricted comparison. A componential definition is a device for elaborated comparison.

Definitions are important in PBE reporting of ethnographic techniques for two main reasons. Definition is the pivot of explanation. Meaning, comparison and contrast, important qualities of good ethnographic reporting, cannot be achieved without capable and imaginative definition.

Different Ways of Seeing: Additional Commentary on General Research Approaches in Practitioner-Based Enquiry

We are wary of the tendency in some research textbooks to provide only the most skeletal outline of research approaches, accompanied with a 'thin' example. We presented the above ethnographic account in full to illustrate the totality of the process as constructed by one particular practitioner-researcher. Later in the book we will provide a similarly full but methodologically different account of a realized PBE. It would be nice to illustrate all the conventional approaches to research practice in this way. The neophyte researcher would then have a full compendium of designs and approaches upon which to base enquiries. However, paper space does not permit such a thing, even if the saturation of research design in this way was thought to be a good idea. What is incumbent in this chapter, though, is the need to identify a range of research approaches commonly used by practitioner researchers, to comment on some of the design features of each, and to indicate the sorts of knowledge criteria they try to construe.

Historical and documentary approaches

This type of approach, as the name implies, involves the gathering and analysis of documents. The painstaking and forensic skills of the historian and the archivist may be applied to special collections held in research libraries. Government reports of yesteryear, particularly those released from the restrictions of the Official Secrets Act under the '30 year rule', are of particular interest to researchers adopting this type of approach. Similarly, official collections such as the data from the British Household Panel Survey archived nationally by the ESRC Research Centre for Micro Social Change at the University of Essex may be re-analysed as 'secondary' data using this approach. The following is a protocol for locating and using documentary and archival sources in research.

Using Documents in Research

First: find them via indexes, catalogues, on-line databases and institutional records.

Second: identify which ones are relevant via content analysis, keywords, specialization, etc.

Third: decide on a method of interrogation via paraphrasing, card duplication, keyword searching, etc.

Fourth: recognize documents as secondary data sources prepared for purposes other than your research.

Fifth: establish an access protocol via negotiating ethics committees, gaining necessary permission, pre-arranged visits, etc.

Sixth: ensure orderly record-keeping and means of retrieval for all documentary sources by bibliographic procedures, personalized card indexes, computer-based records, etc.

Content analysis is the generic name given to varied techniques used in the scanning and sorting of documents. It may involve keywords applications, topic classification, time-sequenced listing of documents, or syntactic and semantic analyses. Historical and documentary work always requires the orderly classification of documents. The classification facilitates technical reading and strengthens the more general review of the literature. Lexicons of terms and content analysis dictionaries of the type presented in Chapter 3 (see p. 54) may then be compiled. These may then be used as verifiers of propositional data gathered by other means in fieldwork contexts. The use of content analysis techniques is essentially a process of transformation in which the abstract and practical implications of research questions are selectively controlled by word signs and cues. Content analysis connects the purposes of the research to the messages in documents. This may be particularly significant when documents intended to predict certain futures have, over the course of time, been found to be incorrect in their predictions. Alternatively, 'reactive biases' in documents, such as strong opinions or judgments on a public controversy, may be interrogated through content analysis techniques. Attempts to discover facts and to interpret factual matters as objectively as possible is a feature of the historical and documentary approach.

Approaches involving experiments

In setting up an experiment, usually, but not exclusively, within the framework of disciplines such as physics, chemistry and psychology, the researcher attempts to measure and analyse the effects of one special treatment or change under controlled conditions. When the target of the experiment is a group of people with defining characteristics, for example, a particular learning disability or the same socio-economic status, the experimental or control conditions are so established that they can be manipulated to measure their effect or influence on the target group. The target group, or sample, are equivalent in all respects prior to the experiment. This helps to minimize the effect of external influences or 'sources of variance', as they are often called. Experiments have to meet strict design criteria. In the case of experiments conducted in laboratories, these criteria may well be expressed in printed guides for the setting up of equipment, attention to safety rules and the timed monitoring of observable changes in the objects of the experiment. Experiments carried out as part of fieldwork – that is, in discrete social and geographical locations selected because of the relevant features they offer to the experiment – are often conducted according to elaborate lists of procedures. Laboratory experiments usually operate to relatively short, fixed time-frames. Fieldwork experiments tend to operate with more extended time-frames. Experiments invariably attempt to measure testable hypotheses. The word 'testable' is important here: it suggests a measurement quantity or 'variable' that the researcher is interested in. This is usually called the 'dependent variable'. The testable hypothesis also includes a measurement condition or 'independent variable'. The manipulation of this according to the controls established ought to produce some noticeable change or effect on the dependent variable. When the change is in the direction predicted, the hypothesis may be said to be verified. When there is no change, or change is not in the direction predicted, then the hypothesis is not verified. The verification of hypotheses under controlled conditions is often a function of the 'repeatability' factor. That is, if the controlled experiment is repeated and the exact effects on the dependent variable are the same as previously, then the possibility for formulating explanatory theory is enhanced.

Of course, PBE approaches using experiments do not always need a strictly testable hypothesis. The device of the hypothesis is, though, a useful tool to focus data collection and analysis. But as we commented in our earlier remarks on the expression of purposes, the formulation of a hypothesis needs considerable attention to variables of the dependent and independent kind, the sorts of relationships that might be envisaged between variables, and the linking words or conjunctions needed to properly express the predicted relationship between 'X' and 'Y'. To begin with a hypothetical statement such as: 'Teaching in small groups is better than mass lectures' is useful only to a point. This hypothetical statement needs further work in respect of the predicted effects of teaching, the type of taught experience undergone, and the establishment of an indicative subject context for both small groups and mass lectures. In PBE we find it helpful to think of hypotheses as devices to encourage precision in thinking. Where the generalities of an 'itch', 'made' or 'given' problem confound the articulation and expression of purpose, the specification of hypotheses may help to unstop the 'blockage'.

Survey approaches

Whilst the term 'survey' is most often associated with paper and pencil questionnaires in social and educational research, the term is really a generic one taking in a whole range of information-gathering techniques for use with representative groups of people. Such people are classed as 'informants' or 'respondents' and, because they demonstrate such similar characteristics, they may be termed a 'survey population'. Official censuses, Gallop polls of voting intentions, job preference inventories, postal questionnaires on consumer purchasing habits are all examples of survey procedures. A key feature of the survey is the attempt to generate classifiable, possibly standardized, information about the theme, object, or idea or group of people under investigation. Surveys are often conducted at particular and opportune points of time, perhaps when public interest is at its highest (e.g. just before an election) or when specific opinion on a crucial matter is required. A national referendum on the desirability of the Euro would be a large scale example of the latter.

Tools used in surveys tend to be highly structured. Much dependence is placed by the researcher on the capacity of instruments selected to explain themselves in terms of adequate wording, to generate interest on the part of the respondent, and to be so carefully structured as to precisely pinpoint the information required. Much attention is given in surveys to sampling techniques. The right kind of survey population has first to be identified. Then the correct proportion of the total to be surveyed has to be calculated. This will be influenced by the kinds of analytical treatments to be used on the data. Similarly, proportionality and stratification rules may be developed to provide limits to indicators of generalizability. A random stratified sample is one in which, first, an arithmetically adequate number of respondents from the survey population is computed. This sample is then further stratified proportionally on the basis of imperative measurement characteristics, for example, 10 per cent of all 17-year-old males in 10 per cent of sixth forms in public sector maintained secondary schools in England. An essential characteristic of survey work is the requirement for the selected samples to be representative in terms of the theorized or predicted qualities of the survey population as a whole. Surveys tend to generate very large datasets which can be subjected to different analytical and statistical treatments. The aforementioned British Household Panel Survey 1990–2 is a case in point. The report on this survey (Buck et al., 1994) shows how researchers are able to postulate confidently on policy-related matters such as household and residential mobility, family and work 1990–2, stability of voting intentions and income, welfare and consumption patterns. Researchers tend to be more confident about drawing conclusions and making recommendations for policy when they have large amounts of survey data to support the case.

We have provided an example of survey instrumentation in Figure 4.1.

Figure 4.1 Opinion inventory

SCHOOL SYSTEM OPINION INVENTORY TEACHER FORM

A survey of views about aspects of school life in Queensland State Secondary Schools

This inventory provides an opportunity for teachers currently working in Queensland state secondary schools to give their opinion about various aspects of school life.

If the community is to improve its understanding of the problems and prospects confronting schools, it is vital that they should know the views of practising teachers.

In this inventory you will find statements about school life that have been derived from sample studies previously conducted in Queensland schools. Please read each statement carefully and indicate your agreement or disagreement.

Complete confidentiality will be maintained; no attempt to identify particular individuals will be made. I would like to take this opportunity to thank you in advance for your cooperation and interest.

SECTION A

You will find below a number of statements that have been derived from information provided by teachers in sample State Schools in Queensland. Please indicate your *agreement* or *disagreement* with these statements by *ticking one* of the boxes on the right-hand side of the page.

strongly agree

agree

disagree

strongly
disagree

1. Teachers in State Secondary schools are best thought as public servants working in a special kind of service organization.

☐ 1 ☐ 2 ☐ 3 ☐ 4 (1:10)

2. Corporal punishment should be retained in Queensland state secondary schools.

☐ 1 ☐ 2 ☐ 3 ☐ 4 (1:11)

3. Compulsory Teacher Registration in Queensland represents unnecessary interference in selection for entry to the teaching profession.

☐ 1 ☐ 2 ☐ 3 ☐ 4 (1:12)

4. ROSBA (Review of School Based Assessments) is likely to benefit the community by making teachers more responsible for their actions.

☐ 1 ☐ 2 ☐ 3 ☐ 4 (1:13)

5. Transition education activities such as STEP (Secondary Transition Education Project) are an adequate response to the problems faced by those students soon to leave school.

☐ 1 ☐ 2 ☐ 3 ☐ 4 (1:14)

6. Schools are poorly organized to deal with the increasing numbers of students returning to commence Grade 11 studies.

☐ 1 ☐ 2 ☐ 3 ☐ 4 (1:15)

7. Religious instruction should be a compulsory component of the curriculum in state high schools.

☐ 1 ☐ 2 ☐ 3 ☐ 4 (1:16)

8. Pressure groups have a disproportionate influence on the educational process in state schools.

☐ 1 ☐ 2 ☐ 3 ☐ 4 (1:17)

9. Parents and Citizens Associations should be more directly involved in the formulation of school policy.

☐ 1 ☐ 2 ☐ 3 ☐ 4 (1:18)

10. There is a lack of certainty in the goals of secondary education.

☐ 1 ☐ 2 ☐ 3 ☐ 4 (1:19)

11. The professional development of teachers is hindered rather than helped by the involvement by combined organizations such as QINSEC (Queensland In-Service Education Committee).

☐ 1 ☐ 2 ☐ 3 ☐ 4 (1:20)

12. Student achievement in school is significantly related to the home background of students.

☐ 1 ☐ 2 ☐ 3 ☐ 4 (1:21)

13. To be a judge of a teacher's effectiveness in the classroom is a legitimate role for school inspectors.

☐ 1 ☐ 2 ☐ 3 ☐ 4 (1:22)

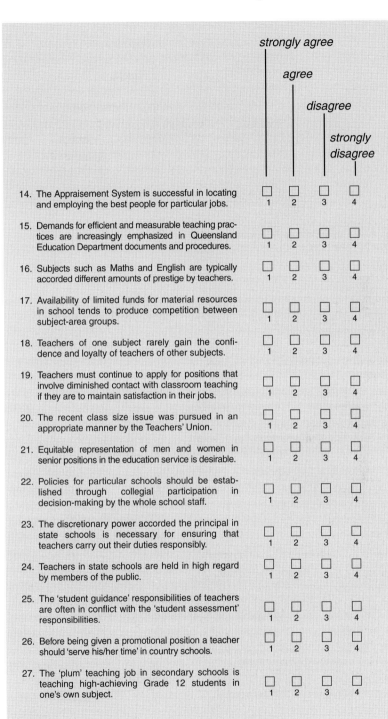

strongly agree

agree

disagree

strongly disagree

14. The Appraisement System is successful in locating and employing the best people for particular jobs.   1   2   3   4   (1:23)

15. Demands for efficient and measurable teaching practices are increasingly emphasized in Queensland Education Department documents and procedures.   1   2   3   4   (1:24)

16. Subjects such as Maths and English are typically accorded different amounts of prestige by teachers.   1   2   3   4   (1:25)

17. Availability of limited funds for material resources in school tends to produce competition between subject-area groups.   1   2   3   4   (1:26)

18. Teachers of one subject rarely gain the confidence and loyalty of teachers of other subjects.   1   2   3   4   (1:27)

19. Teachers must continue to apply for positions that involve diminished contact with classroom teaching if they are to maintain satisfaction in their jobs.   1   2   3   4   (1:28)

20. The recent class size issue was pursued in an appropriate manner by the Teachers' Union.   1   2   3   4   (1:29)

21. Equitable representation of men and women in senior positions in the education service is desirable.   1   2   3   4   (1:30)

22. Policies for particular schools should be established through collegial participation in decision-making by the whole school staff.   1   2   3   4   (1:31)

23. The discretionary power accorded the principal in state schools is necessary for ensuring that teachers carry out their duties responsibly.   1   2   3   4   (1:32)

24. Teachers in state schools are held in high regard by members of the public.   1   2   3   4   (1:33)

25. The 'student guidance' responsibilities of teachers are often in conflict with the 'student assessment' responsibilities.   1   2   3   4   (1:34)

26. Before being given a promotional position a teacher should 'serve his/her time' in country schools.   1   2   3   4   (1:35)

27. The 'plum' teaching job in secondary schools is teaching high-achieving Grade 12 students in one's own subject.   1   2   3   4   (1:36)

		strongly agree	agree	disagree	strongly disagree	
28.	As a general rule, the total student enrolment in a state high school should not exceed 700.	□ 1	□ 2	□ 3	□ 4	(1:37)
29.	Whilst most teachers prefer to teach able and achieving students there is pressure to treat all stu-dents as if they were of comparable ability.	□ 1	□ 2	□ 3	□ 4	(1:38)
30.	Differentiating subjects on the basis of complexity (e.g. advanced, ordinary, general mathematics) is an appropriately practical response to different student abilities.	□ 1	□ 2	□ 3	□ 4	(1:39)
31.	The idea that teachers are a group of 'autonomous professionals' is a myth.	□ 1	□ 2	□ 3	□ 4	(1:40)
32.	Decisions about appropriate ways of disciplining students in schools should be the prerogative of teachers.	□ 1	□ 2	□ 3	□ 4	(1:41)
33.	Political influences on the employment conditions of teachers are likely to increase in the future.	□ 1	□ 2	□ 3	□ 4	(1:42)
34.	A system of school-based assessment for Year 12 students is more satisfactory than a system of externally set and marked examinations.	□ 1	□ 2	□ 3	□ 4	(1:43)
35.	The Queensland state high school is generally successful in satisfying the needs and aspirations of students.	□ 1	□ 2	□ 3	□ 4	(1:44)
36.	Grade 11 and 12 students should not be compelled to wear school uniform.	□ 1	□ 2	□ 3	□ 4	(1:45)
37.	A clear and common set of values should be taught in every Queensland state high school.	□ 1	□ 2	□ 3	□ 4	(1:46)
38.	Public speculation about educational activities is frequently ill-informed.	□ 1	□ 2	□ 3	□ 4	(1:47)
39.	In a democracy, parents should have the right to have their children educated according to their cons-ciences.	□ 1	□ 2	□ 3	□ 4	(1:48)
40.	The content of the subjects I teach is frequently subject to scrutiny, challenge, change.	□ 1	□ 2	□ 3	□ 4	(1:49)
41.	Short in-service courses frequently fail to meet the needs and aspirations of teachers.	□ 1	□ 2	□ 3	□ 4	(1:50)

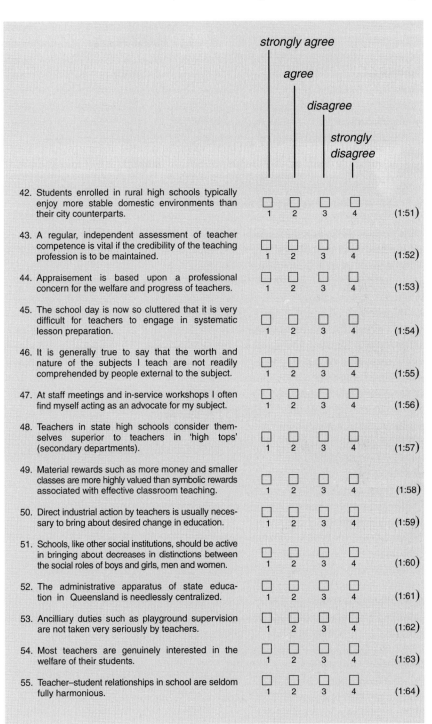

strongly agree

agree

disagree

strongly
disagree

42. Students enrolled in rural high schools typically enjoy more stable domestic environments than their city counterparts.
☐ 1 ☐ 2 ☐ 3 ☐ 4   (1:51)

43. A regular, independent assessment of teacher competence is vital if the credibility of the teaching profession is to be maintained.
☐ 1 ☐ 2 ☐ 3 ☐ 4   (1:52)

44. Appraisement is based upon a professional concern for the welfare and progress of teachers.
☐ 1 ☐ 2 ☐ 3 ☐ 4   (1:53)

45. The school day is now so cluttered that it is very difficult for teachers to engage in systematic lesson preparation.
☐ 1 ☐ 2 ☐ 3 ☐ 4   (1:54)

46. It is generally true to say that the worth and nature of the subjects I teach are not readily comprehended by people external to the subject.
☐ 1 ☐ 2 ☐ 3 ☐ 4   (1:55)

47. At staff meetings and in-service workshops I often find myself acting as an advocate for my subject.
☐ 1 ☐ 2 ☐ 3 ☐ 4   (1:56)

48. Teachers in state high schools consider themselves superior to teachers in 'high tops' (secondary departments).
☐ 1 ☐ 2 ☐ 3 ☐ 4   (1:57)

49. Material rewards such as more money and smaller classes are more highly valued than symbolic rewards associated with effective classroom teaching.
☐ 1 ☐ 2 ☐ 3 ☐ 4   (1:58)

50. Direct industrial action by teachers is usually necessary to bring about desired change in education.
☐ 1 ☐ 2 ☐ 3 ☐ 4   (1:59)

51. Schools, like other social institutions, should be active in bringing about decreases in distinctions between the social roles of boys and girls, men and women.
☐ 1 ☐ 2 ☐ 3 ☐ 4   (1:60)

52. The administrative apparatus of state education in Queensland is needlessly centralized.
☐ 1 ☐ 2 ☐ 3 ☐ 4   (1:61)

53. Ancilliary duties such as playground supervision are not taken very seriously by teachers.
☐ 1 ☐ 2 ☐ 3 ☐ 4   (1:62)

54. Most teachers are genuinely interested in the welfare of their students.
☐ 1 ☐ 2 ☐ 3 ☐ 4   (1:63)

55. Teacher–student relationships in school are seldom fully harmonious.
☐ 1 ☐ 2 ☐ 3 ☐ 4   (1:64)

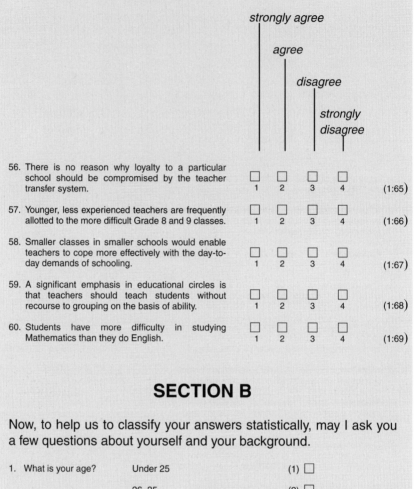

56. There is no reason why loyalty to a particular school should be compromised by the teacher transfer system.

☐ 1 ☐ 2 ☐ 3 ☐ 4 (1:65)

57. Younger, less experienced teachers are frequently allotted to the more difficult Grade 8 and 9 classes.

☐ 1 ☐ 2 ☐ 3 ☐ 4 (1:66)

58. Smaller classes in smaller schools would enable teachers to cope more effectively with the day-to-day demands of schooling.

☐ 1 ☐ 2 ☐ 3 ☐ 4 (1:67)

59. A significant emphasis in educational circles is that teachers should teach students without recourse to grouping on the basis of ability.

☐ 1 ☐ 2 ☐ 3 ☐ 4 (1:68)

60. Students have more difficulty in studying Mathematics than they do English.

☐ 1 ☐ 2 ☐ 3 ☐ 4 (1:69)

SECTION B

Now, to help us to classify your answers statistically, may I ask you a few questions about yourself and your background.

1. What is your age?

Under 25	(1) ☐	
26–35	(2) ☐	
36–45	(3) ☐	
46+	(4) ☐	(1:70)

2. What is your sex?

| Male | (1) ☐ | |
| Female | (2) ☐ | (1:71) |

3. What is your marital status?

| Married | (1) ☐ | |
| Single | (2) ☐ | (1:72) |

4. If you are married, do you have children?	Yes	(1) ☐	
	No	(2) ☐	(1:73)
5. What is your religion?	None	(1) ☐	
	Christian	(2) ☐	
	Other (specify)	(3) ☐	(1:74)
6. How many years have you been teaching?	Under 1 year	(1) ☐	
	2–3 years	(2) ☐	
	3–4 years	(3) ☐	
	5 years	(4) ☐	
	5 years +	(5) ☐	(1:75)
7. How many years have you been teaching in this school?	Under 1 year	(1) ☐	
	Second year	(2) ☐	
	Third year	(3) ☐	
	Over 3 years	(4) ☐	(1:76)
8. What type of school are you currently teaching in?	Grade 1 High School	(1) ☐	
	Grade 2 High School	(2) ☐	
	Secondary Department	(3) ☐	(1:77)
9. Have you taught in Brisbane High Schools?	Yes	(1) ☐	
	No	(2) ☐	(1:78)
10. What position do you currently hold in this school?	Principal	(1) ☐	
	Deputy Principal	(2) ☐	
	Senior Mistress	(3) ☐	
	Subject Master/Mistress	(4) ☐	
	Teacher	(5) ☐	
	Other (specify)	(6) ☐	(1:79)

11. Do you have any pastoral care responsibilities such as Form Teacher or House Coordinator?

Yes (1) ☐

No (2) ☐ (1: 80)

12. What subject(s) do you mainly teach at this school?

English	(01)☐	(2:10,11)
Mathematics	(02)☐	(2:12,13)
Social Sciences	(03)☐	(2:14,15)
Science	(04)☐	(2:16,17)
Commercial	(05)☐	(2.18,19)
Art	(06)☐	(2:20,21)
Music	(07)☐	(2:22,23)
Manual Arts	(08)☐	(2:24,25)
Home Economics	(09)☐	(2:26,27)
Physical Education	(10)☐	(2:28,29)

13. What subject(s) would you prefer to teach at this school?

English	(01)☐	(2:30,31)
Mathematics	(02)☐	(2:32,33)
Social Sciences	(03)☐	(2:34,35)
Science	(04)☐	(2:36,37)
Commercial	(05)☐	(2.38,39)
Art	(06)☐	(2:40,41)
Music	(07)☐	(2:42,43)
Manual Arts	(08)☐	(2:44,45)
Home Economics	(09)☐	(2:46,47)
Physical Education	(10)☐	(2:48,49)

14. Do you consider yourself to be appropriately qualified in the subjects you mainly teach at this school?

Yes (1) ☐

Partly (2) ☐

No (3) ☐ (2:50)

15. What is the highest qualification you have obtained?

Higher Degree	(1) ☐	
Degree	(2) ☐	
3-year Teaching Certificate/Diploma	(3) ☐	
2-year Teaching Certificate/Diploma	(4) ☐	
Other (specify)	(5) ☐	(2:51)

16. Please indicate the location of the Institution at which you gained your highest qualification.

University/Queensland	(1) ☐	
University/Interstate	(2) ☐	
University/Overseas	(3) ☐	
College/Queensland	(4) ☐	
College/Interstate	(5) ☐	
College/Overseas	(6) ☐	(2:52)

17. If you have teaching experience in schools outside Queensland, please indicate where this experience was gained.

Schools/Interstate	(1) ☐	
Schools/Overseas	(2) ☐	(2:53)

18. What percentage (approximate) of your time is spent teaching the following grades?

Grade 8	under 20%	(1) ☐	
	20–50%	(2) ☐	
	over 50%	(3) ☐	(2:54)
Grade 9	under 20%	(1) ☐	
	20–50%	(2) ☐	
	over 50%	(3) ☐	(2:55)
Grade 10	under 20%	(1) ☐	
	20–50%	(2) ☐	
	over 50%	(3) ☐	(2:56)
Grade 11	under 20%	(1) ☐	
	20–50%	(2) ☐	
	over 50%	(3) ☐	(2:57)
Grade 12	under 20%	(1) ☐	
	20–50%	(2) ☐	
	over 50%	(3) ☐	(2:58)

19. Which grade would you most prefer to teach? (*select one*)

Grade 8	(1) ☐	
Grade 9	(2) ☐	
Grade 10	(3) ☐	
Grade 11	(4) ☐	
Grade 12	(5) ☐	(2:59)

SECTION C

This section is optional – you do not have to complete it. However, any additional information you can give will be most welcome.

1. If there are additional comments you would like to make about items 1–60 in Section A of this inventory, please use the space below.

. . . .

. . . .

. . . .

. . . .

. . . .

. . . .

. . . .

. . . .

. . . .

. . . .

2. This research focuses upon the constraints and learning in Queensland State Secondary Schools. It would be most useful if you could *specifically* identify those features of school life that make your teaching and related responsibilities perhaps more difficult than they might otherwise be.

. . . .

. . . .

. . . .

. . . .

. . . .

. . . .

. . . .

. . . .

. . . .

This instrument is technically described as an 'opinion inventory'. Notice that we do not refer to it as a 'personality questionnaire' or an 'attitude survey'. Technically, this instrument was designed to operate largely within the cognitive or knowledge domain of the targeted respondents, i.e. teachers in public sector secondary schools in Queensland, Australia. The instrument contributed to the construct validation activity that produced the content analysis dictionary in Chapter 3 (p. 54). This was a theoretical function of the instrument. It also produced categorical information in its own right, as well as testing opinions about a range of ideas and constructs central to the purposes of the investigation in question. We will now identify some measurement and procedural characteristics of the instrument (Table 4.1) (see also Figure 2.2):

Table 4.1 Constructs representing normatively produced constraints on Queensland State high schools

Theoretical constructs	*Explanation of the meaning of the constructs*	*Empirically derived key indicators of the constructs*	
		Teachers	*Students*
1 Statutes	Constraints on teacher–student behaviour arising from laws and regulations enacted in the parliament of Queensland and proclaimed by Governor-in-Council, Education Act 1964–74, Public Service Act 1922–78.	(i) Process of teacher registration and some of its consequences for professional autonomy. (ii) Regulations made under the Education Act 1964–74. (iii) Legal provisions for corporal punishment and response of teachers to these.	(i) Compulsory attendance under section 28 of Part IV Education Act 1964–74. (ii) Student support and opposition to corporal punishment on sex and age lines.
2 Achievement orientation	Powerful pressures that society exerts on the education system in order to ensure trained manpower for an increasingly complex and specialized economy balanced against the need to provide equal opportunity for all school incumbents.	(i) Procedures for school-based assessments. (ii) Relevant programs for students returning to year 11. (iii) Transition courses and the 'at risk' student in year 10.	(i) Selection of appropriate subjects coping with assignment work and the pressure to consistently produce good grades to reflect in a high TE score. (ii) Year 10 elective course subjects involving 'academic' or 'vocational' emphasis.

Theoretical constructs	Explanation of the meaning of the constructs	Empirically derived key indicators of the constructs	
		Teachers	Students
3 Lay politics	The increasing intrusiveness of value judgments of parents, community associations, vested interest groups and the general public into educational matters, which must be acknowledged by the education system in organized ways, but may remain unexplicated.	(i) Complex of diffuse teacher responses to pressures for increased community involvement. (ii) Intervention of P & C associations in schooling and teacher ambivalence to these. (iii) Caution towards public speculation on educational matters.	(i) Parental direction of subject choice particularly in mathematics. (ii) Moderate to strong parental interest in the schooling of their children. (iii) Parents and community seen as arbiters of morality and good behaviour and school as an endorsing agency.
4 Goal inconsistency	The lack of clarity and consistency in the purposes of education and the resulting problem for an increasingly volatile democracy of relating educational ends and means.	(i) Lack of certainty in the goals of secondary education. (ii) Religious instruction as an exemplification of the dispute over values in education. (iii) The specification of objectives for curriculum subjects as problematic.	(i) Student purposes and spontaneous interests are often at variance with schools' formal goals. (ii) Subjects informally ranked in terms of their usefulness, degree of abstraction, work loads, etc. (iii) Work experience programs and matching of subjects to job aspirations.
5 Central authority	Teachers and students act in schools in rule-bound ways which are in large part a function of the centrally organized, vertically administered legal rational procedures of the Queensland Dept of Education.	(i) The position of teachers in a stratified and inflexible employment system. (ii) The appraisement system and responses of teachers to the revised functions of the inspectorate.	(i) School as a system of authority relationships in which students are always subordinate. (ii) Prefectorial system and student responses to involvement in school governance.

Theoretical constructs	*Explanation of the meaning of the constructs*	*Empirically derived key indicators of the constructs*	
		Teachers	*Students*
6 Status group competition	The conflicting demands and divided loyalties faced by teachers and students in subject groups, pastoral-care arrangements, professional associations and social relationships based on age and experience.	(i) Subject loyalties and curriculum prestige and specialization in school. (ii) Allocation of material resources and ensuing sectorization.	(i) House system and pastoral-care arrangements. (ii) Subject pecking orders based on perceived prestige of academic subjects. (iii) Informal interest groups of diffusely competitive kinds.
7 Occupational status	The position of teachers and students in the rank order of power and prestige in the school and the perception of rewards and obligations associated with the position.	(i) Competition between material and symbolic rewards in teaching. (ii) Career progression from classroom via classified position to administration. (iii) Proportional representation of men and women in certain subjects and positions of seniority.	(i) Age–sex position in school and associated sex-role expectations. (ii) Placement in mathematics classes and perceptions of reward for achievement in this subject. (iii) Year 11/12 academic and non-academic strands.
8 Collegiality	The sense of corporate membership that teachers and students have of their school, particularly as this is exemplified in the presence or absence of discretionary power to influence school governance.	(i) Felt lack of trust and delegated responsibility to make effective decisions. (ii) Teachers' images of themselves. (iii) Interaction between bureaucractic demands and volatile social relationships that schools produce between teachers and students.	(i) Student corporate membership of school under control of teachers and parents. (ii) School uniform, student opinions and unity within student populations 'against' teachers.

Theoretical constructs	Explanation of the meaning of the constructs	Empirically derived key indicators of the constructs	
		Teachers	Students
9 Positional authority	The roles that teachers and students occupy in school and the bases of judgment used in guiding the individual's conduct of the role.	(i) Teachers as examiners, counsellors and instructors – bases for role conflict. (ii) Accountability and teaching preferences. (iii) Instabilities produced by the teacher transfer system.	Expectations of conformity to teacher defined standards. (ii) Sex-related opinions on treatment of students by teachers. (iii) Concepts of seniority in students' peer affiliation and rivalry.
10 Regimentation	The conventional and institutionalized features of school organizations such as classes organized by age, timetables, bells, parades, rule and rituals that create order and predictability.	(i) Tyranny of timetable. (ii) Difficulty of responding to differentiated student abilities. (iii) Press of organization.	(i) Day-to-day routines and classroom requirements. (ii) Impress of school rules exemplified by 'punctuality'. (iii) Student conceptions of their ability and opinions about school's treatment of it.

La Piere (1967) makes the point that questionnaires and inventories are useful in survey research if it is recognized that what they produce is primarily a verbal response to a symbolic situation. An important consideration in the construction of inventories is that they should not be regarded as instruments capable of determining particular patterns of behavioural adjustment in particular settings for action.

This recognition of a fundamental weakness of opinion inventories enables the recognition of a fundamental strength. The sum content of an opinion inventory is representative of the empirical indicators, the variable structure, underpinning theoretical assumptions and premises of research. This is a basic structural feature of the inventory exemplified here. 'Variables' embedded in the inventory are what Lazarsfeld (1959, p. 64) refers to as the 'empirical counterparts of conceptual imagery'. Thus the empirical indicators or variables embedded in declarative statements in the opinion inventory bear an inferential relationship to the underlying conceptual factors sought. A main aim of this inventory is to help in the detection of relationships defining theoretical concepts. The inventory is not concerned, as in other forms of survey research, to identify the correct classification or 'score' of each informant against each variable. The declarative statements used in the main part of the inventory evoke a response; they are not statements requiring verification of what is already known to be factual. Indeed, the content of the inventory is largely derived from theoretical notions empirically confirmed via other measures in sample schools and related venues. The statements in the inventory use terms such as 'should', 'more', 'seldom', 'most', etc. to evoke individual and group opinions.

The declarative statements in Section A are established in the Likert (1967) format. This requires a mixture of positive and negative statements to minimize the possibility of inducing response sets. Opinion statements worded positively or negatively do not reflect, of course, a positive or negative evaluation of the theoretical objects of the statement by the researcher. Similarly, single item statements are usually required in the Likert format. However, some of the empirical indicators generated previously could not be separated from their context. This may be carefully contained by the use of 'double-barrelled' statements. There are also issues of vocabulary complexity here. The wording of the inventory aims at a verbal level that is marginally lower than the general verbal level in the group of teacher respondents.

The Likert statements are accompanied by 'closed' response categories which control recall and memory, require no writing and assure measurement. Also a 'closed' approach ensures that the responses of groups studied in earlier fieldwork situations can be compared, for it is known that these groups have studied the same universe of content. For example, it is posited that teachers varying in occupational status terms will respond differentially. The absence of a middle or 'neutral' response category means that this instrument is of the 'Likert forced choice' type of inventory. That is, in omitting the neutral category the researcher directs or forces the respondents answer towards one end of the score continuum or the other. In layman's terms, the respondent is forced to make a choice. In statistical parlance, this is a source of systematic measurement bias. Being known and decided upon by the researcher, it must be explained in the theoretical rationale for the methodology. Tolerance of systematic measurement bias is usually justified as necessary for theoretical insights that forced responses usually generate. Arithmetic and measurement limitations are important elements in the construction of Likert-type instruments. Oppenheim (1972) provides a useful discussion and commentary on these elements and the more general issues of measurement underpinning questionnaire construction. The researcher has to remain aware of statistical limitations and mathematically imposed constraints on questionnaire-style instrumentation.

The section of declarative statements established in the Likert format is accompanied by a section of direct questions about relevant classificatory variables such as age, sex, type of school, and so on. This Section B, a normal feature of survey instruments, produces information useful in its own right, but it also produces subgroup indicators against which the responses from Section A may be classified. Following conventional Likert theory (Edwards, 1957; Andrich, 1978), names for the extremes of the response continuum are immaterial. The important point is that the statements in Section A, worded and balanced to produce a response that is more towards one end of the response continuum, should do so in a modal sense with the groups represented by clusters of classificatory variables. More simply, the classificatory variables permit quantitative discrimination amongst responses to declarative statements.

Two other features of Section A are worthy of comment. Statements 1–60 are controlled by 'split half reliability' That is, whilst the words are different, questions 1–30 are substantially the same as questions 31–60 (in terms of the underpinning ideas). If this instrument is 'reliable' in the statistical sense, then, scores on the first part of the inventory should be close to scores on the second part. This design feature avoids the need for 'test-retest' use of such instruments – something difficult to organize with survey populations of limited availability. Also, as each declarative statement is, for measurement purposes, a single 'variable', the numbers in parentheses to the right of each response category are provided for ease of computer coding. Consecutive numbering of variables means that they are easy to enter into a computer database and are ready for logical permutations such as rank ordering of data, cross tabulations and more inferentially based statistical analysis.

The final section of the inventory (Section C) is open, permitting respondents to introduce new or additional information or to qualify the pre-coded questions previously encountered in Sections A and B. Consistent with most survey instruments of this genre, the inventory (and its parallel form for use with pupils) pays attention to letter size and parsimony. Instructions are reduced to a minimum to put respondents at ease whilst at the same time convincing them of the value of the survey. Also, the survey population is clearly identified in the instructions but the confidentiality of responses is guaranteed. The inventory can be completed in 30 minutes and in its original user form was given an alphanumeric designation (Form LMT-1983) to protect future copyright and to facilitate identification. It was also colour printed (green, for the teacher version; yellow, for the pupil version) for ease of visual identification and to be user-friendly.

Mathematically, it should be understood that Likert scales are not strictly metric or interval measures. However, the literature on this type of very popular survey instrumentation does indicate that Likert scales differentiate between groups and within groups and that percentile norms and standard deviation norms can be calculated if the sample size is large enough. This is statistically advantageous in PBE approaches using survey methodologies.

Approaches based on the concept of 'Case Study'

Case studies are the detailed analyses of singularities: a person, an event limited in time, a specific department within a larger organization, a particular form of occupational practice, an administrative subsystem, or a single institution with clearly defined boundaries. The case study investigator tries to give a detailed and fair account of the unique features of what or whom is being investigated. In this task, the case study investigator tries to present an objective view and provide sufficient qualifying information about the stance taken and the methodology used so as to enable a reader to make a judgment about the adequacy of the enquiry and the particular interpretation made by the investigator.

More formally, we may say that the purpose of case studies is to identify, reveal and explain the unique features of the case. In respect of persons, this might include their occupational roles, duties, powers, perceptions and motivations in a particular work setting. In the case of events, it might include the date, place and time, the personnel involved, the duration of the event, its purpose, the technology and equipment used, and the outcomes. In the example of a bounded institution, it might include staff profiles, work schedules, timetables, office practices, organizational subunits, throughputs and communication channels.

A key feature of case studies is observation. This may mean the active deployment of techniques such as participant observation and direct observation. It also means the use and application of other data-gathering techniques such as interviews, content analysis of documents, anecdotal data gathering, discourse analysis and ethnography of the type we have previously displayed. Thus the 'case study 'does not employ a single data-gathering technique. It employs selected techniques: those that best fit the facts of the case and the purposes of the enquiry, and which help to *tell the story*.

Case studies tend to reflect the personal style and preferments of the investigator. The main advantage of case studies is that they can be excellent for uncovering unique patterns and features of social interaction within small groups. They are, however, susceptible to intuitive biases and anecdote. Details gathered in and about a case permit generalizations to be made about the case. Accumulated case studies within a subject field permit generalizations to be made about the class of cases. *Generalizability*, though, is a limitation in case study work.

In-depth portrayals and descriptions produced through case study add to the stock of public knowledge about the person, the event or the institution under scrutiny. The credibility of such portrayals and descriptions is based on the idea that the interested reader or lay person will 'connect' the details of the case to what he already knows of specific and general human situations. Case studies assume that the world experienced by people is meaningful. The function of case studies, therefore, is to explain how 'meanings' are shared, especially in the workplace. In this sense, case studies are sociological in character. They assume that the orderly events of daily life are readily known and understood by the person experiencing them, but not necessarily known, recognized or understood by third parties. Such 'third parties' are sometimes referred to as 'outsiders' or laymen. The ultimate responsibility of the case study researcher is to render the events of daily life comprehensible to interested 'third parties'.

Approaches based on systematic description

The word *description* is sometimes treated with scepticism by scientists, even social ones. Somehow, it is taken to connote lack of rigour, analysis and prediction in the conduct of research enquiries. There can, of course, be extremely rigorous descriptive studies. Indeed, research and fieldwork in classical anthropology is governed by rules for description and analysis. The methods of the ethnographer, as we implied earlier, are essentially descriptive, but they are no less respectable for being so. We do not wish at this juncture to return to debate which we outlined in Chapter 2 and which is at the heart of questions about the credibility of descriptive techniques. Rather, we wish here to identify a broader range of descriptive techniques and to comment on some interesting aspects of them. As we have already dealt with ethnography, we will not include a further consideration in this section.

In social and educational research, systematic description is usually used in two ways. First, to describe the features of the research venue or setting prior to the collection of data but after the research purpose has been established. Second, in the data analysis phase of a research report, where the description of the performance behaviour of research subjects, the occurrence of critical incidents, the results of an experiment, etc., require detailed recording and accounting.

It is in this phase of research reporting that the conjunction between data-gathering technique, methodological orientation and data analysis is achieved. There is, here, an underlying tension between 'methods' and 'methodology' which we say much more about in the next chapter. At this point it is sufficient to say that systematic description functions in the form of data-gathering instruments and as a system of analysis. Approaches used may include: various kinds of ethnography; direct observation schedules; life cycle biographies, episodic and ethogenic accounts (character studies primarily based on an analysis of language) and personal construct theory.

Each of these approaches is generic. There are many different kinds of observation schedules (see Foster, 1996). Alternatives and variants are available for each approach. Users need to be clear about the intellectual origins of a technique, as well as practical rules for its use in fieldwork settings. As Boehm and Weinberg (1977) point out, observation is influenced by both the objective and subjective character of what we see. In their example of observations of a supermarket scene (p. 7), they suggest rules for how the objective features may be seen, counted and agreed upon by two or more observers. Similarly, they propose a rule for the subjective features of the supermarket, apparent behaviours of people at the checkout, which involves perception, interpretation and inference-making immediately after the act of observation. Two or more observers may be less likely to agree about the subjective features and their meanings in this supermarket environment. Similarly, the obligations to, or 'ownership' of, a technique by a discipline-based paradigm ought to be recognized. Descriptions based on 'grounded theory' are, for instance, rooted in the Symbolic Interactionist paradigm of sociology. Users also need to be conversant with the methodological limitations and controls on scope that are an inescapable part of the technique. The version of ethnography that we exemplified earlier, ethnographic semantics, is heavily dependent upon the verbal utterances of informants. It is also useful for a user to know a little of the controversies that surround any techniques selected. So-called *ethogenic* approaches (described in full in Cohen and Manion, 1994, ch. 10) are indicative of research preferments that rarely shake off searching questions about the validity, meaning and significance of highly subjectivized personal experiences offered as primary data in research reports. However, ethogenic approaches have an ideas and procedural base that attempts to be justificatory in its own terms. First, they have a concern for how social institutions and practices come into being. Second, they dissect the character of such institutions and practices at points in historical time. Third, they apply the postulate that social interaction in institutions is meaningful in ways localized to the institution but generalized to the culture. Thus, slang expressions used by police officers when describing the criminal underworld to each other are more generally indicative of the shorthand, explanatory function of slang in wider society. Fourth, and like ethnographic semantics, ethogenic approaches tend to be very interested in the wider functions of language. *Speech acts* as they are termed, are examined for how they make thought and action intelligible. The so-called *common sense* in everyday behaviour is unpicked for its origin, evolution and institutionally bounded character.

Amongst descriptive approaches 'grounded theory' has proved seductively popular in PBE work in recent years. The fullest exemplification, the seminal work if you like, of grounded theory and its descriptive techniques is the Glaser and Strauss text *The Discovery of Grounded Theory* (1980). In this book, as in subsequent texts by the same authors and other tomes enthusiastic about such an approach, the core idea is broached: data is collected to generate explanatory theory. As information is collected and analysed, explanations emerge which have the status of substantive 'grounded' theory. The explanations are 'substantive' in that they apply to a carefully defined area of social behaviour, such as the initiation rites of Hell's Angels. The explanations are 'grounded' in that they emerge inductively from data actually produced by the membership of groups such as Hell's Angels via descriptive and recording devices – for instance, action summaries, informal interviews, indirect observations and member diaries.

The accumulation of data to produce 'grounded theory' is described in the book by Glaser and Strauss as 'the constant comparative method of qualitative analysis'. Our interpretation of this is that it is not a specific method at all. Rather, it is a set of principles for orderly description and analysis. The principles do not have an intrinsic discipline like ethnographic semantics. They are rules of interrogation for use with primarily descriptive instruments such as observation schedules, critical incident analysis pro formas, aides mémoire, interview transcripts, and so on.

These 'rules' operate as follows. As incidents occur in a behaviour setting they are recorded. As the stockpile of incidents grows like is compared with like. Similar incidents are grouped under category labels. Separate incidents form unique categories. If there is doubt about the meaning of incidents, a separate memo is written for each. As category labels accumulate, their definitions and meanings are checked with members of the behaviour setting and/or other researchers. Where an incident can be recorded in more than one data format (word – picture – graph) the permanent record consists of one illustration only. A continuous narrative 'story' is written including each separate illustration of an incident. The story has the character of an ongoing serial. The story eventually becomes 'theoretically saturated'. That is, many incidents and their explanatory categories telling the full or almost the full story of the activities and behaviour of members of the group under investigation during the period of research, comprise the narrative. The details of the narrative can then be compared with concepts and explanatory theories to be found in the published literature about the same behavioural setting. When additional data fails to produce new categories or add to the 'story' theoretical saturation is said to be complete and the process of data acquisition ceases. The narrative concludes with a summary: maximizing different behavioural responses of individuals and subgroups; and, abstracted statements about the uniqueness of the categories produced from the incidents that is readily comprehensible to laymen interested in the behaviour setting.

Figure 4.2 (p. 118) shows data gathered by a descriptive device, a structured classroom observation schedule, contributing to a narrative on the constraining conditions of classroom life. This observation was number 17 in a series of 50 conducted in secondary schools. The key feature of the unfolding narrative is 'expressive events'. That is, the depiction of events in which the key occupants of classrooms – teachers and students – express themselves in an emotional and personal manner. Other key features of the narrative included 'normative' or rules-related events and 'instrumental' or curriculum-related events. The direct observation of classroom activity in this way had two main functions. First, the observations produced information to help verify a range of social influences postulated to influence the in-school behaviour of teachers and pupils. More simply, the observations provided visible evidence of norms in schools and classrooms. Second, the observations produced information that is explicable in terms of the impact of these norms – that is, their effect in shaping the evaluative behaviour of pupils and teachers in classrooms. This, in turn, helped in the construction of a narrative about school life revolving around a grounded theory based on three explanatory constructs: instrumental, expressive, normative events. This three-constructs theory could then be reinterrogated against extant positions in the social science literature on these broad ideas for construing social life. It should be noted that in devising this observation instrument a technical problem had to be surmounted. This was whether to record unstructured observations and to construe them retrospectively. The preferred alternative was to allocate observed phenomena to categories judged to be relevant to broader theoretical explanation at the time of the observation. This, and similar technical dilemmas, is the sort of decision-making conundrum that routinely faces descriptive data gathering associated with 'grounded theory'.

Interview-based approaches

Interviews represent possibly the most respectable data-gathering technique in qualitative approaches to social and educational research. They are certainly among the most widely used. Interviews come in different shapes and sizes: informal, with hardly any control; 'grand tour', relying on responses to a single 'big' question; semi-structured, in which interview questions are largely based on predetermined ideas or theory held by the practitioner-researcher, but which are sufficiently 'open' to allow a respondent to develop a point of view; fully structured, in which the questions define a tight universe of content and which force the respondent to remain 'on task' and to give specific answers throughout the duration of the interview. Fully structured interviews are often check-list based, where the interviewer simply ticks boxes as the respondent replies.

Interviews permit the exploration of topics in depth. They are rather more effective at this than other techniques. Questionnaires are 'shallower' by comparison. Other advantages include the opportunity on the part of the interviewer to explain the research and the purposes of questions in the face-to-face situation. They are highly adaptable and the practised interviewer can make full use of the responses to mediate the interview as it progresses. Interviews also permit the manipulation of motivation and satisfaction

Figure 4. 2 Expressive event sequence in mathematics

VENUE: School B   GROUP: Year 12 Mathematics
LOCATION: Room C9   N = 16 (6F; 10 M)
OBSERVATION NUMBER: 17   OBSERVATION NUMBER PER GROUP: 5
                                              LESSON DURATION: 40 minutes

1   The teacher is wandering about the room. Students sit in clusters at
     small tables.
     Teacher: 'Everybody ready for the fray? Peter, recapitulate the proba-
     bility theorem, the proof of probability.'

2   Peter: 'If you have three envelopes and three letters and you put one
     letter in one envelope and two letters ...'

3   Sylvia (interjecting rapidly and waving hand): 'The theorem not the
     example dummy: he (teacher) wants P (A or B or C) = P (A) + P (B) +
     P (C).'

4   Teacher (feigning irony): 'Is that what I want Sylvia? Stephen, write the
     theorem on the board please and then explain it.'

5   Stephen (resignedly) writes the theorem on the board and says: 'It's in
     the book, about page 30, and check the multiplication principle while
     you're at it.'

6   Teacher: 'Stephen I asked you to explain the theorem not sermonize.'
     Stephen then pedantically explains the theorem.

7   Teacher: 'A tennis club has twelve members and four courts therefore
     the probability that one court ... ladies (to a group of three girls sitting
     together on the far side of the room and who have taken no part in
     proceedings so far) are you watching over there?' One of the girls
     nods, the other two flush and then stare at the teacher in a manner
     bordering on hostility.

8   The teacher abruptly walks to front of the room and draws the following
     Venn diagrams on the blackboard. He says: 'This shows the problem and
     its nature, the circles intersecting may be thought of as the theorem. The
     theorem of course can be put to the probabilities of anything.'

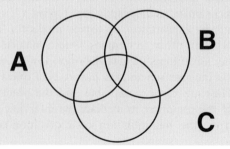

9   'Not bad', says the teacher, admiringly surveying his own handiwork. He now moves towards the group of three girls he had earlier remonstrated with. He sits on an empty chair alongside the girls and studies their exercise books. The rest of the class appear nonplussed and some make half-hearted attempts to continue studying textbook problems. Cursorily, and over his shoulder, teacher says: 'It's Maths week. Do the problems for homework.'

10 Sylvia indignantly and with heavy sarcasm snaps: 'Do we get a prize', and then turns to engage two other girls in private conversation.

11 Stephen, standing by the blackboard, looks at Sylvia, at the teacher, at his work on the board. He says nothing, throw his hands in the air and rejoins three of his grinning, male classmates at a hexagonal table at the side of the class opposite to the spot where the teacher is now preoccupied.

12 The remaining eight minutes of lesson time are taken up with four sets of group activities: Stephen and his group, Sylvia and her group, the teacher and his group, and the remaining male students, Peter amongst them. The bell rings and, without teacher prompting, the students leave the room as separate groups. The teacher and his group remain long after the bell.

variables allowing the emergence of information concerning negative aspects of self and feelings towards others. Interviews can be an important control on reliability when data gathered via other means, but from the same universe of content, is compared with the interview responses.

Disadvantages with interviews are well known; they include response sets where the interviewee seeks to please the interviewer. The tendency for interviews to descend into argument is another problem. Interviews cannot be effectively conducted by non-practised interviewers. It is really a technique that requires systematic training. Other problems are the assumption that the language and wording in the interview schedule will be appropriate to the vocabulary limits of interviewees. Interviews may be conducted for a variety of reasons. The technique may be used for assessing a person's judgment of their own performance. Occupational performance 'appraisals' are of this type. Sampling opinions about a range of matters is often the characteristic of market-research interviewing. Testing preconceived notions is, perhaps, a more subtle and demanding form of interviewing. Providing information that only the respondent holds or has access to, especially if he or she is a specialist in some field, is possibly the most powerful use of the interview technique in social and educational research. Our final exhibit in this chapter is an interview schedule of this type (see below). It is a semi-structured directed interview with a particular role holder in the educational

(Australian state schools) system. The interview, designed to last a maximum of one hour, contains questions that are designed to 'tap' into the specialized knowledge and role of this respondent. Questions of this type usually impress a respondent. In seeing that his world is recognized, he is likely to provide discrete information as well as an evaluative judgment from his professional standpoint of that information. The variability in the questions should be noted: some provide stimulus material to respond to, others seek an opinion; still others lead into trends that the researcher wishes to pursue. In total, the ten questions cover the universe of content (assessment

Directed Interview Schedule with District Moderator – Mathematics

1 What are the major constraints on maths teaching in state high schools?

2 Mathematics is one of the few subjects differentiated by complexity in the syllabus. Why has differentiation occurred in maths and not in other subjects?

3 In a 1982 edition of the journal of the Maths Teacher Association, a leading article called for a return to externally set and marked examinations for Year 12 students. What does this represent?

4 A recurrent source of concern during the 10 years or so of the Radford Scheme centred about the issue of 'moderation'. From your standpoint as district moderator what would you see as the problems of moderation?

5 Is ROSBA* an appropriate development of the Mark I version of Radford?

6 What administrative problems does ROSBA pose for ordinary maths teachers?

7 Is the compilation of TE† scores in any way influenced by a student's selection of subjects in Year 12?

8 My research tends to indicate that students in high school even the bright ones, perceive the maths that they are taught as abstract and inferential. Is modern maths abstract to the point where it is alienating students?

9 Teachers, parent and students frequently accord more prestige to maths than to other school subjects. What are some of the consequences of this?

10 How will maths teachers accommodate the increasing numbers of 'non academic' students returning to studies in Year 11?

* ROSBA = Review of School-Based Assessments, a statewide evaluation of the system of school-based assessments in Queensland.

† Tertiary Entrance Score = A numerical total assessment score used for university entrance purposes.

in mathematics education in Years 10–12 in high schools) in which the researcher is interested.

Classifying the purpose of an interview is a most important part of the research task. Conducting it is equally important. Attention to venue, time and means of recording information should be given priority. Ideally, interviews should be audio recorded and the tape transcribed. However, some interviewees are resistant to audio recording and this should be accepted. An interview is an intensely personal and ethically problematic encounter. For that reason we offer the following list of good practice points:

- Prior to the interview engage the respondent in casual small talk for a few minutes to establish a rapport.
- Assure the respondent that all information will be treated with the utmost confidentiality.
- Avoid cross-examination. The interview venue is not a court room. Pause after the respondent has completed each answer to a question then follow up carefully if required.
- Do not contradict and do not argue against respondent views. It is not the prerogative of interviewers to make moral judgments about respondent answers.
- If a respondent appears threatened by a question pass over it, or change the subject.
- Beware the leading question. That is, any question that, because of its phrasing, leads the respondent to consider one reply more desirable than another – for example, 'In view of the dangers of centralized control, do you feel government financial aid to state schools is desirable?'

Given that interviewing can be a highly subjective technique, a careful pilot study is the best insurance a researcher has against bias and ineffectiveness. A pilot study should test the adequacy of wording in questions; whether the respondents to be selected have a common frame of reference; the degree of interest in the topic represented by the range of questions; motivation to comply with the researcher's procedural requirements; the balance between structured and open questions; the practicality of recording methods and planned analysis. It should be noted that even a 30-minute interview may produce a typed transcript of upwards of four pages in length (see the example provided with the ethnography). Only a fraction of the information can be used in a report.

In this chapter we have considered some implications of the term 'research design' for PBE. We used analogies in this process. Explanation and knowledge criteria were offered as critical illuminators of research design. A full example of a PBE based on a methodology known as ethnographic semantics was then provided to illustrate design in actualization. Following this example we provided shorthand accounts of approaches to educational and social research that are commonly drawn upon in PBE. An emphasis here was on the character and practical features of these approaches. There is always the danger of oversimplification in this. We wrote this section in the manner noted in an attempt to explain the relationship between design as data gathering and design as data analysis. This conjunction is difficult to write about and difficult to achieve in the conduct of practitioner-based enquiry. It is a conjunction that cannot, however, be shirked. For this reason we now turn in Chapter 5 towards some of the ontological and epistemological tensions that surround this conjunction. In short, we theorize further about methods and methodology in PBE.

5   Contriving Methodology
Bringing Unity to Knowing and Doing in Research Activity

The construction of our argument so far about PBE is that it is a relatively unique form of research. The term 'research' is itself contested and used to describe a range of activities that differ in the sorts of ways we have outlined in the previous chapters. Variations and differences tend to create disagreements about what does and does not count as research. We want to emphasize the point in this chapter that this is more than esoteric debate. The label 'research' affects peoples' perception of an activity and any claim to worth or knowledge that accompanies that activity. The appellation 'research' tends to bestow credibility on an activity that may, on closer scrutiny, be undeserving. We have sought to relate PBE to the criteria of credibility and admissibility by identifying it as a process that involves systematic data gathering, a process of analysis that leads to the production of factual rather than fictitious information, and a process that is useful to the practitioner-researcher in his or her occupational context. In the sections that follow we want to examine further the justificatory character of this orientation.

Part A: PBE – Method or Methodology?

Practitioners who are relative newcomers to educational research often rely on standard textbooks for guidance. Some of these we have identified in context in our chapters. Others we list in our bibliography at the end of this book. Some of these books are clear in the information they provide and literate in the sense that the language of explanation they use is comprehensible. Other works are opaque or dense in the messages they attempt to convey. Sometimes, the language used, particularly when it ventures into the domain of social philosophy, is abstract to the point of incomprehensibility. Numerous outcomes are possible with books of this type. Some people are intellectually intimidated or alienated. The tacit message is taken to be: You are not smart enough to understand my argument. Consequently, people put the book down and never approach educational research again. Some people take the opaqueness to be an indicator of profundity. The interpretation is: I can't really understand the author but he must be very clever. The tendency is to 'join the club', to use the language and ideas of the original without really understanding them or examining them for meaning. Still other people find their itch being scratched by such works. The tacit response is: This guy is on to something that bugs me. I need to know more.

One of the problems with research literature is its tendency to conflate or use interchangeably two terms: methods and methodology. Schratz and Walker (1995; p.12) have this to say:

> The significance of the term 'methodology' is that it requires an argument to connect the choice and practice of particular methods to the way that the problem is conceived and the utility and limitations of the outcome. It is in this sense of the term, as requiring a critical justification for the adoption and practice of particular research methods, that we claim that our concern is with 'methodology' rather than with methods alone.

Initially, this citation may seem to belong to the 'opaque school of explanation'. Not so. The description of 'methodology' as a 'critical justification' for the adoption and practice of particular research methods is consistent with the representation of the PBE enterprise that we wish to purvey. However, two further conceptual points need to be introduced at this stage to clarify the emerging distinction between methods and methodology. These points are embedded in two words that appear in many textbooks on social and educational research: *ontology* and *epistemology*. The latter we introduced previously. The former we have tried to avoid saying anything about until it is unavoidable. Ontology refers to questions and assumptions concerning the nature of being human and located in a social world. (Sometimes described as a metaphysical concern.) Epistemology, as we have suggested, concentrates on the nature of knowledge: good, bad, fact, value, ideology, possible, impossible, science, folklore, true, false, religious, voodoo, subjective, objective, subjective, and so on. Epistemology tries to answer (or at least explore) the question: What does it mean to know?

The word 'methodology' is indicative of the unity of ontology and epistemology in any act purporting to call itself research. That is, methodology or the total process of a research enquiry, will reflect a fusion in the researcher's mind of what he or she thinks is the essence of human nature with ideas on the tangibility and origins of knowledge, and the appropriateness of data-gathering techniques implied. Ontological assumptions will give rise to epistemological assumptions which have methodological implications for the choice of particular techniques of data collection. This is the voice of Hitchcock and Hughes (1989, p. 15), it is the voice of Hammersley (1993), and in 2000 it is the voice of Murray and Lawrence in this volume. In a broad theoretical sense, it is – what is.

Now that we have made everything clear about Big Questions let us say a bit more about methodological issues in the context of PBE. These are defined by: How? That is: How were the research questions formulated ? How was a particular theory applied? How was a particular data-gathering technique employed? Thinking ontologically and epistemologically in this way about what one is doing and why helps to reduce the tendency to grab the security blanket of an 'ology'. Because it is tempting to think of methodology in terms of what the 'ologies' offer by way of a menu or recipe, or to be persuaded by pragmatic concerns such as cost, time, resources, availability of a sample, etc., it is easy to lose the more abstract frame of reference. If it is lost, then the justificatory basis for PBE as 'good research' is somewhat weakened.

We are not arguing for metaphysical digressions here. Neither are we arguing for people to do courses in analytical philosophy before they can do PBE. We are arguing for a consciousness about the distinction between methods and methodology. Methods are perhaps best thought of as the tools of the trade. It is possible to use 'antipositivistic' techniques with a positivistic framework. Similarly, it is possible to quantify material gathered ethnographically. The Ethnograph for example (see Tesch, 1990, p. 251), is elaborate software that takes text as scripted data from interview transcripts, segments, codes, collates it and offers numerical options for analysis of the treated data. The program can flaunt its statistical elegance in basically qualitative work to count the number of times a respondent or informant made a precise utterance. Our argument therefore suggests we should acknowledge and be clear about the status of use of a particular data-gathering technique (method) within an overarching framework for action and explanation (methodology). In this day and age, it is no longer sufficient (if it ever was) to compile a questionnaire and semi-structured interview schedule and automatically assume we are marching on the 'Yellow Brick Road to Truth'. Recognizing the problem solving (eclecticism? perhaps, but not quite) approach in educational research is laudable and potentially very productive.

Indeed, a problem-solving approach is the defining feature of many excellent examples of practitioner-based enquiry. In the real world of social and educational research, methodological choices are often a compromise between explicit preference, expedience, default factors arising out of the conditions pertaining in the research venue, and so on. It is helpful, therefore, if researcher and audience are of one mind about procedural decisions and their attendant assumptions. To consider the whole research process rather than applying discrete methods according to rules of application set out in the standard text is, in our scheme, to be setting about better research practice. If budding practitioner researchers try to enact the principles of PBE that we introduced in Chapter 1, then methodological anarchy or methodological stereotyping stands a chance of being avoided. That is, frequent return to the principles will help to preserve the intellectual clarity and orderliness of selected research procedures.

Towards Unification of the 'Divided Mentality'

Following the argument presented in Chapter 2, it ought now to be clear that groups of methods and groups of methodologies cluster in two broad membership categories: normal science or interpretive approaches. Recognising this membership orientation is the first step towards achieving a unification of the 'divided mentality'. A second step is the *interchangeability of terms* factor. Normal science may variously be referred to as 'normativism', 'positivism', 'the scientific method', 'the dominant paradigm' and 'quantitative methodology'. Interpretive approaches may be variously referred to as 'qualitative methods', 'antipositivism', 'postmodernist theorizing', 'interaction-ism', 'ethnographic modelling' or even 'social phenomenology'. Needless to say, there is potential for confusion over terminology alone. Sorting out one's terminology means sorting out ontological and epistemological positions. If this can be done with one's own methodology then, again, there is some advance towards methodological unity and integrity.

Whilst we were critical of the 'divided mentality' in Chapter 2, we revisit it here because of its deep and pervasive influence in social and educational research. Astute observers of research activity and its reporting are aware of the problematic distinction in the use of the first person (I/we) rather than the third person (it/they). In a sense, this problematic symbolizes the character of research reports produced within the 'camp' of normal or interpretive science. We do not wish to exaggerate the significance of heuristic devices for they take the argument away from research methodology and more into the area of language use, syntax rules and sociolinguistics. It is hard to actually find binding rules on the use of pronouns in report writing. It is much easier to find evidence of 'tendencies' that reflect the broad membership orientation we have outlined. What do these tendencies imply?

The use of the third person in writing signifies objectivity. It is a requirement of the natural sciences. Usage connotes a complex of assumptions about the scientific status of the social and natural world as viewed from this membership vantage point. Indeed, it may be possible to say that the assumption of no distinction between the social and natural worlds is made via this device in use. The social world is therefore amenable to the methods of the natural sciences. Just as the application of heat to water will create observable and quantifiable change, the application of a psychological factor will cause observable and quantifiable behaviour. Third person writing may also sometimes seem preoccupied with large data-sets. This is because of the need to be nomothetic: that is, explanation (theory) should be applicable to a large number of cases. There may also be an emphasis on law-like statements, statistical probabilities and patterns indicative of regularity and predictability. The consensus and conflict accounts of society, previously discussed, are indicative of this writing tendency.

In contrast, the subjectivisation in the writing tendency of interpretive science (I/me/we) is a *cri de coeur* that people are not things. They do not blindly react to external (societal) forces. They construct, reconstruct and negotiate social situations. The new teacher meeting a class for the first time does not simply follow the NUT rule book. The country parson alters his sermon according to the mood of the congregation. Roles are not predetermined. Social life is constantly changing and meanings are created, destroyed and recreated. This view is perhaps the most prized intellectual possession of the phenomenologist. If a researcher practitioner is people-oriented in his work, it is not surprising to find a writing style characterised by first person usage. This is a signification of a dual ontological kind: people first in the research and researcher as 'person-first' in writing about people in research.

Choice, Bias and Research Methodology

Some people undertaking practitioner research remain sublimely unaware of ontological and epistemological baggage. Even at the conclusion of a PBE project, the more profound implications of the work may not be recognised. Other practitioner researchers veer towards the other pole: that is, the work for the PBE because of its intensity and proximity to self, tends only to confirm in the researcher's mind the veracity of his own ontological preferences. There are very real dangers in this. At the least harmful end, where the PBE has no consequences for anyone but the person doing it, it can lead to a kind of reified orthodoxy where the methodology of the PBE becomes the only one used in the future. At the other end, where the PBE is publicly touted to have consequences for research practice as well as public policy in an area of educational endeavour, it can lead to the adoption of an ideological mindset that gradually becomes intolerant to other ontological alternatives.

Methodological choices may be based upon pragmatism: Have I the time to commit to this enquiry? Are sufficient resources available? Have I got the statistical knowledge to do a quick 2×2 contingency analysis? What research method can I pluck off the shelf to do the job? In truth though, methodological choices involve ontological and epistemological preference as well as technical expertise at data gathering. Preference for techniques and forms of explanation means that *bias*, the skewing of an enquiry in a particular direction, will always occur in some form. Systematic bias is where the enquiry is known and planned to lead in a particular direction. Some techniques such as the forced choice Likert-style response format in questionnaires (see the example provided in the previous chapter) control 'bias' through mathematical rules under levels of measurement. Where 'unsystematic bias' or 'extraneous variance' occurs as a function of ontological preferment, an enquiry can become seriously distorted in its explanations. This is why limitations and delimitations are so important. Knowing the material to be manipulated in an enquiry is a step towards minimizing inaccuracy. Achieving balance in regarding detail as important to self but less important to significant others will also help. Similarly, attention to detail in checking and rechecking the enquiry process as it proceeds will also help to contain bias.

Criteria for Assessing Practitioner-Based Enquiry

Below is our 'checklist' for assessing the worth of a particular PBE, the validity of its claim to knowledge when set against conventional academic expectations in the university environment and for minimizing inaccuracy and bias. The criteria are not the only criteria. They are not necessarily the 'best' criteria. But external examiners repeatedly tell us that they are 'good' criteria. We have used them routinely in the academic mode to mark PBEs submitted for academic credit. Perhaps, more importantly, we have used them in an evolutionary way to construe the creature of PBE. Some of the criteria are unremarkable and will be found in any assessment specification for assignment work. Some are rather more 'slippery', exploring the ontological and epistemological possibilities that PBE approaches can legitimately pursue.

Checklist for assessing the worth of a PBE

(a) The identification of an appropriate topic to include:
- an adequate and succinct specification of the purpose of the enquiry
- the setting of effective limits to the scope of the enquiry
- the clarification of organizational or institutional contexts from which the purpose of the enquiry derives.

(b) The revelation of significant affective attributes of the topic to include:
- clarification of the social relationships amongst the persons concerned
- analysis of the communication patterns amongst the persons concerned
- examination of the different attitudinal viewpoints of the persons concerned.

(c) Demonstrated evidence of significant and dispassionate reflection on the enquiry undertaken to include:
- information revealing improved knowledge of constraints on teaching and learning
- information that discloses insights into one's own personal motives for the conduct and justification of the enquiry.

(d) Indicators of the use of knowledge and experience of others to facilitate the enquiry to include:
- accounts that evidence the opinions of persons directly involved in the enquiry
- accounts that evidence the knowledge and expertise of persons indirectly involved in the enquiry
- accounts that evidence the use of resource persons, tutors, trainers, advisory teachers, curriculum specialists and other professionals in educational organizations.

(e) Anticipation of the consequences of the enquiry to include:
- the establishment of an ethical framework (see Chapter 2) for the conduct of the enquiry
- consideration of the ways in which the enquiry might help to improve teaching and learning
- showing how the enquiry might eventually contribute to policy development in education.

(f) The formulation of substantive theory specific to the organizational context in which the enquiry is located to include:
- the fitting of theoretical statements to the classroom or instructional venue in which they will be applied
- rendering theoretical statements intelligible to persons working in and around classrooms and instructional venues
- the suggestion of tactics to be drawn from the theoretical statements in order to predict and control events in classrooms and venues.

(g) Comparisons of derived, substantive theory with more generally available explanatory theory to include:
- reviews of the literature to locate existing and relevant theories
- the identification of strengths and weaknesses of substantive theory in the perspective of published works

- reworking and synthesizing substantive theory to accommodate current and established viewpoints.

(h) A coherent plan of the enquiry to include:
- the selection of research instruments appropriate to the purposes of the enquiry
- the establishment of an administrative protocol for the procedural management of the study
- the setting of an effective and realistic time sequence for data collection, processing and analysis.

(i) • Mechanisms to test the effectiveness of the research plan to include:
- comparison of the plan with other plans already established, especially those claiming to be case studies or action research
- consultation with colleagues on the adequacy of the plan
- statements of delimitations to control contingencies such as reliability, sampling and construct validity.

(j) Evidence of effective implementation of the plan to include:
- data gathering, records keeping, document collecting, interim report writing and monitoring and adjusting these processes as need arises
- reporting on the collaborative and participative aspects of the enquiry
- effective closure through data processing, inference making and the formulation of conclusions.

(k) A systematic evaluation of the enquiry to include:
- the devising of mechanisms for the provision of feedback to respondents and persons connected with the enquiry
- ascertaining the effects of the enquiry, especially changes in behaviour and the circumstances in which these occur
- self-assessment to detect changes in one's own behaviour as a result of involvement in the enquiry.

(l) A process of end consultation with other evaluators to include:
- comparisons of one's own evaluative judgements with those made by others
- the seeking of additional external information on the extent to which the enquiry's purpose has been met

- the negotiation of a framework through which confidentiality can be maintained but results usefully disseminated.

(m) Outcomes in use to include:
- final reports and artefacts
- documentation of research findings in a form useful to other educational practitioners and decision-makers
- recommendations for extensions to this enquiry via additional PBEs
- commentary upon the extent to which one's own personal and social development has been advantaged by the enquiry process
- refereed publications deriving from the PBE.

Note: Not all of these criteria will necessarily apply all of the time. However, a satisfactory enquiry will demonstrate most of these elements.

Obligations in Methodology

The practitioner researcher does not simply gain ontological and epistemological wisdom through osmosis or mystical process. The sorts of understandings and technical skills immanent in the above criteria have to be worked towards and arrived at after study, reading and practice of technique in research venues. We now want, therefore, to elaborate further some of the craft aspects or knowledge of research methodology that seem particularly applicable to PBE.

1 Essential considerations in the theory of 'reliability' and 'validity'

'Reliability' is often mistakenly understood as a pure mathematical condition of measurement instruments used in educational and social research. It is not quite so categorical. Reliability is the other side of the coin of 'validity'. In determining the construct validity of a measurement instrument we pursue the truth, meaningfulness and substantive adequacy of the theory underpinning the instrument. Validity is a very complex topic. Ideas such as *intelligence quotient* (IQ), *learning style* and *standard assessment task* (SAT), while in regular terminological use in the education industry, raise difficult questions of meaning. Do these words, for that is what they are, actually represent measurable qualities that they purport to represent? Validity is all about the meaning and character of variables used in research enquiries (see the opinion inventory and its features explained in Chapter 4). In determining the reliability of the same instrument we are pursuing the capacity of that instrument to obtain the same or broadly similar results at different times when used by different people. In order to be able to interpret a test or a measure, quantitative or qualitative, it must be reliable. In this sense *reliability* is at the heart of measurement theory. Question: What sense could we make of a test or measure that produced different results every time it is used?

Reliability as a measure of predictability

Educational and social research often involves predicting the occurrence or influence on educational practices of social and psychological factors such as attitude, sex, personality, age, socio-economic status, etc. A measurement instrument that purports to be reliable would consistently show the influence of the factors when used over and over again with the survey populations for whom it was designed. Question: Why might it not consistently show the influence of such factors with other survey populations? The most rudimentary use of the term 'reliability' is when it indicates the capacity of a measurement instrument to produce the same or similar scores over time.

Reliability as an indicator of measurement accuracy

Mathematicians are often interested in the 'true' scores of people who undertake achievement tests, proficiency examinations, psychometric profiles, and so on. Similarly, social and educational researchers need to be reasonably convinced that whatever the measure used, the scores reported are a 'true' or correct representation of the person's performance. The conventional comparison of results tables is possibly the best example of reliability as an indicator of 'truth' (for an extended discussion see Kerlinger 1986, ch. 26). Consider the following example in Table 5.1:

Table 5.1 Scores for five geography students on an objective test*

A		B		C	
Correct	*Rank*	*Score from reliable test*	*Rank*	*Score from unreliable test*	*Rank*
63	1	66	1	36	4
60	2	61	2	41	3
55	3	57	3	64	2
50	4	52	4	23	5
45	5	46	5	70	1

Source: Kerlinger (1986, p. 406)
Note: *using the procedure of rank order correlation

In this example, the researcher producing the scores for B does not quite hit the correct or 'true' score as represented by A. He does, though, produce the same rank suggesting his reliability or measurement accuracy is high. The researcher producing the scores for C is clearly using an instrument that is unreliable. He has been unable to reproduce the same rank order as A and B.

Reliability as an indicator of error in measurement

There is always error built in to measurement instruments. In the case of the opinion inventory in Chapter 4, the absence of a 'neutral' category in the Likert response format is an example of systematic, though controlled, measurement bias or error. The practitioner researcher needs to know something about the magnitude of error in his instruments and to know enough about measurement theory and statistics to construe it. For example, when an instrument produces scores that skew in one direction there is said to be systematic error or variance. However, it is to be more generally expected that on any measurement instrument scores will vary first one way, then in another direction. This is the phenomenon of random error. It is the product of unknown or random factors at work – the chance element if you like. This may be caused by temporary lapses of concentration in the respondent, particular local conditions that affected completion of the instrument, etc. Here, 'reliability' may be defined in terms of the relative absence of chance or random errors of measurement. Statisticians express these issues under the formal theory of reliability as a heuristic equation. Thus Kerlinger (1986, p. 407) puts it as follows:

$$Xt = Xoo + Xe$$

where Xt represents the sum of the 'true' and 'error' components of the score, Xoo represents 'true' scores (in which 'oo', signifying infinity, is taken as true) for each respondent and Xe represents 'error' scores.

Reliability as an indicator of test/retest consistency

If a test yields a certain rank order of individuals, and the second, third and fourth subsequent administration of the test yields approximately the same rank order, then the test/retest reliability of the instrument is said to be high. The statistical interpretation of this is that the test is able to give an arithmetic indication, by manipulating a correlation coefficient, of individual variation or 'variance', as it is called, through treating each Xoo as the mean of a large number of Xts produced by giving the test to a respondent a large number of times.

Split half reliability

In Chapter 4 we reported a technical feature of the exemplar opinion inventory. We said it was constructed around principles of 'split half' reliability. This is essentially to do with the internal consistency of the test. In survey research, it is often not possible to undertake retest procedures with a survey sample. That is, practical difficulties prevent the researcher from repeating the survey with the same sample, say, six months after the original survey. People move on, conditions change, resources diminish. An alternative technique is to design an instrument so that one set of items within it (the first 30 questions in our exemplar opinion inventory), though worded differently, test the same ideas in the second half (questions 31–60 in Part A of our example). If each respondent's scores on each subset are treated separately, then subset (i) scores can be compared with subset (ii) scores. The average intercorrelation of the subsamples computed under the generalized Spearman–Brown correlation procedure (that is, a standardized statistical measure widely used for this and similar comparisons) produces a measure of the test's internal consistency.

Reliability and triangulation

More measurement sins are committed under the label of 'triangulation' than just about anything else in the measurement box. Cohen and Manion (1994, p. 233) define triangulation as 'the use of two or more methods of data collection in the study of some aspect of human behaviour'. However, we contend that the word 'triangulation' is conceptually elusive and much misused in social and educational research. It is sometimes assumed that using two or more measurement instruments (say, a questionnaire, an interview schedule and a behaviour observation checklist) necessarily makes the testing more reliable. This is not necessarily the case. 'Triangulation' as a process used to explore reliability makes certain assumptions, for example: that different measurement instruments test the same universe of content; that the measurement instruments are broadly comparable in terms of the properties of levels of measurement (nominal/ordinal/interval/ratio); that random error is statistically reduced when two or more instruments are used; that randomness, as a precondition for probability theory to be invoked to establish the statistical integrity of a survey population can be relaxed. All these assumptions are tentative on theoretical grounds and problematic on arithmetic grounds. It is too easy, therefore, to conflate 'triangulation' and 'reliability'.

Validity

Earlier, we began an analysis of reliability by comparing it with construct validity. Validity goes to the very centre of social and educational research.

It is usually defined via a question: Are we investigating what we think we are investigating? We might put the point another way: Do we know what we are talking about? Validity is all about the ideas base of research design. The opinion inventory introduced in the previous chapter had an ideas base that was all about *norms* or social rules and patterns of expectations governing school life. It is important to grasp the multidimensional character of validity. Tests and scales are designed to measure particular ideas bases that are theorized or posited to exist. Thus, the concept of 'personality' is explored by reference to extraversion and introversion in the Eysenck Personality Inventory (EPI), whereas the same concept (personality) is represented by no less than 16 ideas in the Cattell 16 Personality Factor Inventory. Clearly, there is a fundamental difference between Eysenck and Cattell about the nature of 'personality'. Both instruments are technically sophisticated, statistically reliable and standardized to large populations. Who is right therefore about personality? The answer is that within the limits of theory and measurement they are both right. The ideas base (theory of personality) arrived at by a long process of study, conjecture and analysis for each instrument is different but said to be internally valid. The applicability of these inventories, though, to generalized populations of adults, is locked to the notion of 'external validity' and 'representativeness'. Question: Can a personality characteristic such as 'extraversion' be adequately measured by a pencil and paper test?

Constructs and concepts

Validity is usually 'captured' in social and educational research through constructs and concepts. These have similar but not identical meanings. A concept is a generalizing idea or term, useful for classifying phenomena. Concepts are generally regarded as in the public domain and often make up the structure of a subject or discipline. In geography, for example, concepts such as scale, location, distance, direction, contribute to the structure of that subject. In medical science, terms such as sutures, prognosis, care plans, medication, perform a similar function. Constructs are contrived concepts. They may not necessarily be in the public domain That is, they are ideas consciously and systematically thought up by researchers which are used for specific purposes of explanation (theory) or measurement (empiricism). Behavioural scientists and educational researchers frequently derive and use constructs such as school aptitude, educability, creativity, professionalism, attainment, etc. Constructs are often used in a jigsaw fashion to produce sophisticated conceptual schemes of the phenomena under investigation. Consider Table 4.1 (p. 107). This is a detailed elaboration of the constructs appearing in the 'lower half' of Figure 2.2 (p. 39). Notice how these constructs are defined or 'operationalized'. Question: Why is it necessary to have 'empirically defined key indicators' for these constructs? This conceptual scheme is the underpinning theorem of the opinion inventory in Figure 4.1 (p. 97). The constructs are reflected in, and 'tested' by, questions 1–60 in Part A of that inventory. A constitutive construct is one defined by another construct – for example, 'height' can be substituted by 'altitude'. Being able to substitute one idea for another makes clearer the properties embedded in the idea. Constitutive constructs are seen as crucial in the development of explanatory theory for they have the in-built capacity for self-explanation.

Operational definitions of constructs

An operational definition of a construct is one which assigns special meaning to a word or term. Usually this is done to show the manner in which the idea will be tested or measured. Thus 'attitude' may be measured by a pencil and paper test, by observation of behaviour in discrete behaviour settings, or by reference to a horoscope. Operational definitions may also be used to connote in relatively precise form the complex properties of abstract ideas. Thus 'reasoning' may be defined as the capacity to think independently, to read and understand written instructions, and to predict outcomes once instructions are enacted. Operational definitions are crucially important in research. They act as a bridge between original hypotheses and working propositions and actual practical activities of measurement and observation. It has to be remembered, though, that the relationship between the definition of phenomena and measures of indicators of phenomena is an inferred one, i.e., a presumption is made that behaviours recorded or observed may be adequately described by the definitions established. Indeed, it may be helpful to think of constructs as 'nonobservables' and operationally defined constructs as 'observables'.

Constructs as independent and dependent variables

We have previously used the conventional research terminology of *dependent* and *independent* variables. It is appropriate to offer a little more explanation on this useful dichotomy. The terms 'dependent' and 'independent' derive from mathematics where phenomena are assigned arithmetic values and located on 'X' (or abscissa) and 'Y' (or ordinate) axes. The independent variable is a presumed cause and the dependent variable is the effect; independent variables are antecedent to dependent variables. Usually, a researcher is trying to explain the dependent variable. For example, 'attainment' is often regarded as a crucial dependent variable in educational research. The *dependency* of attainment *or* its relatedness to other factors requires these factors to be classed as *independent* variables. Their magnitude of influence on attainment varies independently. For example, independent variables known to be related to attainment, and which may be manipulated by the researcher, include socio-economic status, gender, reading age, IQ, and so on. It is possible, of course, for an independent variable to become a dependent variable to suit the purposes of research. Socio-economic status or gender may be held as constants while a researcher probes the ins and outs of attainment.

Attribute variables

These are usually thought of as human and social characteristics such as sex, age, weight, height, religion, ethnicity, marital status, and so forth. As it is not really possible for a researcher to manipulate these (sex can only have two values 0 = male, 1 = female), they are useful for classification and description purposes, particularly with large data-sets. Attribute variables are said to be categorical. This refers to the type of measurement they permit. Categorical variables belong to the nominal level of measurement in which members of a subset are named the same (nominal) and assigned the same numeral as in '0' for male and '1' for female. In this way 'male' and 'female' are the categorical subset variables of the attribute variable 'sex'.

2 Essential considerations in the theory and practice of observation

In social and educational research, observation – that is, the systematic visual scanning of research subjects by the researcher or a team of trained observers – is a regular part of many data-gathering processes. Much research in the social and behavioural sciences could not proceed without observations of one kind or another. The process of 'seeing' and then 'interpreting' is tacit to, and inevitable in, any enterprise calling itself scientific enquiry. Indeed, the ontological preferments we debated earlier suggest a propensity for 'seeing' and 'interpreting'. In many cases, though, particularly qualitative research designs, observational activity as a means of data gathering is formalized in varying orders of magnitude related to, and informed by, the purposes of the research. This may well incur a 'training' element in the observation techniques to be used, a basis of selection for a particular style of observation, and strict adherence to protocol (when in the observation setting) established for the particular observation instrument.

Unstructured observation

This is where the observer has no significant scheme to guide his observations. What is seen is what is recorded. Having amassed a series of observations in shorthand written form, the researcher – who may not have actually been the observer – has the difficult *ex post facto* task of 'unpicking' them or explaining their significance. As we pointed out earlier, this will be difficult without some rules for observing and isolating the objective and subjective features of environments. Diaries are frequently full of unstructured observations. Personal accounts of what is seen and done in the aforementioned supermarket may be rich in descriptive detail but lacking in structure. The application of an observation instrument to a social setting based on preconceived notions of *instrumental* or curriculum related events, *expressive* or person/emotion-related events, and *normative* or rules-related events (as in Figure 4.2, p. 118), is very difficult from jottings, anecdotal records, casual field notes, and sensory impressions not disciplined by an exact purpose for observation.

Participant observation

This is where an observer actually joins or becomes a member of a group under investigation. Here the researcher wears two hats: one as an indication of group membership and the obligations that this entails, and the other as that of researcher in which the activities of the group are studied from the inside. The process may be overt (and is usually required to be so) in which group members understand and accept the functions of the observer. The process may be covert (not recommended) in that group members remain unaware that a member is researching their activities. In either mode, participant observation is notoriously tricky to do. Given that the very presence of a researcher-observer in a behaviour setting tends to alter the behaviour of the group members, the possibility for bias in both recording and interpreting behaviour is high.

Direct observation

This is where an observer is close to, but remains apart from, a nominated group of research subjects. It usually involves the recording of observed behaviours according to predetermined categories, as the example in Figure 4.2 (p. 118) illustrates, or by reference to time sequences. There are numerous examples of direct-observation instruments. It is a requirement for the observer-researcher to know what the observation instrument omits as well as what it includes. Instruments based on principles of exclusion (e.g. where only physical movements are noted) or principles of inclusion are particularly susceptible to rules of observation. In illustrating the latter, the well-known Flanders Interaction Analysis Category (FIAC) schedules (Flanders, 1970) use 10 classifiers of teacher/pupil talk to form the basis of observed (and audibly heard) phenomena. It should be noted that FIAC describes verbal utterances of teachers and pupils rather than visible behaviours per se. A simplified portrayal of Flanderian observation categories is as follows:

Teacher talk

1   Accepts feelings

2   Praises
3   Accepts ideas
4   Questions
5   Lectures
6   Commands
7   Criticizes

Pupil talk

8   Solicited
9   Unsolicited
10 Silence

The classroom use of FIAC often involves a timing device or metronome that beeps every three seconds. The verbal utterance occurring at that moment in time is entered on a record sheet for subsequent analysis. The code number (1–10) representing the precise utterance is the figure entered. A matrix completed for a 30-minute lesson may yield some 600 codings. The matrix of observed and recorded codes may be analysed in a number of ways depending upon the purposes of the researcher. A common analysis includes teacher talk termed 'indirect' (categories 1, 2, 3 and 4) with teacher talk termed 'direct' (categories 5, 6 and 7). Various judgments about *teaching style* based on patterns of utterances may be formulated.

Observations as revelatory technique

Observations are designed to provide visible and confirmatory evidence of something. One therefore needs to be knowledgeable about what that 'something' is. Is it to do with furniture arrangements in laboratories? Is it a theory of control in the classroom? Is it about the skills of apprentices in workshops? Observations produce information that is explicable in terms of the evaluative behaviour of people. Having observed such behaviour, it still has to be explained and interpreted. In the case of laboratory furniture, this may have to do with theories of posture at the bench. In the case of class-room control, it may have to do with the optimum conditions for motivating learning to occur. The whole question of observer inference has to be squarely confronted. It should be noted, however, that observations can produce categorical information that can easily be rechecked – for example, the number of people in the room at the time of observation, numbers of females and males, the type of event timetabled (e.g. a demonstration session for trainee physiotherapists), and the artefacts or equipment being used or manipulated. Categorical information gathered via observation can acquire the status of objective archival (i.e. historic) records of people and objects in context.

3 Essential considerations in the theory and practice of sampling

PBE, as with any form of satisfactory social and educational research, needs to pay considerable attention to sampling. That is, if the research purpose is targeting people, much thought has to be given to who these people are, their common attributes, why they are of interest to the practitioner researcher and their degree of representativeness of larger populations. Results of research are easily compromised if insufficient attention is given to sampling. Much depends on selection and justification, especially in PBE where sample sizes are usually small. Perhaps the ideal situation in small-scale research is where the researcher has good access to a research venue, that venue contains all the people and resources that the research purpose is directed towards, and the possibility exists for the researcher to know all the relevant information about the subjects under study. Rarely is the ideal realized. Social and educational researchers have to work within the operating limits of educational institutions. For this reason, as well as for reasons based on probability theory, research work is usually conducted with small groups of informants – the 'sample' representing the larger collectivity.

Samples need to be carefully defined at an early stage of the research. The order of procedure is usually to consider the total population(s) of interest. The total population for the opinion inventory in Chapter 4 was all teachers in state high schools in Queensland. The total population for the student version of the inventory was all Year 10 and Year 12 students in state high schools in Queensland. Having identified the total population, it then becomes possible to identify and select the attributes of members that the research will investigate. Examples of these are fully shown in Part B of the inventory. They include subject responsibilities, type of school, age, classified position, and so on. Part A contains different 'attributes' of the population. That is, opinion statements known to define the occupational and learning world of teachers and students are listed. Such statements have a dual function. They define (theoretically) the universe of content for the research. They also define the shared professional knowledge, or 'attribute', of the population of teachers and students. Having identified and justified the measurement attributes (or 'variables', as they will become) of the population, the final step is to isolate a representative proportion of the population that is capable of practical management. Generally, the larger the proportion the better, as this minimizes what statisticians refer to as 'sampling error'.

In survey research, samples of less than 30 respondents are usually regarded as not satisfactory. Under probability rules, it is difficult to apply worthwhile inferential statistics to small samples. It is also difficult to study and/or manipulate sub-groups with small samples. Many PBEs, of course, cannot be conducted according to mathematical strictures imposed under the theory of the 'normal curve of distribution'. Thinking about sampling in small-scale research involves thinking about non-probability sampling as well as thinking about probability sampling.

For the purposes of this account, *probability sampling* is the process of drawing a proportion of a survey population so that all members of that population have an equal mathematical chance of being selected. *Non-probability samples* are deliberately selected members of a survey population who are chosen on the basis of the relevance of the features they exhibit to the research in hand. Such examples may or may not be considered mathematically indicative of the survey population as a whole.

Convenience and opportunity sampling

As the name implies, convenience and opportunity sampling is where the researcher chooses the most convenient group of people who collectively demonstrate the characteristics and attributes in which the research is interested. A key feature of these samples is 'access' – that is, required groups are available and willing to participate in research. PBEs tend to make great use of opportunity samples. However, the possibility of generalizing from such samples is limited.

Purposive sampling

A development of convenience sampling, purposive sampling is when the researcher makes a precise judgment about a feature or features of a group of people. Selection of a sample, therefore, is based on the pervasiveness of the feature of central interest to the research. Girls underachieving in mathematics, tutors of modern foreign languages, adults with low levels of literacy undertaking City and Guilds WordPower courses are indicative of how purposive sampling focuses on a measurement attribute of a restricted population.

Quota sampling

In this type of sampling selections are made on the basis of categories studied. Correct or matching numbers of respondents might be sought for the categories 'male' and 'female', '10 years teaching service' and '5 years teaching service', 'RSA certification and non-RSA certification', etc. The notion of 'quota' is the notion of matching totals so that these numerically equivalent groups can be compared. Much research manipulating variables such as attainment, ethnic background and intelligence quotient (IQ) is dependent on quota sampling.

Dimensional sampling

This is a more refined and technically sophisticated form of quota sampling. It invokes the idea of 'multivariate research design'. It is unlikely to characterise PBE, being suggestive of complex and composite variables, tiers and matrices of relationships, and patterns of analysis based on inferential statistical procedures such as Factor Analysis and Analysis of Variance (ANOVA). For example, if we were studying the effects of vocabulary on hand–eye coordination during word-processing exercises at a computer keyboard with five groups of students A, B, C, D and E, a procedure is needed for simultaneously testing the *mean performance* scores of these groups. Such procedure is the basis of analysis of variance. It is important for practitioner researchers to know something of dimensional sampling as many research enquiries reported in the literature and analysed as background information to PBE make use of this technique.

Snowball sampling

Snowball sampling is a technique often used by ethnographers and qualitative researchers. Key individual respondents are identified; they are observed and usually interviewed or questioned informally. As an anecdotal aside, they are asked to suggest a further respondent who might provide confirmatory information on the same topic, or who could provide alternative and additional perspectives on the topic. That person is then followed-up, interviewed and asked to name a further respondent, and so on, until the researcher is satisfied he has contacted enough people or evolved a 'representative' sample. This procedure is fairly 'loose' in a strict methodological sense, but it is always interesting, widely used and can be surprisingly effective. The procedure is analogous to that of the chain letter.

Probability sampling

If the research design meets the requirements of probability theory, and the possibility to sample a large survey population is real, then a precise sampling frame for the total population can be constructed. This frame can then be used to generate one or more of the classic sample types. A random sample, highly desired by social and educational researchers, is when everyone in the sampling frame has an equal chance of being selected. The presumption is that the randomly drawn sample is completely representative of the total population. The '10–20 per cent threshold' – that is, the survey sample constitutes between 10 and 20 per cent of the total population – is often an arithmetical feature of random samples. The systematic random sample is premised on the idea of recursiveness. For example, every seventh or eighth person is selected until an adequate number is reached. Adequacy is understood and expressed as a principle of both constancy and randomness. A stratified random sample is a variation on this theme, except that here there is an attempt to preserve proportionality. The survey population is divided into subsets relevant to the purposes of the enquiry. Exact proportions of each subset are then randomly selected. In the case of the survey sample for the student version of the opinion inventory (Chapter 4), the 'strata' included sex (male and female), year group (Year 10 and Year 12), and 'spearhead' curriculum subjects (English and mathematics). In order to fill each substratum, the enquiry sought to allocate 10 per cent of all 15–17 year olds in state high schools in Queensland.

In many enquiries, where there is geographical and occupational dispersal of the total population, the logistics of simple random sampling may prove difficult. Cluster sampling helps to surmount some of the difficulties. For example, if it was wished to study all the trainee nurses in a large regional health authority, a number of teaching hospitals could be randomly selected rather than nurses throughout the region. Then all the nurse trainees within these selected hospitals could be surveyed. Cluster sampling sometimes requires second-tier work, or multistage sampling – that is, from nurses surveyed in teaching hospitals, a further sample of male nurses only is taken, followed by a further sample of those on learning contract arrangements, and so on.

4 Other essential considerations

There are many features of the methodology of social and educational research which are beyond the scope of consideration of this book. We highlighted sampling, reliability and validity, and observation because they are germane to any enquiry purporting to call itself 'research', and because we believe that they are prerequisite considerations to PBE. They are also useful 'levers' for construing methods and methodology. There are several other considerations that we feel require further noting.

Pilot study

Research which does not test its own methodology can hardly be called 'reflective'. Research which takes its own presuppositions to be self-evidently true is likely to prove disappointing. The purpose of a 'pilot study' – that is, a small preliminary examination of methodology and the use of planned data-gathering techniques with a restricted sample – is to provide information about the adequacy of research design overall and the functionality of data-gathering techniques in particular. PBE and similar research should always be trialled so that difficulties and problems can be anticipated and planned for. There will still, of course, always be the unforeseen eventuality. In the case of survey instruments and self-constructed opinion inventories, it is particularly critical that these are rigorously tested beforehand. It should be understood that, in general terms, pilot studies do not produce information to be included in the substantive conclusions of an enquiry.

Scales and standardized tests

Over many years, the discipline of psychology in particular has been active in the development of scales and test instruments, often requiring written answers, for a range of attitudinal, ability, personality and organizational adjustment variables. Some of these instruments have become 'standardized'. That is, their reliability and validity has derived from large populations to the point where the instrument has public confidence in its use. The British Picture Vocabulary Scales (BVPS), the culture-free self-esteem inventory (CFSEI-2),and the Stanford-Binet Intelligence Scale (fourth edition) are tests of this type. The term 'standardization' also infers the internal frame of reference and its underlying construct structure (see the foregoing section on validity). Results from these tests are typically expressed as raw scores or scale points which can then be statistically compared to norms or averages computed for discrete populations over time. This then permits individuals to be classified against the particular measurement trait such as anxiety, self-esteem, aptitude, extraversion, and so on. It is important to understand that the wide use and acceptance of a standardized test does not close down the debate about what the test claims to measure. In psychometric measurement terms, British and American ability scales measure ability very well. They do, though, measure it 'differently' and debate continues about the underlying properties (theory/constructs) of these instruments.

In our view, inexperienced postgraduate students should only use standardized tests under the supervision of registered or professionally competent users of such tests. Indeed, some professional organizations, such as the British Psychological Society, proscribe the use of psychological tests by non-registered or non-approved groups of people. Similarly, the National Foundation for Educational Research has a registered user scheme for the large range of tests it carries. The question of usage is illustrated by the difficult concept of 'attitude' – something notoriously difficult to conceptualize and quantify, and yet something routinely talked about by the man in the street. Many researchers appropriate this concept, but their measures of it are susceptible to criticism on grounds of validity and reliability. In general meaning, attitudes are part of a person's total personality, a learned disposition to respond to objects, people, situations and ideas. Attitudes are inferred from a person's verbal and non-verbal behaviour, are evaluative and vary in intensity and direction. They have much to do with the emotional make-up of people, sometimes referred to as the 'affective' dimension of personality.

You will note that our opinion inventory in Chapter 4 is called an 'opinion inventory' and not an attitude scale. It is designed to explore the cognitive/knowledge/belief dimension of persons' responses rather than their emotional reactions.

Scaling techniques – in which words and phrases taken as indicators of *behavioural predispositions* (attitudes) and *psychomotor capacity* (abilities) are reduced mathematically to 'best fit' a model of people behaviour – provide the means to quantify attitudes and abilities. This is a highly technical procedure and interested readers are asked to consult a psychometric measurement text. Of more general concern in the perspective of PBE, is the need to recognize the deceptive simplicity in the construction of even the most basic questionnaire. Considerations of item selection and analysis, grouping of items, the selection of a response format such as the Summated Rating Scale (Likert) or the Equal Appearing Interval Scale (Thurstone), and other psychometric features, will have to be made.

Review of the literature

We have referred previously to the aspect of research and reporting called the 'Review of the Literature'. This is a most important part of any research enquiry. Through it, intellectual control over methodology is usually attained and maintained. We emphasize that the review is not an arbitrary description of books read. It is part of the database and part of the mindset of the practitioner researcher. The title of a PBE should give some cue as to the orientation of the literature review. Putting the study into its intellectual and perspectival context is an important function of the review. It is necessary to revisit what has been said and done by others to gain accumulated wisdom, to identify any needless repetitions (avoiding 'reinventing-the-wheel' syndrome, as it is called), and to place your own enquiry on the continuum of research and development in the substantive area. Ideally, the research questions in a PBE come at the end of what is already known and reported upon. This helps to clarify the claim to knowledge that the PBE is trying to make. In reading widely about the substantive topic, the researcher more fully understands the character of the research problem as it has crystallized over time. More simply, the contemporary relevance of the problem is made clearer. Paradoxically, this involves discounting some of what is read, criticizing some of the remaining literature and recording in detail only that which has met the criteria of admissibility to the enquiry.

Part B: An Exemplification of Methodology

We have now covered in some detail arguments defining the intellectual separation of methods and methodology. We have elaborated further on those selected elements which we judge to be high priority in the PBE enterprise. In the remaining part of this chapter we present our second detailed example of a PBE, the report of which reveals many of the preferred elements of methodology welded into a holistic story. We believe this to be an intellectually and methodologically 'honest' PBE. The research in geographical education and information technology skills reported in the PBE are as much an elucidation and verification of assumptions underpinning PBE rather than a 'stand alone' investigation of those two subject fields.

Many teachers and tutors will recognize and empathize with the imperative character of the school-related constraints outlined. They will also acknowledge the 'tension' that exists between the conduct of an enquiry into school practices for pedagogical and organizational improvement with study for a higher degree (for which the PBE was originally submitted) and its associated rigours.

Information Technology and Geographical Education

Background curriculum imperatives to the research

Recent developments arising out of National Curriculum consultation reports in particular have focused on the place of information technology skills in the school curriculum for the late twentieth century and early twenty-first century. The essential thrust of these developments is that IT skills of pupils in British schools must be improved across the board if the nation is to remain economically competitive (and, by implication, socially cohesive). 'Technology' has come to crystallize as a subject in the National Curriculum, loosely synthesizing craft, business education, design and information processing skills. At the same time, and parallel to this, other conventional curriculum subjects have come to attend to and acknowledge the cross-curricular relevance of information technology. In geographical education, Lidstone (1989) has formulated a model expressing the purposes of information technology. Also, difficulties in using software to enhance keyboard skills are analysed. Unwin and Maguire (1990), Fitzpatrick (1990) and Butt (1992) have explored the categorization of software such as database simulations and the impact of computer-assisted learning in geography in both secondary and higher education. Kent (1992) and his colleagues have provided some early responses to the resource implications of IT in the National Curriculum in geography.

Further work includes that of Fitzsimons (1989) on the appropriateness of type faces to construe basic geographic terminology, Rudnicki (1990) on the tactical use of spreadsheets in population geography classes and Rice (1990) who has included computer-drawn maps in attempts to analyse the difficulty in teaching about distortion in map projection when traditional Mercator approaches depict a round world on a flat surface. Finally, the recognition of geographical educators to keep their pedagogies both contemporary in terms of delivery skills, and relevant in terms of geography's evergreen interests such as landscape, environment and settlement, is clear in the impressive symposium papers brought together by Gerber and Lidstone (1988) and the synthesis provided by Robinson (1986) on teachers' reflections on development indicators. The account of the World Development Database Exercise that follows should be understood in the context of the above curriculum and research trends.

Planning the World Development Database Exercise

The World Development Database Exercise was conducted with 89 children in an Isle of Wight middle school during 1990 and 1991. All children had attained the 13th birthday by 31 August 1991.

The World Development Database is a computerized version of *The Development Data Book*, a summary for student use of social and economic statistics on 125 countries compiled by the World Bank. The book lists statistical data on 15 indicators of social and economic development using figures obtained over the 1960–81 period. It considers spatial distribution of five of the indicators, briefly summarizes main worldwide trends in the post-World War II period and offers a categorization of world countries on the basis of their state of development. In its introduction it makes a relevant point:

> Many aspects of economic development cannot be measured by statistics. Examples are the attitudes and feelings of people, their values and ideas, their political systems, and the history and culture. So, while statistics can tell much about economic development, there is much they do not tell.
>
> (World Bank, 1984, p. 2)

The listed indicators of development closely compare with those postulated by Lacoste (1976), although not all of his 14 groups of indicators are statistically quantifiable.

The user guide (Segall, 1987) for the World Development Database functions as a link between *The Development Data Book* and the data handling package itself. Apart from listing useful technical data on the GRASS and QUEST database management systems and the file details, a brief case study is included. This summarizes Walton's introduction of the database to his class of 8–10 year olds, together with suggestions for its use with older students. An inherent advantage of the World Development Database is its flexibility. Its mode of use is not predetermined by its originators, but it may be structured to suit the requirements and inclinations of the user. The purposes to which the database was put in this exploratory study are expressed as follows:

1   To provide an example to geography teachers and general subject teaching that IT can be effectively employed in schools in the teaching of a subject other than technology.
2   To explore the feasibility of delivering aspects of the IT programmes of study through geography.
3   To provide personal experience of planning and managing such an activity.
4   To indicate the potential for assessment of IT capability as delineated in the National Curriculum document for technology.

The decision to utilize the World Development Database was influenced by the imperative nature of the following classroom considerations of the case study group.

Continuity

A module could be devised as an effective conclusion to Year 8 geography work in the academic year 1990/91. The work for the year began with a module on weather and climate, followed by one studying contrasting climate patterns through production and comparison of graphs showing temperature and precipitation through the year for selected places. Each pupil then completed a case study of a farming community in Australia, Brazil, south India, Japan or Nigeria, the intention being to further the understanding of the influences of factors such as latitude, topography and climate upon ways of life. While the case studies were under way, work on underdevelopment took place in economic awareness lessons. The medium used was a series of video programmes, *The Foundations of Wealth*, which studied, through cartoon material, documentary film and simple statistics, the problems of underdevelopment and the theoretical processes by means of which communities can move from a subsistence economy towards a developed, economically dependent society.

Quality of decision-making

It was considered important that these children, on the threshold of moving to higher schools, should have the experience of acquiring data which was not the subject of 'right' or 'wrong' decisions, but was rather the foundation upon which informed judgments and opinions could be based. These pupils had only one previous experience of using a database during their time at the school, and that had related to facts rather than opinions. Three years previously, shortly after their entry to the school, each child had, as a class-based mathematics exercise, completed a personal profile (e.g. boy/girl, birthday, number of brothers and sisters, number and type of pets) for inclusion in a simple database leading to the plotting of bar graphs.

Relevance to national and local initiatives

At the time of planning this unit of work, indications were that the definitive National Curriculum document for geography and the Isle of Wight strategy for responding to it would include some work on development. This was subsequently confirmed when the statutory orders became available some five months later. Although the Programmes of Study therein contained few direct references to IT, work done with the World Development Database closely relates to a number of statements of attainment.

Extension of general world place knowledge

Present geography schemes of work in schools are thought to be deficient in transmission of world place knowledge. Proposed work with the World Development Database, as it related to political and economic geography of the world, was expected to go some way to redress such imbalances.

Disruption of the timetable

The summer term in 9–13 middle schools is, especially for Year 8 pupils, a time of frequent disruption of the timetable as special end-of-year events, residential visits, summer sports fixtures and preparations for transfer of pupils to high schools all intrude into the normal course of lessons. It is a time, too, when motivation is apt to decline and standards of discipline tend to slip. With these points in mind there were benefits in using a largely practically based unit of work and one, moreover, which could accommodate some disruption to the normal flow of lessons. The World Development Database appeared to meet these requirements.

School characteristics and constraints

Detailed planning of the exercise had to take account of constraints and limitations of available equipment and the physical surroundings. Year 8 comprised 89 pupils aged 12–13 years, organized in four classes: 8D, 8F, 8P and 8T (each taking the initial letter of the class teacher's surname). Class sizes ranged from 20 to 23 children. Geography lessons took place on Monday to Thursday afternoons from 14.30 to 15.40. For the purpose of the exercise, access to the seven BBC computers located in an area adjacent to the school library was a prime consideration. Unfortunately, this area did not have the space to accommodate the whole class: a classroom for use as a base area for some of the activities was a necessity. Moving the computers to the class base was not a viable option, nor was there much scope to exchange classrooms for the duration of the exercise. On Wednesdays and Thursdays the classrooms used were adjacent to the computer area. To avoid a long trek through other classrooms, Tuesday lessons took place in the craft room, close to the computer area but cramped for space, while on Mondays the best compromise was to use part of the dining area, fairly close to the computers but open to other users and to through traffic; it was also quite noisy. The division of pupil activities between the class base and the computer area was unavoidable, but certainly acted as a major constraint on the case study.

The memory limitations of the BBC microcomputer, which limit its suitability for handling databases, is known to teachers and regular users. The machine is working close to its limits in operating the World Development Database. The number of records (i.e. 125 countries) and the amount of stored data (i.e. fields, being the indicators of development) are of course interrelated. Discussion with the school's in-house computer expert led to the decision to use GRASS as the database management system and also, on advice, the pruning of the list of countries. Some (e.g. Kampuchea – No. 111) were excluded on the grounds of the limited data provided, others (e.g. Bhutan – No. 104) because of their small population and remote location. With hindsight, it was a mistake to exclude Somalia (No. 91) as it exhibits an interesting comparison between its low life expectancy figure and its higher than expected adult literacy rate. In world political terms, it is also highly topical. The list of countries was thus reduced to 118 and a special file (Yr8geog) created on the World Development Database disk. It should be appreciated that the information upon which the database is founded is essentially captured at a point in time; hence, like atlases, it is quickly outdated. For instance, data on Germany reflects its pre-unification state; also, Upper Volta has been renamed Burkina Faso.

The World Development Database exercise was planned in two phases: a core unit which all children would follow, then a range of follow-up tasks in which an element of choice would be allowed.

Phase 1: Core unit

For the first phase, four fields were selected for study from the 16 available on the database. All four are indicators of development and link with those in Lacoste's (1976) list. They were:

1   Life expectancy (1981 figures): The average number of years newborn babies can be expected to live if health conditions stay the same.
2   Number of inhabitants per doctor (1980 figures): The population of a country divided by the number of its physicians.
3   Gross national product (GNP) per capita (1981 figures): The US dollar value of a country's production of goods and services in that year divided by its population.
4   Adult literacy rate (1980 figures): The percentage of people over 15 who can read and write a simple letter.

The intention for the first phase of the exercise was that pupils of each class would cooperate to produce a master map of A3 size for each of the four chosen fields. Apart from blank A3 maps, sufficient maps for each pupil were also produced at A4 size, the source in each case being the blank map included in the user guide. A procedural guide for accessing the database and a list which grouped the 118 countries studied into groups of five or six were also produced. Pupils within each class worked in pairs to prepare the class master maps: each pair were allocated a group of countries from the list and, using the procedural guide, accessed the database to obtain data for the field in question. Depending upon the value extracted, the countries in the group were filled in (in the appropriate colours) on the pupil's individual maps (felt-tip markers were provided to ensure uniformity of colouring). Pupils then checked each other's work for accuracy (i.e. correct country coloured in the correct colour) before the countries were coloured in on the class master map. The pair of pupils then chose another group of countries and repeated the procedure until that class master map was completed. It was assumed that during and at the end of this phase pupils would be able to address the following key issues:

(a) meaning and significance of indicators used to measure development/underdevelopment among the nations of the world;
(b) limitations and shortcomings of such indicators;
(c) the processes of judgment making leading to the classification of countries as developed or underdeveloped/Third World/First World.

Phase 2: Elective analyses

For the second phase of the exercise, a number of developmental alternatives were presented. Pupils were asked to pursue a course of action from the following:

1 After study of the patterns emerging from the completed master maps, pupils to be encouraged to formulate hypotheses regarding the development state of countries/groups or countries/continents, and then to test these hypotheses by accessing other fields (i.e. other development indicators) through the database.
2 Pupils to be given a choice of any of the fields on the database for investigation, leading to production of their own world maps. These maps were then to be compared with the existing master maps.
3 Having defined, on the basis of investigations through the database, world areas of underdevelopment, and using library sources to obtain pictorial and descriptive accounts of the inhabitants' way of life, findings to be compared possibly with the generalizations made on the *Foundations of Wealth* videotapes.
4 Comparison of the geographical case studies made earlier in the year with World Development Database information to judge whether the settlements studied were typical of their countries as a

whole. As the case study material predated the database information, indications of trends might possibly be detected.

5   Further investigations through library sources and additional database fields of countries which, on the basis of the original class master maps, showed an unclear picture of their states of development.

6   Selection through the database of fields for which two sets of figures were available (for 1960 and 1980 or 1981), e.g. life expectancy, infant mortality rate, primary school enrolment ratio. From this data trends in development states could be determined and then mapped in suitable ways.

Evaluating IT Capacities

Operation of the World Development Database exercise in the perspective of organizational constraints

Reference has been made earlier to the tendency (in middle schools, at any rate) for the summer term to be a time of disruptions to the normal timetable. In January 1991, when this exercise was planned, known disruptions were a block of time for residential visits (10–24 May), two staff development days and the May Day bank holiday. The previous unit of geography work was expected to be completed during the first two weeks of the term: in the event, some of this time was able to be used in preparatory work. This included explanation of the aims and form of the exercise, recapitulating earlier work relating to development, and leading discussion and explanation of the indicators of development which would be used. What was unforeseen at the time of planning, and underestimated at the commencement of the summer term, was the variety, extent and impact of other disrupting events, some of which were foisted upon the school with little prior warning.

As noted previously, the exercise took place in a split-site situation: a classroom base and the area where the computers were located. This imposed severe restrictions on the controlling teacher's freedom to operate as a participant observer and, consequently, on the volume and nature of the data which could be collected. The impossibility of observing all the pupils for all of the time precluded attempts at structured data gathering. Nevertheless, there were no realistic alternatives to this situation, which had to be accepted as an inevitable limitation upon what was attempted and how it was done.

The observer/evaluator sought for patterns of pupil behaviour across the four class groups by comparing one group with the others, identifying measurable phenomena in one class, then seeking its reappearance elsewhere, transferring a technique learned by members of one class into the others and then seeking comparable outcomes. On the odd occasion even these modest aims proved unworkable in practice. The nadir of the whole experience was Monday, 22 April, when, as the first practical session with 8B, it was planned to re-show the first *Foundations of Wealth* video programme as a recapitulation of the essential elements of underdevelopment, and then allow pupils free access to the database, using the procedural guide to help them extract whatever information they wished. The evaluator had only 15 minutes warning that 8B's eleven participants in the French exchange would be bringing along their guests (who had arrived the day before) and whose afternoon programme had been suddenly changed.

Despite the organizational constraints, the process of observation suggested the following as recurrent and stable behaviours – or, to put it another way, 'signposts to IT literacy':

1 Growth of operating skills The rapidity with which all pupils came to terms with the operation of the World Development Database was particularly noteworthy, notwithstanding the fact that a wide range of individual capabilities and speeds of working existed within all classes.

2 Patterns of adaptation The development sequence of adaptation to use of the database was broadly comparable in all classes. Initially, there were observable signs of apprehension in some pupils, notably among girls, but nowhere was there observed a refusal or extreme reluctance to use the computers. Common to all groups was an initial tendency to set the user guide to one side and to try to muddle along without it. This was a phase of the exercise when calls to the teacher for help were frequent and repetitive. The commonality of this pattern to all groups tends to suggest that this is an inevitable, perhaps necessary, stage in the accommodation of these (to the pupils) new skills. However, by the end of the first lesson the majority in each class were observed to be gaining confidence, relying heavily upon the user guide and speeding up in use of the keyboard. Noticeable here was the mutual help and support for slower working children which came from those more capable pairs of pupils who, gaining confidence, appeared keen to share their developing expertise. From the third week onward, the user guides were referred to less and less, to the point where, in the concluding weeks, hardly anybody even bothered to collect one. It was in the third week that the teacher/evaluator observed the development of an alternative searching strategy to that shown on the user guide.

Emma and Gill, girls in 8T, had discovered a time-saving short cut. Having followed the user guide to access the first country on the list, if at stage 10 the option 'Add to the search' was selected, remaining countries on the list could be accessed by successive cycles of stages 4 to 10. The girls had also noted that when the records were displayed at the conclusion of the search, data was not shown in the order that countries had been accessed, but in numerical order of map number. This technique began to filter through 8T to the point where approaching half of the pairs of pupils used it regularly. When, however, this technique was transferred into other classes, take-up was smaller. When the new technique was publicized, one or two other pairs of pupils in each class stated that they had developed their own search technique already. These all proved to be the less sophisticated technique of selecting the option 'Display all records', where each successive touch of the space bar displayed information on the next numerical country. This technique only saved time when accessing a group of countries with relatively low map numbers. Curiously, in contrast to children's willingness to share their growing facility with the database, as noted earlier, new searching techniques were seldom shared by pairs of pupils, hence the decision to publicize them by the teacher/evaluator.

3 Variation in work rates As previously noted, all pupils quickly gained confidence and speed at the keyboard, and individual rates of working varied markedly within each class group. A measure of this variation was obtained by checking on the number of countries each pair of pupils had accessed and coloured in on the class maps by the end of the third session. In 8T, numbers varied from 6 to 27, and in 8F from 6 to 37. It was found that in the case of the lowest scores, these children had been obtaining far more information than was required.

4 Motivation Motivation for all classes rapidly improved after the uncertainty at the start of the first practical session, and thereafter remained high until the end of the exercise. Pupils came to lessons eager to begin at the computers, took pride in the accuracy of their class maps and, in several cases, were reluctant to pack up at the end of the lessons.

5 Gender-related working practices   Reference has been made to the greater apprehension initially observed among the girls early on in the exercise. Towards the end of the experience it was possible to pick out one or possibly two pairs of children in each class who appeared less confident, were slower in their working and were more prone to make mistakes. In three out of the four classes, these were pairs of girls. On the other hand, the majority of girls compared very favourably with the boys in general capability (subjectively judged on observations of confidence, speed of working and minimal error) and the most capable pairs of pupils were all girls. When watching one of the capable pairs, it was possible to observe efficient division of labour in action (e.g. one partner remaining in the class base to complete the colouring of the class master map, while the other one copied down the next group of countries, collected the program disk, loaded it into the computer and began accessing the database until joined by her partner). These groups also displayed signs of better motivation and appeared less easy to divert from the task in hand. In all the class groups in week 5 it was found that the two fastest-working pairs of pupils in each class were girls. The conclusions, based upon these observations, were that the strengths of these working groups of capable girls were their ability to evolve more efficient strategies of working, and their interest and concentration upon the task in hand.

6 Need for organizational changes   Instances of resentful behaviour were noted among the children on occasions and could be traced to two causes: when they discovered that information they required was not available on the database and also when they accessed a group of countries and extracted the data, only to find when they came to colour in the class map that another group of pupils had already completed that task for those countries. While the exercise was in progress, organizational strategies were developed to try to eliminate the latter cause of frustration. In the initial stage of the first lesson when the first master map for each class was begun, the teacher personally allocated groups of countries to pairs of pupils. When a pair had extracted the data they required and coloured in those parts of the class map, they came to the teacher for another group of countries. Clearly this restricted teacher freedom to move between the working areas and to observe the pupils, so a simple self-help strategy was developed. A copy of the list of countries was displayed in the classroom with a sliding arrow marker clipped to its edge. When they required another group of countries, a pair of children would copy down the group opposite the arrow, then, before going to the computer, move the marker down to the next group on the sheet. This speeded up the rate of working and gave the teacher/evaluator more freedom of operation. On occasions people forgot to move the marker, leading to duplication of effort and frustration. In week 5 the teacher copied the groups of countries on to separate cards and made a three-compartment box to hold them. By this stage of the exercise a class was capable of completing one map and filling in 50–75 per cent of another in one double lesson. Country group cards were placed in the front compartment of the box, together with a marker showing the title of the current map. Pairs of pupils collected cards from the front compartment and, when the task was finished, placed them in the middle compartment (which had a marker describing the next map to be coloured); they then took another card from the front compartment. When all cards had been taken from the front of the box, work transferred to the next map using cards taken from the middle compartment, and these were placed in the rear compartment when they had been used. This system successfully eliminated unnecessary duplication of effort, but it was necessary to note the stage a particular class had reached at the end of a lesson and then to set up the box to an identical state at the commencement of the next lesson.

7 World knowledge Although no attempt was made to test or quantify this in a formal sense, impressions were that the general world knowledge of the pupils improved through participation in the exercise. No obvious difficulties were observed in children matching accessed data to that country on the map, while, in the short group-discussion sessions with which lessons usually began and sometimes ended, children seemed more capable at naming and identifying particular countries as the exercise progressed. Very few pupils could not identify North American countries, and most European and major Australasian countries at the commencement of the exercise. Following media coverage of the Gulf War, it was understandable that most Middle Eastern countries were known. North and central Africa (with the exception of Ethiopia), South America and South East Asia were largely unknown territories.

Few errors were detected in the colouring of class maps: five instances in 8B, three in 8F, two in 8P and one in 8T. Most errors occurred shortly after a new map was started, indicating organizational rather than geographical shortcomings. Further observations, common to all classes, were that Alaska was rarely coloured in with the rest of the USA, the constituent islands of Indonesia were never identified without help and peripheral islands were usually not coloured in with the parent country (e.g. Tasmania was not identified as part of Australia or Novaya Zemlya with the then USSR). A common question was 'Who owns Greenland?'. In every case, after considering its tiny population, it was left blank.

8 Understanding and recall   There was wide variation in the quantity and quality of contributions made by pupils during the initial lessons with each class, which recapitulated upon past experiences and knowledge of development and also explained the indicators of development which were used in the exercise. While the majority could recall factual details from the *Foundations of Wealth* video programmes which had formed the core of the economic awareness lessons of the early part of the spring term, this appeared to be beyond about 10 per cent of the year group, who had little recall of what had been covered. On the other hand, about two or three individuals in each class were particularly stimulated by these lessons. Most noteworthy was Chris, a clever loner in 8T. When the indicators of development that were being used were introduced, Chris immediately challenged gross national product per capita as being 'inaccurate'. In response to encouragement to develop his statement, he cited a dictatorship in which most of the wealth was concentrated in the hands of a few. Before the teacher could respond, Chris thought for a moment, then said 'But that's probably true of any country'. This led to a critical appraisal of all the chosen indicators through class discussion in which Chris dominated but to which well over half the class made active contributions. Other classes did not reach these heights, but the impression was left that, at least at the commencement of the practical work, over half of the year group had a concept of the indicators of development as flawed measuring instruments, but the best available and capable of giving acceptable descriptions of a country's state of development.

Conclusions

It would be nice to say that the exercise was brought to a tidy conclusion, full evaluations written up and the children 'signed off', so to
speak. This would not be true. Planned follow-up work had to be
severely curtailed on account of the degree of disruption to the
timetable. Although not every class map was fully complete, sufficient
information was there to enable them to be used in the concluding
sessions in which they were compared, discussed, and from which
patterns were recognized. The generalization of one boy, which he
based upon the life expectancy map, that 'Your state of development
depends upon your latitude' was recognized as over-simplistic, but
containing an element of truth and serving as a useful starting point
from which his class could progress. All classes proved capable of
recognizing the following patterns of development:

1   South Saharan and central African countries which scored consis-
    tently low on all the indicators of development studied.
2   Developed countries of North America, Europe, Japan and
    Australasia.
3   A 'second tier' group of countries (Central and South America and
    South Africa) which matched group 2 (above) in some respects
    (notably adult literacy rate) but were rated lower on some indicators.
4   High population areas (e.g. India and China) which rated fairly high
    on all indicators except GNP/capita.
5   High income (oil-based) countries of the Middle East.
6   Numerous (often Communist bloc) countries for which GNP/capita
    figures were not available.

During times when significant numbers of pupils were absent (e.g.
French exchange, 11–18 June, and high school induction time, 2–5 and
9 July) those pupils present were given the option of either selecting
one of their individual maps for completion, or of choosing to prepare
a world map for any of the other development indicators included on
the database. With the exceptions of Sarah and Lucy (8P), who
worked on a map of infant mortality rates, and Ian and Luke (8T), also
Tom and Keith (8B), who chose to investigate energy consumption,
everyone chose the first option.

> Regrettably, there was never a suitable opportunity to evaluate pupil comprehension through a concluding written exercise, nor even to bring the experience to a clean definite end, as disruption of the timetable continued into the concluding weeks of the term. Such is the reality of experimental teaching and small-scale applied research in schools.

In this chapter we have smoothed potential confusion in using the terms 'method' and 'methodology'. We suggested that confusion was possible because researchers approach their enquiries from an ontological and epistemological standpoint. The potential for confusion is particularly great when these propensities are unacknowledged – either by those conducting research or by those reading and using research. It was our contention that ontological and epistemological tensions resulted in a further polarization in the 'divided mentality' that we first construed in Chapter 2. In attempting to heal this 'divided mentality' we offered thirteen criteria against which PBEs could be assessed. That is, we provided a template for a check on the ontological and epistemological orientation of PBE. We subsequently enriched this analysis by explaining further some of the essential features of research methodology. Finally, we have reported a PBE in full. This was in order to reveal its ontological and epistemological preferments, its holistic approach to methodology, and its value as a model for further work likely to be conducted under the same sorts of constraints. We have now concluded our three-part exposition of the conduct of PBE. In Chapter 6, we will round this off by discussing the essentially technical matters of data analysis and report writing.

6 Analysing and Writing – Writing and Analysing

Prior Thoughts

The research design of a PBE should have demonstrated that the data-gathering strategies fit their settings. Similarly, this planning principle ought to have led in the direction of systems of organization of data to make its retrieval for analysis as easy as possible. It is generally not a good idea to collect large amounts of data and then look for ways of deciphering it at a later date. Data analysis is, along with the formulation of conclusions, the culminating feature of the research process. It is designed to bring order, coherent patterns and meaning to data accumulated. The data analysis process can be thought of in terms of steps. First, raw data collected from questionnaires, survey instruments, interviews, observations, etc., has to be tabulated on charts, spreadsheets or other aggregating devices. The data is then subject to a process of reduction into meaningful bits. Categories are sought and allocated, relationships are tested, qualitative data is examined for meaning, statistics are computed, and so on. In reality, if the data-gathering instruments have been well prepared, the data should sort itself or at least point towards a sorting path. The classroom observation featured in Chapter 4 is both a recording and an explanatory device. The series of observations makes up the dataset and is available for analysis and interpretation by reference to the underlying theory.

As data is reduced and analysed the process of interpretation occurs. This is the process whereby warranted conclusions about the meaning of the data are drawn. Interpretation may be thought of as a reading, thinking, inferring and concluding process. It may involve the technical editing of field notes, decisions to use verbatim statements from interview transcripts, the application of a particularly searching inferential statistic, the matching of data to a hypothesis, and so on. The process of interpretation is an active intellectual one, and is now considerably aided by the availability of sophisticated computer software; more will be said about this later. Processes central to data analysis are coding and categorization. This is especially true of qualitative datasets such as extensive interview transcripts. We have already seen how, under the rules of grounded theory, the categorization process occurs. Coding is a similar process whereby numbers, words or alphanumeric codes are assigned to particular themes or pattern indicators. The dataset is then checked for the occurrence of these and their frequency of incidence recorded against their code. Analytical codes are usually specific to the research, though numerical coding based on the binary logic of computers is now universal. Coding and categories are the technical counterparts of analy-tical thinking. Whatever the dataset, during the process of analysis the researcher has to remain sensitive to explicit and tacit meanings, to subtle possibilities for typologizing as in the ethnography in Chapter 4, to nuances of language, and to cross-classification of ideas. It is most important that codes, categories and other measurement controls should be indicative of naturally occurring variation in the datasets.

Research reports tend make effective use of data in two main ways. The first is presentational in which data is represented in abbreviated visual form outwards to impact immediately. The second is analytical in which data is commented on at length in writing in the body of the report. However, it is important at this juncture to state that the presentational and analytical dimensions of a research report are mutual and complementary rather than exclusive and opposed. We shall now discuss selected data analysis and presentation formats.

Graphical and Statistical Representations of Data

Data is often presented in statistical (tabular) and graphical (figurative) form. Such representations are particularly useful for ordering data, for expressing complexity in the simplest possible terms, for positing logical and testable relationships and so on. Diagrams, tables and charts leave a strong visual impression and are able to communicate their information quickly to the senses, rather more quickly than the printed word. Such devices also have a powerful summarizing capacity. Consider Figures 6.1, 6.2 and 6.3. These diagrams are useful for representing the concept of *school organization*. In School A the hierarchical character of comprehensive school organization in the UK is illustrated. Management roles are shown in *line responsibility* order and are identified by labels. The labels are essential signifiers of both authority and function, e.g. 'head teacher' and 'deputy head curriculum'. There is allusion here also to the most striking feature of school organization, separation of students into age or year groups, and curriculum provision based on subject departments. Such features are much more overt in the diagram for School B. This school is classified as a Grade 2 state high school by the Queensland Department of Education because of its enrolment size (less than 700). The seven subject departments are identified but there are only three designated *subject masters* or *mistresses*, as a function of the school's small size, and analogous to heads of subject departments in School A. Student year groups are clearly indicated and the *form* or *tutor* group designations based on the initial of the appropriate teacher's surname is also a feature. Student participation in school governance is indicated by the identification of a *house* and *prefectorial* system. The presence of a *senior mistress* in this school's hierarchy is indicative of special responsibility for the welfare of girls.

The diagram for School C is different again. Here the concept of organization is expressed less in hierarchical terms and more in terms of mutual *reciprocity* and *interdependence* . There are seven teachers and only two of these hold classified senior positions. Organization is flat rather than hierarchical and more suggestive of the *family character* of primary and junior schools. Pupils, rather than subjects, are central to the learning task in this 5–12-year First and Middle school. The label 'Voluntary Aided' says

Figure 6.1   School A organization

Type: Maintained 11–16 (age range) co-educational secondary school in Hampshire. UK enrolment 1300

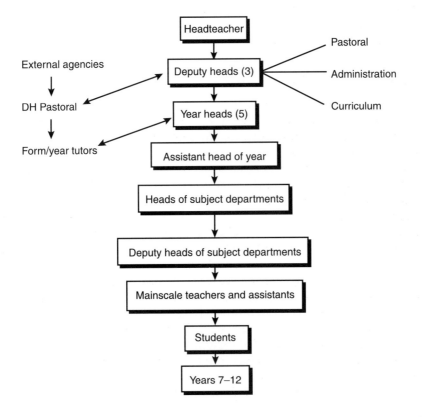

Figure 6.2   School B organization

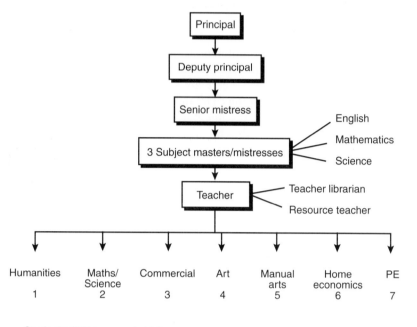

Type: State high school – Grade 2. Enrolment less than 700
Queensland, Australia

Students (410 boys and girls)

Form Structure (Number of classes per year)

Year 8	8R	8P	8K	8B*			(110 students)
Year 9	9WH	9WT	9T	9CU	9CD		(110 students)
Year 10	10T	10S	10R	10O	10CW	10CH	(100 students)
Year 11	11T	11M	(55 students)				
Year 12	12W	12M	(35 students)				

* Designates initial of form teacher's surname

Student council: None
Prefects: 6 girls and 6 boys elected from year 12 by teachers and students
House system: Condamine-Beauraba-Yandilla

something of the accommodation reached by Roman Catholic schools with the state in the UK in the matters of ownership, organization and function.

Using diagrams such as these on a comparative basis enables the concept of *school organization* to be expanded and developed. Whilst not every feature of school organization is depicted by the diagrams, there is sufficient information to indicate that schools are a special kind of organization: they are populated by two groups, teachers and pupils, an adult–child cleavage unusual in work organizations, and where the children are subordinate to the adults. The school

Figure 6.3   School C organization

Type: Voluntary–aided (RC) first and middle school 5–12 (age range) – inner city UK.
Enrolment 240 in a 7 form entry

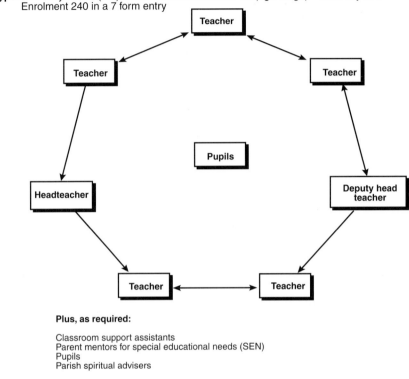

Plus, as required:

Classroom support assistants
Parent mentors for special educational needs (SEN)
Pupils
Parish spiritual advisers

can also be understood as a special kind of *social system* in which the incumbents occupy *roles* and *statuses* based on age, function, subject specialism, and so on, and that there is a rational basis to the organization.

Sophisticated theories, generalizing propositions, inferential relations between measurement variables and warranted conclusions for a complete research project are all capable of summarization via a series of tables and figures. The uses to which graphical and statistical representations of data are put is a function of the expressed purpose of the research, the feasibility and desirability of converting information into visual form, the arithmetic values ascribed to datasets, and the location of these on the aforementioned measurement scale.

Categorical tables

These report the attributes of a survey population or a categorical (factual) relationship. They are often used in educational research to depict such things as sex, length of service, formal qualifications, posts of responsibility held, etc. Where one categorical variable is linked to another – for example, sex with length of service – the process is known as cross tabulation. Table 6.1 is an example of a categorical table. It reports factual information for eight deputy heads of junior schools in the south of England. The four categories of information, or *variables*, are able to be reported numerically. Thus, for deputy head teacher 6 we note that this person has 18 years of teaching experience, has been in the post of deputy head for the relatively short time of 15 months, is currently placed in a school with a pupil enrolment of 95 and is one of 4.5 teaching staff. Simple arithmetical operations may be conducted on such a table. Totalling the number of years teaching experience and dividing by 8 gives the average (17 years) for that category variable. Categorical tables may also be noted for what they omit as well as what they include. For example, the addition of gender/sex information – 1 = male; 2 = female – might have added additional explanatory power to this type of statistical array.

Percentages and frequency counts

These are non-inferential statistics that show broad score patterns in raw data in respect of some theoretically meaningful measurement criterion. An example might be the proportion of secondary school teachers supporting the retention of corporal punishment. Another example might be the percentage of post-16 female trainees on word-processing courses run by local education authorities and who had gained GCSE grades A–C in five subjects. Yet another example might be the numbers of parents of school-aged children supporting the retention of grammar schools and who voted for the Labour Party at the last general election.

Table 6.1 Selected characteristics of eight (8) deputy heads of public sector junior schools in the south of England

Occupational characteristics	Deputy head (DH) respondents							
	1	2	3	4	5	6	7	8
Number of years teaching experience	16	20	15	20	15	18	20	12
Length of time in post of deputy head	4 months	3 years	1 year	3 years	1 year	15 months	13 months	2.5 years
Number of pupils in current school	96	110	180	140	139	95	130	70
Number of teaching staff in current school	5	55	8	6	6	4.5	5.5	4

A frequency table is essentially a device for arranging individual respondents to a survey on a quantifiable characteristic. It is particularly useful when the number of respondents is large, say, upwards of 100. Table 6.2 is a frequency table reporting teacher responses to selected opinion statements on school life. This table was compiled from responses to the opinion inventory presented and explained in Chapter 4. The teacher sample of 102 responded to 15 items representing validated viewpoints on school life. Percentage scores are provided for each of four strength-of-agreement categories. Responses are classified by gender – male and female teachers. For item 2 on *corporal punishment* it will be seen that 55.4 per cent of male teachers strongly agree with the statement that corporal punishment should be retained in Queensland state secondary schools. This compared with 28.9 percent of female teachers. If both agreement cell scores are combined – that is, the scores in the 'strongly agree' and 'agree' categories – then strong evidence emerges from the sample of teachers for the retention of corporal punishment. At the time of the survey, the situation in Queensland was unusual in that corporal punishment of the approved kind was legal for boys but not for girls.

Table 6.2 Teacher responses to selected opinion statements on school life – by sex

Item			Strongly agree %	Agree %	Disagree %	Strongly disagree %
			Strength of teacher opinion			
Teachers in state secondary schools are best thought of as public servants working in a special kind of service organization.	1	M	12.5	51.8	26.8	8.9
		F	8.9	57.8	24.4	8.9
Corporal punishment should be retained in Queensland state secondary schools.	2	M	55.4	39.3	3.6	1.7
		F	28.9	64.4	4.4	2.3
A system of school-based assessments for Year 12 students is more satisfactory than a system of externally set and marked examinations.	3	M	19.6	41.1	26.8	12.5
		F	11.1	42.2	28.9	17.8
The Queensland state high school is generally successful in satisfying the needs and aspirations of students.	4	M	1.8	50.0	44.6	3.6
		F	0	53.5	37.2	9.3

Item			Strength of teacher opinion			
			Strongly agree %	Agree %	Disagree %	Strongly disagree %
Parents and citizens' associations should be more involved in the formulation of school policy.	5	M	17.5	49.2	22.8	10.5
		F	4.5	52.4	38.6	4.5
Public speculation about educational activities is frequently ill-informed.	6	M	35.7	60.7	1.8	1.8
		F	37.8	55.6	4.4	2.2
There is a lack of certainty in the goals of secondary education.	7	M	10.5	63.2	21.1	5.2
		F	11.1	55.6	31.1	2.2
A clear and common set of values should be taught in every Queensland state high school.	8	M	14.3	44.6	26.8	14.3
		F	15.6	51.1	24.4	8.9
The appraisement system is successful in locating and employing the best people for particular jobs.	9	M	5.3	21.1	47.4	26.2
		F	0	16.3	60.5	23.2
Subjects such as Maths and English are typically accorded different amounts of prestige by teachers.	10	M	14.0	70.2	15.8	0
		F	22.2	55.6	22.2	0
Policies of particular schools should be established through collegial participation in decision-making by the whole school staff.	11	M	29.8	57.9	10.5	1.8
		F	31.1	60.0	8.9	0
Before being given a promotional position a teacher should serve his or her time in country schools.	12	M	30.4	30.4	28.6	10.6
		F	25.0	54.5	13.7	6.8
Equitable representation of men and women in senior positions in the education service is desirable.	13	M	12.3	57.9	19.3	10.5
		F	31.8	59.1	9.1	0
While most teachers prefer to teach able and achieving students, there is a pressure to treat all students as if they were of comparable ability.	14	M	8.8	54.4	35.1	1.7
		F	13.3	57.8	24.4	4.5
Smaller classes in smaller schools would enable teachers to cope more effectively with the day-to-day demands of schooling.	15	M	46.4	50.0	3.6	0
		F	50.0	40.9	9.1	0

Notes: N = 102

Similarly, scores for all other items in the frequency table can be examined either selectively or collectively. The *variable content* of the opinion statements may be examined by whatever nominated classificatory indices are to be used. In social and educational research these often include such things as age, sex, marital status, current definitions of socio-economic status and level of educational qualifications. The nominated classificatory indices for the teacher sample in Table 6.2 as well as sex, include age, classified position, subject commitments, preferences for teaching year groups, highest qualification obtained, and number of years teaching. The interested reader will find the full list of classificatory indices in Section B of the opinion inventory presented in Chapter 4.

Linear diagrams and theoretical models

These are abbreviated technical drawings that visually reveal complex relationships and interconnections between variables and/or the subjects of investigation. These figures usually include a primary title that spells out the purpose of the graphic, and subtitles that indicate subordinate links within the overarching framework.

Graphics of this type invariably express principles of hierarchy, ranking, logical interconnection and linearity. They are simplifications of real life and are *ideal types*, an abstract approximation of complex realities. Two or more graphics may stand in explanatory relationship. Table 4.1 (p. 107) in this text is an 'exploded' or amplified version of the lower half of the theoretical model represented by Figure 2.2 (p. 39).

In Chapter 2 we used this *orienting theoretical model*, Figure 2.2 to assert some intellectual control over what is termed the *action-structure dilemma*. Whilst the primary function of the model was intellectual, its *stylistic character* is such as to show a hypothesized *causal chain* for the behaviour of teachers and students in an organization that we happen to call 'school'. A broad range of social influences, identified by construct labels such as *achievement orientation* and *status group competition*, are traced in the model from their point of origin in society. These influences combine to exercise a shaping effect on the psychological and pre-dispositional attributes of teachers and pupils. The totality of sociological and psychological influences goes a long way to explaining *behaviour* in schools. However, though a theoretical model may appear to be a clever drawing, it is only useful as a device of explanation if its underlying ideas are validated – either by explanation of the validating processes in text, or by way of additional diagrams that amplify the original, or, in this case, orienting theoretical model. Thus Table 4.1 is an essential accessory to Figure 2.2. Here, theoretical constructs are formally defined, arranged into a posited inclusive hierarchical order and validated by the presentation of empirically derived key indicators of each of the constructs. As they apply to teachers and students. Thus from the standpoint of data analysis, Figure 2.2 and Table 4.1

are necessary and, hopefully, sufficient. Diagramming ideas in this way helps in the task of analysing and writing about complex reality.

Other forms of proportional representation

Graphs, bar charts and pie charts investigate and report on the concept of proportions. They are designed to permit immediate internal comparisons of divided datasets – for example, the numbers of pupils taking school meals, numbers of pupils paying for school meals, numbers of pupils claiming free school meals. Such forms of representation often show change over time in respect of some interesting trend or concept. Examples might include 'poverty increases', 'population of working age', or 'government expenditure on education for the period 1971–2000'. These forms of representation are not very useful with small population samples or datasets.

In the following example, two forms of proportional representation are presented for the variable 'highest educational qualification'. This variable is one of some 18 listed for and used in the British Household Panel Survey (Rose and Sullivan, 1996, p. 226). Other variables listed in this important national survey include: job satisfaction, Registrar General social class categories, age, sex, housing tenure, marital status, political party supported, and so on. The sample used in the BHPS includes 2540 adults randomly selected to represent British 'households'.

The exhibits include a frequency table for some 15 sub-categories of 'highest educational qualification' for the 2540 survey respondents (see Table 6.3). Once calculated, these frequencies may be represented diagrammatically to create an immediate visual impression of the proportionate character of the labelled sub-categories. For the purposes of illustration we have included two representational forms, the bar chart (Figure 6.4) and the pie chart (Figure 6.5). Both readily illustrate the dominance of the sub-categories 'GCE O Levels' and 'no qualification' in this sample. It is a moot point as to which representation form is more effective than the other. The pie chart presents data segmentally as part of the 360-degree character of a circle. The bar chart, which may have either vertical or horizontal bars is arguably better at representing data by numbers of respondents.

Bar charts are also doubly helpful in that 'trend lines' can be graphed across the top of the bars. However, the multicolour print capacity of modern computer printers means that coloured pie charts, faceted graphs, composite tables, etc., can be produced to a high desktop publishing standard. Graphical forms of proportional representation are widely used in the analysis and reporting phases of social and educational research. Once data is aggregated into some kind of visually coherent pattern, it tends to become easier to write about it. That is why the written analysis sections of research reports are often illustrated by visual representations. The use of such devices is also an important aid to brevity in writing-up research findings.

Table 6.3 Frequency table for 15 sub-categories of the variable 'Highest Educational Qualification' for 2540 survey respondents

Statistics

	Valid	Missing	Mean
		N	
Highest educational qualification	2540	0	7.88

Highest educational qualification

		Frequency	Percent	Valid percent	Cumulative percent
Valid	Missing	8	0.3	0.3	0.3
	Higher degree	30	1.2	1.2	1.5
	First degree	158	6.2	6.2	7.7
	Teaching QF	67	2.6	2.6	10.3
	Other higher QF	283	11.1	11.1	21.5
	Nursing QF	45	1.8	1.8	23.2
	GCE A levels	268	10.6	10.6	33.8
	GCE O levels or equiv.	557	21.9	21.9	55.7
	Commercial QF, no O levels	86	3.4	3.4	59.1
	CSE grade 2–5, Scottish grade 4–5	107	4.2	4.2	63.3
	Apprenticeship	73	2.9	2.9	66.2
	Other QF	12	0.5	0.5	66.7
	No QF	843	33.2	33.2	99.8
	Still at school, no QF	5	0.2	0.2	100.0
	Total	2540	100.0	100.0	
Total		2540	100.0		

Contingency tables

These are amongst the more sophisticated forms of statistical representation and most typically take the form of a '2 × 2' where two dependent variables are statistically compared with at least two independent variables. Contingency tables employ inferential statistics which examine the chance

Figure 6.4 Representation as a bar chart

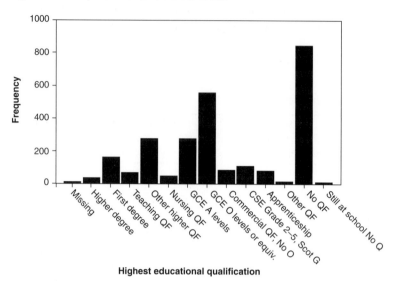

Source: Derived from data disc in Rose and Sullivan, 1996

Figure 6.5 Representation as a pie chart

Highest educational qualification

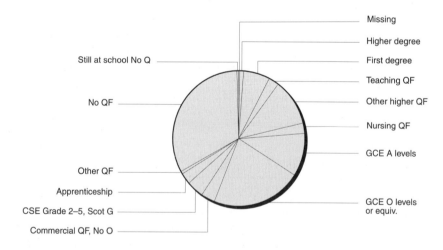

Source: Derived from data disc in Rose and Sullivan, 1996

happening of a relationship between variables thus pointing in the direction of causality. Statistical manipulations of this type enable a researcher to measure the strength of a relationship, thus giving analytical weight to theoretical explanation. Contingency tables are more powerful than frequency counts and descriptive statistics.

Electronic Tools and Data Analysis

Earlier in this book we have provided methodological commentary that has been illustrated by a variety of forms of data analysis. Indeed, we have provided two PBE 'reports', an ethnography and a school-focused case study that show how two particular practitioner-researchers have recorded, analysed and reported their data. That data was qualitative in kind. Under the rubric of PBE, as we have constructed it, most data is qualitative. Observations, interviews, case descriptions, small surveys, etc., tend to produce detailed written material of an explanatory kind. However, as the practitioner-researcher becomes more conceptually and methodologically sophisticated about datasets, it becomes increasingly necessary to apply the tools that contemporary electronic hardware has to offer. That was one reason why we began this chapter with a basic consideration of graphical and statistical representations of data. Another reason is our belief that studying a few statistical/quantitative procedures helps in learning more about qualitative ones. While the typical practitioner-researcher may be put off by the very thought of statistics and graphics, it is in these domains that electronic tools for analysis have long been pre-eminent. Computers, though, offer the researcher many possibilities to facilitate the task of data analysis and interpretation. In the qualitative mode it is difficult to escape from longhand record-keeping and analysis. That is, piles of unedited interview transcripts, copious field notes, completed observation schedules, incident logs, and so on, constitute both the record and the dataset. In some ways, longhand records are the 'burden to bear' of the practitioner-researcher.

These are laborious to assemble and often hard to analyse, especially if 'methodology' is slippery. Interview transcripts, in particular, are deceptive in respect of what they contain and how the information can be used. Study the example of the interview transcript that accompanies the ethnography. Note the type of questions asked. Note the character of the interviewee responses. Note the total amount of information generated. Note how, under the rules of ethnographic semantics, the author uses interview information to construct typologies (explanatory classifications) to explain debating and to construe informant utterances.

The detail required for recording and reporting in ethnographic semantics is considerable. The advent of word-processors, text analysis packages, bibliographic software tools and spreadsheets is therefore highly advantageous to this type of research fieldwork. Computer technology is best regarded by the qualitative researcher in the following terms:

(a) As an effective vehicle for records keeping.
(b) As the means by which 'holding programmes' such as spreadsheets and word-processors permit data to be manipulated.
(c) As the device best available to achieve variable transformation economically in terms of time and analytical complexity.

Variable transformation is the essential principle of data analysis in social and educational research. It includes written accounts of variables, listings and annotations of ideas, graphical representations of data and computations (both quantitative and qualitative) of inferred cause and effect. This principle is at the heart of data analysis packages that are routinely available for microcomputers. These include Minitab, Statpack, Statview, and the 'industry standard' of SPSS – Statistical Package for the Social Sciences.

Minitab is representative of smaller-scale data analysis packages for use with personal computers. Like most other packages of similar size it provides a *data analysis environment* consisting of the following:

*   A *worksheet* into which data is first entered.
*   A *data window* that displays data in an orderly, usually *columnar*, form.
*   A variety of *menus* that contain commands for data manipulation, statistical analysis and *data transformation*. Items on menus can provide direct commands or they can open *dialogue boxes* permitting a researcher to choose from a more detailed array of analytical tools.
*   A session window displays results of data manipulation.
*   Graph windows provide for high resolution graphical and tabular representations of data that may be printed in several colours.
*   An information window displays a summary of the initial worksheet.
*   A history window lists commands for activities conducted during a data analysis session. These can be copied into a command line editor that permits the researcher to edit and re-execute session commands.
*   Accompanying Minitab is a context-sensitive Help facility. This provides overview information, explanation of session window commands and helpful advice on how Minitab may best be used to analyse the data inputted to it.

Historically, SPSS was a mainframe system devised to handle the very large datasets routinely analysed by social scientists. Census data, Gallup Polls, attitude surveys and other forms of trend analysis data were all handled by SPSS from the late 1960s onwards. In recent years, emergence of the PC version of SPSS has placed considerable analytical capacity within reach of small-scale research. Information and operating procedures on the PC version of SPSS can be found in Kinnear and Gray (1995).

What does SPSS do?

It enables data from surveys, experiments and other information-gathering devices to be stored electronically. It permits the researcher to undertake sophisticated statistical and related analyses of any data that is stored. It provides a permanent record, known as a datafile, of research information that can be added to or deleted at will. It also allows data stored to be transformed and represented in words, numbers, graphics and tables that can be printed out to desktop publishing standard, with colour options if required.

What does SPSS teach the researcher?

It teaches the researcher how to collect raw data in a form that can be coded into numeric and alphanumeric form. Following that process, it enables the researcher to enter numeric and alphanumeric data into a computer and save it. The researcher is next able to define the entered data as a datafile or dataset by means of annotated descriptions and labels. In doing this, the researcher is taught how to construe meaning for measurable items by devising variable names and value labels. Finally, SPSS helps the researcher to understand the nature and significance of statistical tests in the production of research reports.

Why is SPSS advantageous to the social and educational researcher?

It has the capacity to store large numbers of records in different formats. Through subroutines such as 'frequencies' and 'cross-tabulations' it provides listings of scores and basic comparisons between variables – the first and most fundamental level of social and educational research. Similarly, the requirement to label and define variables and values causes the researcher to understand better the substantive and empirical character of the dataset. Also, the stepwise logic of analysis in SPSS requires research questions to be posited and hypotheses to be formulated that, as they are interrogated via the data, help to unfold the inside story of the research.

AN EXAMPLE

The example that follows is identified by the SPSS nomenclature:

a:\homeless.sav –
    where a = the drive location (in this case a floppy disk); homeless = the file name; sav = the extension convention for SPSS Windows Save File.

Thus Table 6.4 is an SPSS datafile about the effects of homelessness on an aspect of educational performance – social adjustment as measured by the Bristol Social Adjustment Guides.

The dependent variable (see Chapter 4) is therefore 'BSAG' and it is assumed that scores on this will be particularly related to the variables labelled 'house', indicating four possible types of conditions of domicile, and 'moves' indicating the number of moves from one dwelling to another that each respondent has made. 'School' is likely to be an intervening or control variable. There are six schools from which respondents come; the schools serve different catchment areas, are known to vary on the quality of the educational experiences offered and may be used differentially by the respondents. The respondents are children aged between 5 and 10 years, and

Table 6.4 An example of an SPSS numerical data file*

	Sex	Age	School	House	Moves	BSAG
1	2.00	6.00	4.00	3.00	1.00	8.00
2	2.00	7.00	3.00	3.00	1.00	11.00
3	1.00	8.00	2.00	2.00	1.00	12.00
4	1.00	9.00	1.00	3.00	4.00	5.00
5	2.00	9.00	5.00	2.00	4.00	5.00
6	1.00	8.00	6.00	2.00	4.00	11.00
7	1.00	6.00	6.00	2.00	4.00	9.00
8	1.00	6.00	6.00	2.00	4.00	12.00
9	2.00	5.00	5.00	1.00	11.00	5.00
10	2.00	7.00	5.00	1.00	12.00	5.00
11	1.00	6.00	4.00	4.00	3.00	8.00
12	2.00	6.00	4.00	4.00	1.00	8.00
13	2.00	8.00	3.00	1.00	11.00	5.00
14	2.00	8.00	3.00	2.00	8.00	9.00
15	1.00	9.00	1.00	2.00	6.00	8.00
16	1.00	10.00	1.00	4.00	1.00	10.00
17	1.00	8.00	1.00	4.00	1.00	10.00
18	1.00	8.00	2.00	2.00	5.00	6.00
19	2.00	9.00	3.00	3.00	2.00	12.00
20	2.00	9.00	2.00	4.00	2.00	11.00

Notes:
*   All other statistical and analytical operations are conducted from this file.
(a)   20 cases or respondents are numbered in the left-hand column; 6 exploratory variables are listed across the top.
(b)   Discrete or continuous scores are reported for each case on each variable.
(c)   The dependent variable is BSAG (Bristol Social Adjustment Guide) score; independent variables are 'moves' and 'house'.
       The basic hypothesis is a high number of moves correlates positively with a low BSAG score.

their parents. The file contains twenty (20) respondents or 'cases' as they are called with equal numbers of boys and girls. It is possible that BSAG scores may vary by sex, but this is not regarded as a potentially critical relationship in the early stage of analysis. Thus the datafile (Table 6.5) has the following character:

The basic research hypothesis that we could use this datafile to test is that a high number of moves would correlate positively with a low BSAG score. This type of datafile teaches us that when using a computer in data analysis a variable list comprising variable names, definitions, short labels and numerical values should always be written up prior to entry to the computer. Also, the variable list ought to be written to reflect entry to the computer. In the example, VAR001 is sex, VAR002 is age, VAR003 is school, and so on. The file name should reflect the substantive topic, there should be a brief identification of dependent and independent variables, and a statement of the basic or null hypothesis. Note that the column and row matrix in which raw scores are allocated to a cell is both an input technique and an output display (on screen or printed on paper) in SPSS and is broadly common to other data analysis packages such as Minitab.

Table 6.5 The descriptive characteristics of an SPSS data file

Variable names	Variable definitions	Value labels	Values
Sex	Gender of respondent	male/female	01 02
Age	Chronological age in years	–	–
School	Six schools in sample	A B C D E F G	01 02 03 04 05 06
House	Condition of domicile	Hom = homeless	01
		BB = temporary board	02
		Own = owner home	03
		Lar = local authority rent	04
Moves	Number of moves each respondent has made from home	–	–
BSAG	Scores on the Bristol Social Adjustment Guides		

Internet tools

Data analysis packages for microcomputers represent one set of 'tools' for analysis. A different set of tools, in which information retrieval is accompanied by automatic categorization and storage or downloading, is symbolized by the Internet. This global network of computers provides unprecedented access to thousands of resources and means for categorizing and listing them via electronic mail, file transfer and interactive access. Within the scope of this volume, it is only possible to indicate briefly some of these resources. Information gateways, as they are called, facilitate 'navigation' of the Internet. The Social Science Information Gateway, or SOSIG as it is colloquially named, provides access to OFSTED reports, government documents and data archives around the world. Through the Social Science Information Gateway (at web address: http://sosig.ac.uk/subjects/new.html) the following (indicative) topics may be accessed:

Indicative Information Topics Via the Social Science Information Gateway (Internet)

Department for Education and Employment (DfEE):

Education information
The National Curriculum and the statutory subject orders for England
School and college performance tables

Office for Standards in Education (OFSTED):

The OFSTED 'home' page
Inspection reports for schools and colleges

Publications:

Times Educational Supplement, including current edition, archives and 'hot' news
Education Week – an American site with information about education policy and reform in the USA.

Higher education admissions:

ECCTIS – the national database of university and college courses
Universities and Colleges Admissions Service (UCAS)

Institutional prospectuses
Supporting Bodies and Organizations
National Council for Educational technology
National Foundation for Research in Education (NFER)
Association for Science Education
UK parliament education unit
SENCO Information exchange – for special educational needs coordinators.

Further education:

Books and book equivalents
Educational materials, Apple Virtual Campus, college 'home' pages, alphabetical listings
Governmental bodies such as Further Education Development Authority (FEDA)
Journals in adult and further education, sometimes with full text
Current research projects and centres such as Center for Curriculum Transfer and Technology.

As the manipulation of data records is an important part of qualitative research, the facilities of the Internet and contemporary electronic databases can be summarized for technical use in the following ways:

1   Field Definition:
    • setting up descriptive category names;
    • setting up analytical category names;
    • using text (words) format only;
    • using numbers (numeric) formats only;
    • using alphanumeric (combined words and numbers) formats only.

2   Principles of Order and Organization:
    • by individual record and case number;
    • chronologically by date and time;
    • by author, title of published work, place, publisher and date of publication;
    • by cumulative keyword index;
    • by sequence of manipulation, such as ongoing and inclusive calculation of numerical data.

3   Layout Changes:
- pure text;
- numerical data accompanied by explanatory text;
- columns and rows;
- paragraphing, indentation, italicization, capitalization;
- titles and subtitles;
- deletions and additions;
- placement of visuals, colour shading and underlining;
- appendices, single case reports, cumulative reports of numbers of cases.

4   Storage and Output Options:
- data storage on floppy disks, hard drives and network files
- conventional print output for reports to desktop publishing standards
- mailmerge and labelling facilities for dissemination of letters and circulars
- downloading data to other relevant subfiles or transporting to World Wide Web (www) sites.

Some further advice on procedure for analysing qualitative data

Whatever the data format – interview transcripts, biographical case notes, card summaries of documents, etc. – it is always important to get a sense of the whole. The content analysis procedures that we described in Chapter 4 are attempting to formalize a means of doing just that. However, habits of mind and routine practices are also required with qualitative data. It should become habitual, for example, to read a data record when it first becomes available. It may only be a preliminary scanning kind of reading but it should be done. As the other data records become available they too should be read. During this preliminary reading it is useful to make unstructured notes, possibly in the margins of the actual data reports. We would recommend this practice for at least a quarter of the dataset.

Once a sense of the whole has been gained select any record representing the dataset, but have a reason for selecting it – for example, the shortest, the most interesting, the longest, the most wordy. Read this record in depth. Pay attention to focus, topic and content by mentally distinguishing the three. Note the frequency of topic changes. Use a highlighter to mark any part of the record that is considered to be crux material and which may later be incorporated into a written report. Repeat the process for at least five data records.

When you have read in depth five data records and highlighted crux material, make a list of the topics defined by the crux material. Transfer these to columns on metre-square chart paper, with each column representing a single data record; alternatively, use a spreadsheet. Then:

- Underline topics with a commonality in the same colour ink, e.g. red.
- Underline topics with a uniqueness in colours signifying the character of that uniqueness.
- Repeat for all topics across all columns.
- If the meaning of the topic remains opaque, return to the individual data record and reread it.
- Group topics with a commonality and assign a construct label to that group.
- Repeat for unique topics unidimensionally, that is, one construct label per topic.

Make a rank order of topic clusters on a separate sheet. Adjacent to each rank, write the reason for ordering the clusters in this way – why Cluster1 is at the top, and so on. Abbreviate the topic constructs as codes and apply them to the remaining dataset. The now coded topics should analytically fit (that is, effectively interrogate) much that is in the remaining data, permitting a fairly explicit (and theoretically and judgmentally informed) kind of interpretation. Where incongruities occur (i.e. where the codes do not fit) respondent variance and/or the adequacy of the construct appellations is illuminated. If the new incongruities are judged to be relevant, decide whether or not to assign them new construct labels. Continue to write on 5" × 3" system cards aides mémoire about the data.

It now remains to compile a rank-ordering system for all coded data for the complete dataset. The full dataset is then interrogated by re-theorizing and explaining the content that exemplifies the construct label. That is, the rank-ordered construct labels are 'fleshed out' to provide a template of explanatory theory. (To review an exemplification of the results of this process return to a study of Table 4.1 on p. 107.) As you do the 'fleshing out', keep in mind the original research questions or hypotheses. The explanations of the constructs should harmonize with the expressed purposes of the research as contained in the research questions. With regard to the final list of explanations, it is important to ensure that the 'boundary' between each construct is appropriately defined and understood.

The above process is just one example of coding, categorizing and charting data. There are many other possibilities, but they are likely to have the same intrinsic logic of analysis. Most practitioner-researchers find it necessary and sufficient to devise their own analytical schemes. Whatever scheme is devised it will need to be checked for adequacy through the following questions:

> Have sufficient data records been used to establish a representative dataset?
> Have the necessary and sufficient construct labels been devised for interrogating the dataset?

Are the reasons for rank ordering explicit and justified?

Has the process of item versus item and case versus case comparisons been implemented?

Is the separation of topic, content and focus rational and valid?

A special note on dealing with interview data

At various points in the book we have commented on the data-gathering technique of interviewing. We have drawn attention to some of the advantages and drawbacks of interview transcript material as data. We would like to offer some additional advice about the use and integration of interview data into a final report. The reader will find it helpful to supplement these comments with a meta analysis (an analysis of the analysis) of the interview procedures used by our ethnographer(s) in Chapter 4.

Interviews provide very large amounts of data in the form of typed transcripts of respondent verbal utterances. The real question is what to do with this material because only a fraction of it can be used in a final report. The first obligation (as we have said above) is for the practitioner-researcher to read and know all the interview material. This is no small reading task. It is also an intensely privatized task carrying numerous obligations. What reading predisposition should be adopted? What will be put in the report? What will be left out? How will principles of selection of material be explained to the readership? How will the flavour of the interviews be communicated? All these and other important questions have to be confronted when using interview transcript material.

In our view, interviews that are audio-recorded or shorthand-noted should always be typed up into full transcripts of the verbal encounter. The time, date, duration, and the designation of the interviewer and respondent (coded if so required under confidentiality rules) should appear at the head of the transcript. Factual records of interviews are necessary for several reasons. The order in which interviews are conducted is often important in respect of how the data is to be interpreted. For example, interviews with pupils in schools may be undertaken prior to interviews with teachers on the presumption that the former may be more spontaneously honest than the latter. Similarly, the veracity of interviews may be challenged at a point in the future. The researcher needs to anticipate a need to disarm critics by being able to quote times, places, respondents, and what was said and recorded. Finally, and especially if a respondent has insisted on complete anonymity, if an interview audio recording or transcript is not effectively coded as part of a dataset, human memory being what it is, data will eventually be 'lost' from the emerging account. Good record-keeping is one of the processes required for the orderly treatment of data.

If the transcript is a verbatim (unedited) report of utterances, this should also be indicated. If the transcript is edited, the principles of editing (and later selection of materials) should be clearly stated. If annotations are to be written in the margins or on separate paper, they should be made in red or green ink to identify their separate authorship. The typed transcripts become the data archive of the interviews. This should be available for consultation at future points if: (a) further detailed information is required; (b) a respondent needs a reminder of what he or she actually said; (c) a check is required on the validity of claims for selection of material as used in a final report. The latter point should not be underestimated; the veracity of research reports is often questioned by critics on the basis of what was done in and around interviews. Similarly, it is wise to keep an interview transcript archive for no longer than three years, unless historical documentary purposes decree otherwise. After three years we suggest that the average transcript file should be destroyed as it contains confidential information which people provided willingly at a point in historical time, but do not necessarily want retained in perpetuity. In any case, after three years or so, the information may no longer be relevant. Also, any tape recordings of interviews should be erased once the material has been transcribed.

However, this informal rule may be waived in situations where it is important to archive material for the future. Archiving is a specialist function. In retaining material in archive form a preliminary question has to be faced : Is it the substance of the material that requires to be archived or the respondent's unique conveyance of the substance? If it is the former, then there is no great problem. Substance is extracted and depersonalized. If it is the latter, or a combination of both, then the personalization of the archival record is regarded as important. In such cases, appropriate rules and procedures have to be formalized to ensure confidentiality and proper usage.

In reporting interview data we have already referred to two examples of how this is done. The 'long' way is to reproduce the full interview transcript in script or, more appropriately, in an appendix. Often this cannot be done if the transcript is too long and additional commentary upon it would make for an unwieldy report. Where the transcript responses are abbreviated, as in the example of the (provided) ethnography, and where the methodological posture benefits from it, a complete transcript can be fitted in, possibly two, but rarely more than that. What is provided in the ethnography, bearing in mind it was a three-respondent study, is close to the limit of what is admissible in a 5000–7000-word report. The 'short' way is to use selected verbatim statements (unedited respondent utterances) and to chart or list these in an integrated way into the report. Table 6.6 is an example of this. Note that the assembly of material in this chart is similar in appearance to the '2 × 2' contingency arrangements for statistical tables. Similarly, the principles for selection are governed and indicated by words such as 'typical', 'positive' and 'negative', and classifiers such as 'sex' and 'year group'.

Table 6.6 A selection of typical student comments on aspects of school life – by year group and sex

	Male		Female	
	Year 10	*Year 12*	*Year 10*	*Year 12*
Positive	School is enjoyable if teachers take the trouble to get involved with students. At school you meet new people, fall into and out of friendships and learn new things. School is a place where students learn to be independent from parents. I like the sport and social activities. I particularly like the subjects in which the student must be responsible for doing a lot of work themselves. It is good when students are given the right to decide on matters around school.	Fifty per cent of us are immature or idiots so we need to be in school. I appreciate the dedication and fairness of teachers at this school. The fact that things are organized, especially sport, is good. I enjoy talking to the teachers socially outside the classroom.	School is a place where you can feel safe and secure. Meeting friends every day helps to reduce the pressure from teachers. The work experience programme is great. It is important at school to learn how to treat people differently. Socials and extra-curricular activities make school worthwhile.	It is nice when teachers respect you and treat you as young men and women. Wearing uniforms is good because it allows everyone to exist on a common basis. It is good to be challenged to express yourself in a number of ways. Meeting and making new friends is the best part of school. There is a secure atmosphere because everything is planned for you. Some of the teachers are fun to be around.
Negative	You learn less than you would if you stayed at home and you are treated like a kid. Examinations coming in one block at the end of semester is bad. I hate the teachers, many are too strict. Learning foreign languages is impractical and a waste of time. The seniors here continually gain preferential treatment. There is not enough choice of flexibility in subjects offered.	It's impossible when teachers roar on into new work and you can't understand what you've just finished. The strain is just as great, even greater, having exams and assignments spread throughout the year, as one external exam at the end. Those students who study maths, physics and chemistry look down on those who study art, commerce and geography. Students who could have passed are failing because of the rigid timetable of subjects and the pushing of content masses on students.	I dislike it when teachers force their own opinions on you instead of letting you make up your own mind. Most teachers tend to take notice of the kids who are brainy. Teachers tend to forget that they are not the only ones giving homework. I greatly dislike the jail-like features especially the stupid rules like not being allowed out of the school yard. There are too many assignments; they are often not properly structured and there is insufficient time to complete them.	Some of the teachers don't plan their teaching programmes very well; they tend to put most of the information you need into the last couple of months before the exams. The fact that students have to conform to standards in so many ways makes school life difficult. It's obvious that some teachers haven't got a clue about their subjects and they disadvantage their students. I am appalled by the constant pressure that Grade 12s are put under to succeed and complete their work.

Verbatim statements are useful for they recount the 'story' in the words of the respondent and not in the language of the researcher. However, it is easy to slip into selecting those statements that only prove one's theory or vindicate one's claims. Verbatim statements should therefore be used judiciously. Principles of selection should be made clear in the methodological write-up parts of a report. Selection is usually made on the premise that the statement in question is particularly rich in detail or sound in respect of explaining something. Other statements may be picked for their emotional content in order to jar the reader into mental alertness. Still others may be selected for their capacity to illustrate constructs or coded ideas developing during the analysis. In general, verbatim statements selected for inclusion in a final report should represent the full range of opinions in the dataset covered by the interview transcripts.

Other possibilities for the use of interview data include the extraction and use in script of key statements – if you like, a form of independent citation. In a more categorical- or information-based mode, interview respondents holding specialized positions can provide material or perspective available from no other source. This can be summarized in point form, or paraphrased and inserted into the report in those parts dealing with the characteristics of the sample, as well as in the substantive conclusions. Finally, interview data can be reported as point–counterpoint dialogue to illustrate arguments for and against something. In using interview data the practitioner-researcher has to be particularly conscious of the principle of creative parsimony. By this we mean that a balance has to be achieved in nominating the volume of material to be used, the device by which that volume is represented to the senses (e.g. a visual chart) and criteria of selection which are economical in rendering the overarching messages comprehensible to a critically inclined reader.

Report writing

Once a dataset has been analysed and interpreted, conclusions are drawn. Hypotheses are judged to have been proven or not proven. Research questions are judged to have been answered in full, in part, or not answered at all. If the latter is the case, then the concluding remarks to a research report must either indicate directions for future work or assess the adequacy of the questions in the terms in which they were first presented. Any recommendations that may be made for future practices or educational policy tend to follow these concluding elements. Rough drafts of these elements can then be incorporated into admissible artefacts, especially the written report. In Chapter 1 we referred to the admissibility and character of PBE artefacts. We drew a distinction between a formative working document known as a 'journal' and a technical PBE report. We described the latter as having craft aspects or penmanship features that are relatively unique to the PBE enterprise. Where such reports are submitted to higher education institutions for academic credit, they have the character of summative (capable of being awarded letter grades or numerical marks) assessment devices, judged against the criteria presented in Chapter 5. PBE reports also hold the potential to be 'stand alone' documents – that is, independently contrived pieces of scholarly writing that are capable of transformation into articles for learned journals, chapters for books, and submissions to public authorities. Much of our argument in this book has been about ways of contriving scholarship That is, we have presented PBE – conducting small-scale research, analysing data and writing about it – as a particular genre of scholarly activity, one in which the quality of learning has parity with any importance attached to the findings of research.

The generalized academic genre is to be found in the style guides adopted by universities and colleges (Turabian, 1973; Barzun and Graff, 1977), manuals of government departments and learned bodies (e.g. Publication Manual of the American Psychological Society), and in commercially available publications that tend to offer shorthand and simplified approaches to the task of academic writing (Rudestam and Newton, 1992; Berry, 1994). Usually, candidates on university award-bearing courses will be provided with explicit documentation on the required format for assignments, practitioner-research reports and dissertations. This documentation is often modelled upon, and derivative of, established bibliographical and lexical systems such as the 'Harvard' or 'Oxford' systems, which have achieved high professional visibility and use in the English-speaking world. We have provided a conventional example of this documentation, as used at the University of Portsmouth, in Appendix 2. The sorts of formal features of academic writing and presentation indicated will normally appear in PBE reports. Whether these features are replicated directly or whether they are treated to a derivative format will depend on the extent to which academic institutions require candidates to conform to their published rubrics. All writers and 'doers' of practitioner-based enquiries should, of course, thoroughly familiarize themselves with the academic submission and style requirements of their host institution.

Genre and Drafting Processes in PBE

One problem encountered in conventional academic rubrics for writing is that they do not readily superimpose on to all topics. PBE reports tend to be cast in an evolved genre form that is, in part, necessitated by the topic under investigation. The drafting process, editing and rewriting parts of the paper is as much a process of 'casting genre' as it is a (much more mundane) task of grammatical correction and syntactic ordering. In our extended examples in this book – the ethnographic account of debating and the use of information technology in middle school geography – the issue of genre is well illustrated. The written genre of the ethnography is in significant measure a function of adherence to the 'rules' of ethnographic semantics. By contrast, the PBE report on IT in middle school geography employs a fair amount of factual recounting.

Similarly, the kind of theoretical orientations we discussed in Chapter 2 illustrate how difficult it is to compose a model of report writing that would suit all PBE purposes. In 'postmodernism' especially, the introspective and sometimes anarchic quality of the 'debate' renders the articulation of principles for writing problematic. This seems to be a product especially of those books and tracts which are read by an 'audience' which is not assessing the work for academic credit. Derrida may have said 'there is nothing beyond the text' – but he evolved and was dependent upon a textual genre to say it. The judgment on this 'claim to knowledge' is reflected in the interest shown by the 'lit-crit' industry, the 1001 theses contrived to prove or denounce the claim in university departments, and the jangling of tills in the accounts departments of international publishing houses. Genre can presumably be whatever a writer wants it to be if he or she cares not a jot about audience reaction.

But – and it is a big 'but' – audience reaction is a critical matter in respect of PBE writing. The drafting process has to take account of audience requirements and system expectations – for, as we have argued, PBE is system-based enquiry. The serious point is what Berry (1994, p. 40) has called the 'search for internal form'. It is Berry's belief that 'every topic has a natural form, and it is the business of the writer to explore and clarify this form'. In respect of writing about learning theory, for example, 'natural form' would be discerned from concepts (and accumulated evidence for such concepts) such as stimulus-response, conditioning, reinforcement and habituation. With regard to writing-up historically oriented research, concepts of 'chronology' and 'time' would necessarily steer the account. How could it be otherwise in matter purporting to be historical? As far as the reporting of peoples' experiences of, say, an Information Technology training course for beginners is concerned, consideration would necessarily have to be given in precise order to respondent characteristics (especially any prior experience), the factual events of the learning activities and the verbatim responses of the participants to the learning experience.

Devices to capture genre

(i) Amplifying the use of the direct citation

At various points in this book we have pinpointed and commented upon literary and technical devices that aid in the production of the enquiry and the contrivance of the artefact or research report. A few additional, targeted remarks are of value at this juncture.

To quote other authors' works directly in the body of a research report is, perhaps, the most widely recognized feature of scholarly and academic writing. Writer-researchers should be clear about the advantages and purposes of this. Direct citations are normally selected to provide a definitive enunciation of a key point. Such an enunciation is given status by being drawn from previously published work. Further authority is given to the point if it has been well explained by credible authors and scholars. From the standpoint of the writing task, therefore, this tends to take the idea out of the realm of hearsay, opinion and intuition. The core idea enters and pervades the discourse that the writer-researcher wishes to construe. If the citation is in a word form that cannot be bettered, then it simplifies the task of academic writing. It acts on behalf of the writer to express meaning and capture genre. However, citations have to be husbanded carefully. They should not be overlong (drawing an account towards heavy dependence upon the original author) and they should not appear too frequently in text. Their additional function is, of course, to show evidence of wide reading around a topic and the knowledge gathered during that reading phase.

At a more technical level, and as previously inferred by our consideration of reviews of the literature, citation records are part of the secondary database of an enquiry. They are 'secondary' because the content of the record was not provided first-hand by informants. Rather, it is documented data produced at another time and for purposes unconnected with the current enquiry. It is you, the writer-researcher, who must connect the documented information to your own enquiry. The citation record card (see Figure 6.6) shows how this is an active enterprise. The citation, shown to be a citation by the use of quotation marks, contains the core ideas or 'essences' that the writer has read and wishes to capture and utilize. The insertion of three additional indicators (there may of course be others that could be used) – 'seminal', 'card 1', 'keyword' – are reminders to oneself that the book so recorded is critical to the enquiry and its messages ought to contribute to substance and add flavour to genre. Also, citation records of the type illustrated help to place a written report on the continuum of policy, research and development in the substantive topic area by date order, keyword and title, as well as alphabetically by author, citation and annotation. Such a 'continuum' usually involves a dialogue with books, articles, or the ideas of other authors known to be influential in this field of study.

(ii) The art and science of paraphrasing

Much of the written script in a PBE report ought to be – and probably will be – original, in that the words used are the author's own. However, it is also likely that parts of the script will be paraphrases. Paraphrasing is an acquired skill. It is essentially the summarization of an argument in your own words. It comes with the practice of note-taking. That is, material that

Figure 6.7 A typical citation/reference record card

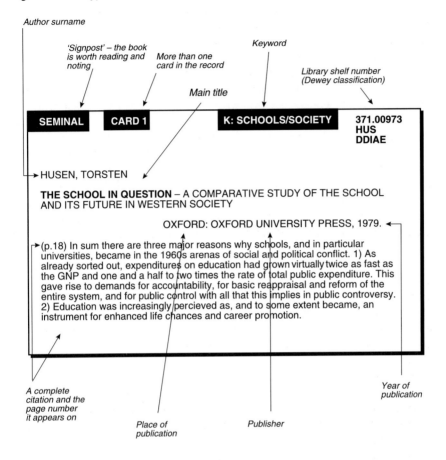

is read or acquired in other ways through the senses, is summarized in note form. The 'B' or reverse side of a system card record may be used for summary notes based on the reading of a source document. Alternatively, perhaps additionally, commentary on or about the citation that appears on the 'A' side of the card may be written. The absence of quotation marks here is a reminder to self that these are your own words. They can thus be inserted at appropriate places in the body of the script forming the report. Depending on how 'raw' the notes are, the key arguments of a particular book or the ideas of a notable author are summarized in as literary a manner as is efficiently possible. These summaries, when implanted in a formal report, may be enlarged as required.

The convention, of course, is always to acknowledge original sources, unless the ideas are fully integrated into the public domain. However, a good review of the literature section in a PBE report is often a series of connected paraphrases. Indeed, writing the review from a series of paraphrased record cards has many advantages over writing direct from text books. In paraphrasing other works, a writer-researcher engages in a kind of literary colonization, incorporating previously published information into the structure and framework of his or her enquiry. We all learn from earlier scholars and teachers. Paraphrasing is one of the literary devices available to systematize this learning into independently contrived scholarship. That is a most important point. Unless we are writing review essays of other authors works, paraphrasing is a means to a separate end; the 'end' of telling a logically congruent and integrated 'story' of a research project. By 'integrated' we mean a fusion of genre, substance and technical manipulation of supportive writing manuals and documentation. Habitual practice with course documents provided by universities, etc., and with standard reference works such as *Roget's Thesaurus*, the *Concise Oxford Dictionary of Current English* (which reached its ninth edition in 1995), and the *Writers' and Artists' Yearbook* (which is published annually) facilitate such a manipulation.

(iii) Knowing the politics of writing

There is the potential for sins of omission and commission in report writing. Knowing something about common errors and 'offences' against scholarly convention is helpful when writing research reports. Understanding that something is frowned upon, inappropriate, unethical or wrong often helps to instil 'avoidance' strategies when at the stage of report writing – a form of mental discipline. In this difficult and opaque area there are 'categories of sinfulness'. Plagiarism, the deliberate and unacknowledged copying of other people's writings and presenting them as if they were your own, is almost universally proscribed in academic institutions. Similarly, strict copyright laws protect authors and their manuscripts. Work written and submitted for academic credit and judged to be plagiarized risks failing grades and severe punitive sanctions. Plagiarism is close to the top of the 'league table' of writing sins.

However, it is the unintended failings or 'sins of omission' that are more likely to detract from a research report. These are numerous and are often commented upon in examiners' reports. They include incorrect nomenclature on cover and imprint pages, typographic errors which change meaning and emphasis (e.g. 'affect' as opposed to 'effect'), punctuation, case usage, grammar and syntax problems, conclusions not warranted by the evidence produced, and the provision of an extended bibliography that fails to be reflected in the text. Similarly, writers of research reports often experience difficulty in 'closing' their arguments – that is, they fail to make an effective terminating statement about what the research was about in the first place. 'Recommendations' become confused with 'conclusions', and vice versa.

To guard against such sins the writer must always retain a keen sense of audience. Knowing what the academy regards as good practice is helpful. It is vital to understand the checklist of assessment criteria that a tutor is empowered to use for judging the adequacy of a PBE report. Knowing what is proscribed in law and under university statute and academic regulations is equally important. All this implies becoming familiar with any printed rules for the submission of PBE reports. It also implies proofreading as the 'twin' of drafting. As a draft is written, it needs to be carefully read and proofed for errors. Preferably, this should be done by a third party who is sufficiently distant from the subject matter. Perhaps surprisingly, the evidence is that such people are often better at spotting errors than the actual writer. Proofreading not only helps in the identification of technical errors, it can also provide insights into how the report actually reads. Its logical congruence or 'flow', the balance of the argument as presented, the constant imposition of personal bias, and so forth.

The 'politics of writing' are analysed in detail by Clark and Ivanic (1997). These writers make it clear that there are governing academic and professional conventions for writing which cannot be ignored. These are of the type outlined in Appendix 2. There is also a 'deeper structure' to academic writing at the level of mores or powerful norms that shape and guide writing practices within a culture. These may be felt and experienced rather than confronted via the stipulations of the institutional handbook. Writing offers the opportunity to engage in word games, plays on abstraction, jargon production and relativistic arrogance – a criticism often made of postmodernist writing. It also offers the opportunity to construct an identity for self and present it in such a way that it is positively misleading. Furthermore, conclusions can be 'manufactured' to induce consent to a spurious claim to knowledge. Some modern research reporting may be interpreted as indicative 'rites of passage' work within and between cultural and educational elites. Writing aimed at publication often has to survive the 'gatekeeping' activities of elder 'statespeople' who control the editorial boards of learned journals. The claim to knowledge in this type of work may be incidental to the task of having it judged worthy of publication. To help writer-researchers judge the adequacy and intellectual integrity of their written PBE reports in the perspective of the above we have provided the following fifteen pointers:

Fifteen pointers for judging professional and intellectual integrity in writing PBE reports

1 Does the title of the report communicate immediately with the intended audience?
2 Are the conventions of standard English, use of tenses, grammar and punctuation adhered to in the script?
3 Does the report conform to assignment writing criteria set and published by an academic or professional institution?
4 Has an abstract been provided (in 250 words or less) to say what was done, why it was done, what was found out?
5 Has a referencing and citation format been appropriately embedded in the report?
6 Is the terminology used both necessary and sufficient to construe purposes and to control abstract explanation?
7 Has appropriate attention been given to the separation of factual statements, value judgments, opinions, warranted assertions, descriptive statements, analytical statements?
8 Is the account in the report conjectural or evidence-led?
9 Given a selected or preferred writing style – continuous prose, technical report, chronological diary, data plus analytical commentary, etc. – does the report unfold a 'story'?
10 Does the report enunciate, and subsequently reflect, a clear sense of purpose throughout?
11 Is the report capable of being used by reader-researchers as an archive document?
12 Is the report capable of functioning as a template for repeatability activities by readers?
13 Does the explanation of methodology avoid lies, licence and larceny?
14 Is the report written with conviction in respect of results and knowledge produced?
15 Has every word in the report been made to count?

Writing and Analysing – Analysing and Writing

Writing a PBE report is part technical routine, part creative composition and part forensic analysis. While it is relatively easy to follow and to internalize the aforelisted academic conventions to produce a competent report, the main text in particular will always require something extra. We doubt if it is possible to give people a formula for writing 'good' research reports. There are many permutations and stylistic variations that can be mobilized for maximum communicative effect. In this book alone, we have reproduced in full two PBE reports that contrast markedly in their report format. In large measure, this is a function of their methodological standpoint. It is also a function of other things such as the mixture of descriptive prose, occasional subjectivization and technical reporting. There is no substitute for practice in writing research reports. They have to be worked at, produced in draft form, revised and edited. Similarly, they require to be oriented towards particular audiences and the judgmental criteria that such people bring to bear when reading. Above all they have to be effectively 'signposted'. At its simplest, signposting is the use of directional phrases, such as 'I will now turn to...' or 'having reviewed the article by Brennan, I will proceed to...', to inform the reader about steps the author is taking to explain the account. At its most subtle, signposting is a key tool for expediting analysis of data, emphasizing limitations, and keeping logical congruence throughout the report. It is sometimes necessary to use signposts that tell the reader what the PBE is *not* about. This makes the reader aware of a writer's conscious decision not to use certain information or techniques. We can illustrate some of the functions of signposting for a hypothetical PBE on the famous UK 'free school' of Summerhill, but before we do this it is worthwhile giving an extra bit of thought to the writing of abstracts.

The abstract

It will be understood that most journal articles, technical reports, some books and other formal documents have, as a kind of frontispiece, an abbreviated abstract. This is a synopsis in about 250 words of the complete report that follows. The abstract may be thought of as the 'critical signpost' to a research report. After the title, it is the first thing the reader sees and reads. Being in 'reported speech' form, it is usually simple to digest and easy to read. Good abstracts appear deceptively simple, but they are not at all easy to write. Compressing what was undertaken in the research, why it was undertaken and listing what was discovered or found out into about 250 words is a painstaking part of the writing task. It is, though, a most important part of that task.

Composing an abstract helps to crystallize the totality of the research project in the writer-researcher's mind. It induces writing discipline that is necessarily focused upon the essentials of the research problem, the design of the enquiry and the data-gathering methods it employed, its main outcomes or findings and the conclusions drawn. The language used has to be clear and direct and uncluttered by quotations or material from 'third parties'. The abstract performs numerous functions for the reader. Most notably, good abstracts achieve 'closure' on the topic *in absentia* of the substantive details. A reader will know when he or she has read a good abstract. They will have a sense of 'knowing' the story to come, they will have picked up on the gist, and they will probably be motivated to read on.

Abstracts, like good novels, are broadly formulaic rather than spontaneous or 'off-the-cuff' summaries. They are crafted to perform technical functions and to capture the reader's interest. They are essentially a device of synthesis. Practised researchers sometimes write an abstract before they commence an enquiry. The idea here is to tell self where to go, what to do, when to stop. Realistically, though, abstract writing is a recursive practice. The final 'published' abstract will almost certainly have been honed, tightened, polished, and be the product of a series of writing episodes that were required for the assembly and composition of the report.

Consider the 'A' version of the following abstract for the PBE (Figure 6.7) and then consider the 'B' version with annotations. In not much more than 100 words, this short abstract is performing at least eight functions for the research report, prominent among which is signposting. It is, perhaps, not too much of a cliché to say that producing a report for PBE is an art, as well as a habitual practice guided by convention. In the PBEs to which we refer in Chapter 7, all the authors have produced PBE reports that are variations on the theme. Their written works, on first encounter, all appear radically different. A closer examination reveals that most of the features described above are appropriated in some way and embedded in the script. In this sense, writing the report is the final step in analysing the data and bringing the research to closure. (See Murray and Lawrence (1995) for an account of how publicly available materials on the ever-popular and ever-controversial topic of Summerhill School may be used to develop PBE skills.)

In this chapter we construed the data analysis process as a series of connected intellectual steps. We have reviewed some of the more common graphical and statistical devices for representing data to the senses. This section was complemented by a concise account of what modern electronic data analysis packages can offer the practitioner-researcher. Further advice was proffered on the procedure for handling qualitative data, especially material drawn from interview transcripts. We then turned to the task of writing PBE reports. We listed an indicative structure for PBE reports based on established academic conventions, and, finally, we concluded by challenging the practitioner-researcher to become author-researcher through a wordsmithing and craftsmanship approach. In the final chapter of this book we return to more general PBE themes and show how practitioner research reports can be used to 'make a difference' to shape and influence educational policies.

Figure 6.7   Abstracts for a PBE

Version A

> Instability in Charismatic Leadership in Educational Organizations: The Case of A.S. Neill and Summerhill School
>
> ### ABSTRACT
>
> This PBE investigates selected dimensions of leadership in educational organizations. Specifically, alternative schools are described as in permanent crisis because their day-to-day administration is subservient to the pervasive ideology of their founders.
>
> The PBE derives a construct of 'charismatic leadership' by analysing the verbal utterances of A.S. Neill and his successors at Summerhill made in a series of sound and vision programmes for public consumption in the period 1950–92. Secondary data on administrative conduct at Summerhill is provided from school documents and written records of 'town meetings'.
>
> The PBE concludes that orderly and rational administration at alternative schools such as Summerhill is compromised because of persistent instabilities generated through dependence on charismatic leadership. Furthermore, as time goes by, instabilities are institutionalized because of the lack of continuity in school leadership roles.

Study this abstract carefully. What functions does it perform? Is it a good or bad abstract?

Version B

Research purpose   Key construct in title   'Signpost'   Indication of case study

> Instability in Charismatic Leadership in Educational Organizations: The Case of A.S. Neill and Summerhill School
>
> ### ABSTRACT
>
> This PBE investigates selected dimensions of leadership in educational organizations. Specifically, alternative schools are described as in permanent crisis because their day-to-day administration is subservient to the pervasive ideology of their founders.
>
> The PBE derives a construct of 'charismatic leadership' by analysing the verbal utterances of A.S. Neill and his successors at Summerhill made in a series of sound and vision programmes for public consumption in the period 1950–92. Secondary data on administrative conduct at Summerhill is provided from school documents and written records of 'town meetings'.
>
> The PBE concludes that orderly and rational administration at alternative schools such as Summerhill is compromised because of persistent instabilities generated through dependence on charismatic leadership. Furthermore, as time goes by, instabilities are institutionalized because of the lack of continuity in school leadership roles.

Presumption of prior knowledge on part of readership   Two substantive conclusions   Generalization beyond the particular case   Method of data collection

Study this annotated version of the abstract. Do the functions highlighted match the one you identified? How might the abstract be amended and improved?

7 Making a Difference
Using PBE to Influence Policy and Practice

In this concluding chapter we draw upon and present some purpose statements of actual PBE work to illustrate how the stable predisposition of tutor as enquirer may actively connect with the real world concerns of education and training. Similarly, these extracts may be taken as indicators of how the assumptions of PBE are made visible and, through their reception and use in the public domain, tested for admissibility. It is here where the meaning of 'applications' and 'implications for policy' becomes clearer. The diversity and range in the educational and training settings that are the sites for these examples helps to make visible the institutional character of the issues under enquiry. PBE is, as emphasized in earlier chapters, system-based and often system-derived. In speaking of the implications of PBE for wider educational practices and policies, even if they are local ones, reference is made therefore as to how institutions might respond to the pressing issues of the day. These are usually two-dimensional: they have a specific and current character that may be defined by government policy or pressing operational requirement. They also in some way illuminate the more abstract developments and cultural changes in the society in which they are located.

Consider PBE Exhibit A, a set of research questions on a highly topical and controversial aspect of police operational practice and the training for that operational practice in a county police force in the south of England:

PBE Exhibit A: Child protection practices in a county constabulary

1   What is the current child protection practice in Midshires constabulary?
2   How do police managers view their role within child protection practice?

> 3 What evidence exists to show that training in child protection
>   practices is required by police managers?
> 4 How can training needs for police managers be identified?

This PBE was undertaken by a serving police officer with delegated responsibility for child protection training. The research was aimed at the rank of detective inspector, the level at which responsibility for operational matters in respect of child protection rests in Midshires. In the face of widespread concern over child abuse, the James Bulger tragedy, the Cleveland enquiry, and Home Office initiatives following the Butler-Sloss recommendations, county constabularies have had to reassess both policy and needs in child protection. The responsibility for undertaking the research into a reassessment of training needs may, as in this example, fall into the lap of a single officer. Although this person may be well experienced in active policing in respect of child protection, the identification of training needs for senior officers is a requirement of a different order. The PBE must set out to discover how Midshires constabulary has equipped its middle management to train and supervise officers working on child protection cases. The PBE is consequentially risky but challenging: risky in the responsibilities it places upon the enquirer, especially in the knowledge that management training has been historically neglected; challenging in the sense that it offers the opportunity to influence new concepts of police operational training in the follow-up period after the publication of national enquiries such as that defined by the Sheehy Report.

In the second example, an adult languages tutor has attempted to clarify the role of the bilingual assistant in primary schools where spoken and written English classes have had to accommodate up to 30 per cent of children from a Bangladeshi minority community. The initiative of provision of bilingual assistants is typical of that taken by local education authorities in large urban areas in response to community needs. The research was driven by the lack of clarity in links between home, school and LEA in respect of language policy and general educational matters, and in the knowledge that approximately 30 per cent of the target community was aged between 5 and 15 years old and spoke predominantly Bengali at home. A bilingual assistant is usually an adult member of the speech and ethnic community from whence these children originate. The task of the bilingual assistant may require physical presence in conventional classrooms alongside a conventionally appointed classroom teacher. In a general sense, activities will include routine translation of complex words, helping children to understand and interpret messages given out in English, and mediating a variety of transactions between pupil and teacher. However, the job may be very much what the individual makes of it. Research, therefore, is useful in helping to identify more formal possibilities for the role of bilingual assistant. Indeed, professionally indeterminate roles such as bilingual assistant tend to sharpen a focus on policy requirements. School language curriculum, LEA resourcing responsibilities and the important matter of the professional status of teachers and ancillaries in the same room are all policy-generating concerns that are likely to be informed by this work.

PBE Exhibit B: The role of the bilingual assistant in primary schools in urban areas

1 What range of tasks must a bilingual assistant routinely undertake?
2 How do bilingual assistants adjust to children whose home language is not English?
3 What language facilitation resources are available for use in the classroom?
4 What personal attributes are demanded of bilingual assistants?

The third example is from the world of nurse education and medical practice. In this example, the enquirer, who is an experienced sister/charge nurse and nurse educator, sought to identify the reasons for the use of certain wound-cleansing solutions in clinical practices in a large London teaching hospital. The premise was that if consistent principles for the selection and use of wound-cleansing solutions could be established, instruction of student nurses in this technique could be simplified and enhanced. It might be assumed that procedures for clinical practices such as this one would be established by regulation or explained chapter and verse in teaching manuals – but apparently not. Custom and practice, it was claimed, not to mention the private preferments of experienced nurses in hospitals, is sufficient to offset any standardized instructions on the bottle or general rules in a nurse education syllabus.

It can be seen at a glance of the research questions, that this research is very important in three respects. First, public confidence in nursing competence may be undermined if there is no agreement about wound-cleansing solutions. Second, the nurse education curriculum of teaching hospitals could be compromised if private preferments and local customs subvert knowledge of best practices. Third, national imperatives for nurse tutors and the competencies they require under Project 2000 of the English National Board for Nursing, Midwifery and Health Visiting (ENB) are compromised. Thus, a clinically specific and institutionally circumscribed investigation can have implications that extend well beyond the first concerns of the practitioner conducting the investigation.

PBE Exhibit C: The identification of influences on the use of wound-cleansing solutions in a London teaching hospital

1   What brands of wound-cleansing solutions are regularly used in clinical areas in teaching hospitals?
2   What regulations and principles govern the use of these solutions?
3   To what extent is the selection of wound-cleansing solutions a function of unexamined personal preferences of nurses?
4   What are student nurses routinely taught about wound-cleansing solutions?

The fourth example is from early childhood education and arrangements for the learning and teaching of reading. Concerns over the language and literacy of young children and their parents possibly reached their greatest public visibility in the UK in 1998. Indeed, the intensity of debates about the teaching of basic literacy skills in young children, reading standards and the implications of poor levels of adult literacy for child socialization has been fuelled by critical media commentary and research reports issued by the National Foundation for Educational Research (NFER) and similar agencies. A political response to this debate was the establishment of the Basic Skills Agency (BSA), separate from the Department for Education and Employment (DFEE), and tasked with the responsibility of raising standards of literacy among adults with known difficulties and their children. While the kindergarten classroom may have the surface appearance of a cosy and insulated world of feelings, the wider political and educational milieu to which it is attached is a turbulent one in the eyes of the early childhood teacher. Crucial decisions have to be taken in respect of children aged 5–7. What to teach? How to organize a reading scheme? What strategies can be adopted to cause reading behaviours to occur? And so on. A recognition of the character of this milieu provided the impetus for the study of twelve (12) children's perceptions of reading.

The fieldwork phase of the study was conducted in a one-form entry infant school in Hampshire with 12 children from two Year 1 and Year 2 classes. The mean age of the children was 5 years 8 months.

PBE Exhibit D: Twelve children's perceptions of reading

1 What do the pupils think their reading capabilities are?
2 Do children have specific views on why they like or dislike reading?
3 What do teachers think the pupils achieve in reading tasks?
4 What are the pupils measured capacities in reading?

Information was gathered from examining progress reports and reading records for each child, teachers verbatim reports, descriptions of the learning environment, Standard Attainment Task (SAT) scores produced under National Curriculum rubrics, and interviews with teachers and pupils on an individual basis (Ralls and Murray, 1997). The relatively unusual stance of this research – to enable children as well as teachers to give voice to their perception of reading ability – provided an additional vantage point on the reading debate. Hitherto, much of that debate had been teacher-centric, adult appropriated and directed towards formal arrangements for the teaching of literacy. Recent 'practice and policy' initiatives such as the basic Skills Agency's literacy demonstration programmes (Brooks, Gorman, Harman et al., 1996) suggest that there is now a more clearly understood empirical frame of reference for the teaching of reading and other literacy processes. At the core of this frame of reference is the child's linguistic relations with parents, teachers and significant others in a speech community. The PBE outlined above recognizes and connects with that empirical frame of reference. In recognizing children's perceptual views as a resource to be used to inform a reading policy, and by analysing such perceptions via low technology research methodologies, the infant school in question joins the national project and debate on literacy.

There is no reason why PBE should be saddled with the label of parochialism. The fifth and final example in this section is an international one. In this example, the researcher, who was working towards an MA at a British university, conducted fieldwork in her native state of Virginia in the USA. The focus of her enquiry was the perennial one of differentiation by ability in Grades 1–5 within three elementary schools in northern Virginia. In a strongly democratic society such as that of the USA, state educational authorities differ in respect of the separation of groups of students for educational purposes on the basis of measured intellectual ability. However, the practices of *tracking* (a term in general use in the USA) and *differentiation* or *setting* (terms that have tended to replace *streaming* in the UK) refer to classroom arrangements whereby pupils of *different abilities* are taught. These arrangements might include tasks of varying grades of difficulty and

assessment practices in which numerical marks and letter grades are cali-
brated to, or scaled against, the measured intellectual capabilities of pupils.
There is an extensive and complex literature on this topic. Research findings
are used and counter-used to support claims for various kinds of policies
with practical consequences. The provision of comprehensive schools is
heavily underpinned by concepts of equality that rest uncomfortably with
differentiation by ability. In the USA, widely practised tracking and
grouping is opposed on philosophical grounds by the John Dewey Society
and by school districts in southern states where social justice is fully integrated into the educational agenda.

**PBE Exhibit E: Elementary school ability grouping – an
examination of practices in a suburban northern Virginia school
district**

Student effects

H1 Heterogeneously grouped students will achieve higher attainment
mathematics scores on the Iowa Test of Basic Skills.

H2 Heterogeneously grouped students will achieve higher attainment
verbal English scores on the Iowa Test of Basic Skills.

H3 Self-esteem scores will be higher among low ability students under
heterogeneous grouping.

Teacher effects

H4 Lesson planning will be less difficult for teachers under homogeneous grouping.

H5 Lesson presentation will be less difficult for teachers under homogeneous grouping.

H6 Maintaining classroom discipline will be more difficult for teachers
of low ability groups under homogeneous grouping.

H7 Overall classroom management will be less difficult under homogeneous grouping.

H8 Professional morale will be lower for teachers of low ability groups
under homogeneous grouping.

The candidate undertaking this work, well aware of the sensitivities
surrounding the issue, considered it wise to phrase her purposes as
hypotheses. While not all of these hypotheses can be considered strictly
testable in the statistical sense, they do exercise some degree of measurement
control on the range of variables confounding accounts of grouping in

schools in the northern Virginia school district. This highly visible school district, adjacent to Washington DC and containing the residences of many of the nation's policy makers, had undergone a significant restructuring in the early 1990s reflecting wider social change in the USA. The school board adopted a heterogeneous cluster grouping procedure in the early childhood Grades 1 and 2 and the upper elementary Grades 3–5. Heterogeneous cluster grouping is a form of organization in which pupils of above average, average and below average ability are assigned proportionally to each class. This change, controversial in social and educational policy terms, reflected a longitudinal shift in Virginia from 1950s–1960s practices which had included classes segregated along racial lines and homogeneous group arrangements where pupils were allocated to classes structured to reflect group performance on standardized attainment test scales and teacher recommendations.

The technocratic character of this enquiry, analysing standardized attainment test scores, making use of teacher interviews, and so on, steered it towards evidence-based conclusions that could be, and were, made available to the northern Virginia school district. In such a way, partisanship was avoided and a genuine contribution to this most intractable of educational issues was made.

Further Observations on the Policy Context of Educational Research

Having connected the practical worlds of trainers and educators to the active process of research, we are now able to make some rather more formal observations about the character of educational policy. The five research exhibits in the previous section show that research occurs in a context. It does not take place in a vacuum. The discerning practitioner-researcher examines the policy implications of his work by reference to occupational demands, to personal goals and motives, academic and professional interests and the wider socio-economic environment within which he lives and works. Recent writings (Whiston, 1992; Rice, 1992) have given an added dimension to this discernment. The long-standing tension between the production of scholarly knowledge for its own sake in universities and what is considered necessary for the solution of practical problems has clarified via five increasingly accepted tendencies, as follows:

- That quality teaching and learning is underpinned by and dependent upon a sound base of research and scholarship.
- That national and international industrial and political alignments and the globalization of competition increases the need for both the practical relevance of local research and the strategic relevance of academic research per se.

- That wealth creation is perceived as causally dependent upon enhanced learning of a continuous, dynamic and lifelong kind.
- That accountability is a multidimensional concept taking in institutional responsiveness to client (e.g. student) needs, value for money in respect of public services 'purchased' especially through the raising of taxes, and is a process increasingly mediated through the ballot box.
- That historical and cultural antecedents which shaped educational and social priorities are now subject to re-examination and reformulation as new technology and the 'knowledge explosion' give large numbers of ordinary people the means to redefine their life chances.

We appear to be living in something of a distinct epoch in respect of educational policies, and this seems to be true throughout the Western world. Education at all levels seems heavily directed towards the driving up of standards, especially in literacy and numeracy, key skills and instrumental competencies, mass participation in higher education, value for educational services provided, and so on. Economic motives appear to be the root stimulus of these epochal trends. The point is made by one perceptive author as follows – commenting on the strategic policy thrust of research across the HE sector in the UK and associated agencies he says:

> The overall policy thrust embracing the above (greater reliance on directive programmes, research council mergers, central control of research funding, and so on), and much else, can be categorized in relation to a perceived governmental need to limit public spending; concentrate and select overall research priorities; increase control of and accountability of the HE sector; increase the strategic relevance of academic research; introduce a much greater directive mode between the Research Councils and HE (mainly the universities); increase or improve academic–industrial collaboration.
>
> (Whiston, 1992, p. 20)

We introduced this book by arguing that arrangements for practitioner-research in award-bearing courses in institutions of higher education could be understood as a visible response to cultural shifts in educational provision related to social change, to the emergence of a loose but discernible 'teacher as researcher' movement, and to changes in the orientation and method of social science leading to paradigm fragmentation. It is a moot point as to whether 'policy' follows these tendencies and their abstract counterparts which we have just discussed. It may be that 'policy', particularly in its most codified form such as an Act of Parliament, functions retrospectively – to 'gather in', 'collect up' and 'colonize' tendencies which are occurring and would occur in any case. Educational policies certainly attempt to prefigure some kind of desired future. They are also, perhaps inevitably, responsive and reactive to events which may have their roots in industrial change, in political realignments – as in the emergence of the European Union – or in demographic movements, etc. With regard to the latter, for example, the Central Statistical Office (CSO) reports in *Social Trends 25* that:

- in 1993 only 7 per cent of households in Great Britain had five or more members compared with 16 per cent in 1961;
- if the divorce rates of 1988/9 were to continue some 24 per cent of children would experience divorce in their family by age 16;
- since 1987 the proportion of single mothers has increased rapidly so that in 1992 almost 1 in 5 mothers with dependent children was a lone mother;
- the percentage of live births outside marriage increased from 8 per cent in 1971 to 32 per cent in 1993;
- there were 102,000 pupils with statements of special needs in public sector schools in 1992/3.

This kind of socio-demographic change within a very short period of historical time has massive implications for educational policy. Indeed, it has massive implications for the ways in which individual teachers can present themselves in a classroom. If it is known that perhaps half of a class of pupils have 'absent fathers', then a young male teacher especially is presented with a demanding task of interpreting his function of that as a role model.

These kinds of social changes enter the political process and the public imagination in a variety of ways. They are often reported on in populist language in tabloid newspapers. They are commented on editorially in the serious press. An abundance of government reports may act as precursors to local planning initiatives or to Parliamentary action. Academics, TV pundits and novelists alike may variously proselytize on such matters as either a curtain raiser for a kind of social apocalypse or as some kind of reconfiguration of society for the twenty-first century. It is thus apposite to turn to a description and analysis of some policy indicators in the UK that have particular resonance for research activity.

Indicators of UK Education Policy

In order to build associations between PBE work undertaken by the single researcher and wider policy-driven project work at an institutional level, it is necessary to know explicitly what current educational policies are and from whence they spring. In the case of the maintained schools sector (England and Wales) policy initiatives are formally expressed through Acts of Parliament. The following is a list of recent criterial pieces of legislation in England and Wales, post-1980, and their special concerns:

- Education Act 1981 – provision for special educational needs.
- Education Reform Act 1988 – National Curriculum, City Technology Colleges, etc.
- Children Act 1989 – redefinition of welfare provisions for children, particularly those under the control of Social Services.
- Education (Schools) Act 1992 – creation of the Office for Standards in Education.
- Education Act 1993 – creation of the School Curriculum and Assessment Authority and arrangements for failing schools and pupil exclusions.
- School Standards and Framework Act 1999 – flagship educational legislation by the Labour government establishing academic attainment requirements for public sector schools, abolishing the previous government's category of Grant-Maintained Schools and redefining the powers of local education authorities.

'Policy' may also be understood as manifesting at various levels. At the level of the 'State', the highest level of institutionalization, policies are expressed through Acts of Parliament, statutes and ministerial instructions. At the level of collective organization – or as we theorized it in Chapter 2, the 'social structural system', to include LEAs, city councils, school boards, metropolitan boroughs, boards of governors, and so on – policies are expressed through by-laws, mission statements, strategic plans, etc. that attempt to regionally construe the national imperative. At the level of the social system – say, an individual school or college – policies are expressed through prospectuses that usually reflect local considerations of client needs.

In a multi-party pluralist democracy it is to be recognized that there are many stakeholders in education policy. The publication in November 1997 of the Qualifications and Curriculum Authority (QCA – the Labour government inspired successor to the School Curriculum and Assessment Authority, or SCAA) draft guidelines on the 'promotion of pupils' spiritual, moral, social and cultural development' clearly understands this proposition. The fact that the QCA documents claim legitimacy by citing a 'MORI omnibus poll of 1544 adults, and surveys of 3200 schools and 700 organizations, with a membership representative of the whole population', is testament enough to the anxieties, sensitivities and controversy that underlies policy making in the subject area of Personal and Social Education (PSE).

Similarly, relatively independent agencies and statutory bodies may attempt to direct a national requirement, the prevailing mood of the general public, or socio-economic policy by articulating a vision of a future society based upon a research agenda. The highly influential research councils are fully implicated in this process through the generation of projects and ideas and the use of public moneys to support them. The Thematic Priorities Document (Update 1997) of the Economic and Social Research Council explains, for example, how 65 per cent of the ESRC training and research budget, taking in both centre and programme activity, is directed by the nine imperative themes it has established. These are listed as follows:

1 Economic performance and development
2 Environment and sustainability
3 Globalization, regions and emerging markets
4 Governance, regulation and accountability
5 Technology and people
6 Innovation
7 Knowledge, communication and learning
8 Lifespan, lifestyles and health
9 Social inclusion and exclusion

It is also worth pointing out here that the ESRC, the research council that most commonly accommodates educational and social research, also has a separate Research Grants Scheme to which individual researchers may bid. ESRC states:

> An important element of the thematic strategy is to maintain at the same time (e.g. in coexistence with large research programmes and centre project activity such as The Learning Society project) an independent and wholly responsive research grants scheme which assesses and funds purely on scientific merit.
>
> (ESRC Thematic Priorities Update, 1997, p. 2)

As we have identified the national research councils as central to any consideration of policy, it is helpful for reference purposes to name the councils at this point. They are:

Biotechnology and Biological Sciences Research Council (BBSRC)
Economic and Social Research Council (ESRC)
Engineering and Physical Science Research Council (EPSRC)
Medical Research Council (MRC)
Natural Environment Research Council (NERC)
Particle Physics and Astronomy Research Council (PPARC)

They are likely to be joined shortly by a new research council for the arts and humanities, which will take over some of the responsibilities in this area that have previously been within the broad sphere of interest of the British Academy. Paralleling the work of the research councils and often challenging official definitions of policy, are charitable trusts and voluntary agencies supporting educational development and research, often in social policy contexts. Many of the voluntary agencies grew out of industry in the nineteenth century and have come to be identified with philanthropic and social justice philosophies. Prominent among these are:

- The Rowntree Trust, based in York, which has a particular interest in housing, welfare and social service.
- The Nuffield Foundation, which has long supported research and development into science education. More recently, it has extended its work into social administration and ageing.
- The Cadbury Trust, which has an extensive portfolio of interests in equal opportunities, civil rights and penal affairs.
- The Calouste Gulbenkian Foundation, which supports research into the social purposes of education, youth alienation and the aesthetic and performing arts.

The Harris Report and related commentaries

When practitioner-researchers undertake research leading to the production of PBE reports and dissertations admissible for credit in award-bearing courses, the written reports fulfil two primary functions. First, they are written to make what may be a unique claim to knowledge. This is an 'educational goal' in its own right, personal, intrinsically satisfying and educational in the fullest sense of the word. Second, they are written to produce a report that will skip over the hurdles of academic rules and conventions in order to acquire institutional endorsement leading to the award of the degree. This second function, largely within the 'gift' of the host institution, has come under intense scrutiny in the postgraduate area in recent years.

In January 1995, the Higher Education Funding Council for England (HEFCE) established a committee to review postgraduate education. The review was impelled by the need to modernize and rationalize postgraduate education and to reconstruct a better relation between research work at the PG level and the more general portfolio of research business that contributes to the lifeblood of many universities. In short, a concerted effort was made to refashion policies for the provision of postgraduate education. The review, sponsored by the Committee of Vice Chancellors (CVCP) and Standing Conference of Principals (SCOP), has led to a series of proposals which may be thought of as prefiguring policy indicators for postgraduate education, and which act to construe the 'gift' of universities in respect of such things as PBE-driven award-bearing courses.

However, the Harris Committee (it takes its title from the name of its chairperson, Professor Martin Harris of the University of Manchester, although the report is formally titled *Review of Postgraduate Education*) was mindful of the nationwide proliferation of postgraduate programmes and associated qualifications. Growth was viewed as related to: the expansion in the range of subjects on offer and the spread of these beyond traditional subject boundaries; more variation in teaching arrangements and the inclusion in these of elements of professional and vocational practices; the impact on course delivery of sophisticated information technology; greater flexibility for on-the-job training in the workplace; more focused involvement in higher education of professional bodies; and changes to both the concept of the 'working week' and the 'traditional academic year'.

The Quality Assurance Agency for Higher Education (QAA) was requested to trial some of these proposals. Consequently, under the aegis of a Steering Committee, a project was established in early 1997 to consider options for a 'typology' of postgraduate qualifications. The word 'typology', coined by QAA, is important for it reflects a core recommendation of the Harris Committee: the establishment of a national qualifications framework. It may be noted at this juncture that the Harris Committee proposals were paralleled by those emerging from the National Committee of Enquiry into Higher Education: Report of the Scottish Committee (*The Garrick Report*) The project was undertaken in nine colleges and universities and the conceptual and development work was taken further forward by QAA Qualifications Frameworks Development Groups in England, Wales, Northern Ireland and Scotland.

In November 1998, the QAA published a 'Consultation Paper on Qualifications Frameworks: Postgraduate Qualifications'. The purpose of the paper is to set out the 'principles for a postgraduate typology' and to generate wide-ranging responses to these. Indeed, the consultation paper comes complete with an attached and structured evaluation document that enables individuals, groups, agencies and educational institutions to indicate the extent of their agreement with the principles and/or to suggest modifications to them. It is the considered position of QAA that: 'The recommendations of, and responses to, the Harris Review, NCIHE reports and the subsequent QAA papers on new arrangements for the assurance of quality and standards within UK higher education have established widespread support for the development of national qualifications frameworks structured in terms of a series of levels [indicating progressively greater intellectual challenge ...] and credit (as a means of identifying the volume of learning achieved at each of the levels)' (QAA, November 1998, p. 3).

The emerging national framework for postgraduate education, therefore, is one in which the practitioner-researcher may well find that his or her enquiries are policy-led from the outset. The Harris Committee called for a breaking of the mould of traditional concepts of postgraduate education. There was an urgent call for more explicit statements of expectations in respect of candidates enrolling for research-oriented degrees. These expectations should include not only the academic research programme, but also a code of practice for students regarding their recruitment, reception and supervision. It was considered desirable to suggest to HEFCE that postgraduate students should only attract research grants in subject areas in higher education institutions which have a pervasive research culture and can provide excellence in research education. The main performance indicator for this would be a Grade 3 or above rating allocated to departments that have participated in the Research Assessment Exercise (RAE).

It was also proposed that the research councils and the British Academy should take a role in shaping research activity by reference to the identification of discrete areas of demand. The inference from this is that the 'free-standing' project beloved by the practitioner-researcher ought to configure more comfortably with HEI subject expertise and research council definitions of supply and demand. More specifically, postgraduate education ought to be capable of classification by 'aim of the course'. The classification would be described by categories such as: 'research and scholarship'; 'preparation for research and deepening subject knowledge'; 'professional and practice related' content. Therefore, practitioner-researchers undertaking award-bearing courses would in reality be 'allocated' to this latter category and all that it implies for technical specialization and career development. The QAA consultation paper expresses principles suggestive of an operational framework for these and other ideas.

Principle 1 defines what postgraduate qualifications actually are. Principles II to VI are about 'levels' – that is, an 'indicator of the relative demand, complexity, depth of study and learner autonomy involved in a programme' (QAA, 1998, p. 4). Levels are not necessarily indicative of years of full-time study. Rather they should be indicative of the intellectual and professional demands of a postgraduate programme and the demonstrated achievements associated with the named qualification. Thus:

> A higher postgraduate level, for example, could be described in terms of the completion of a substantial piece of research or advanced professional project in such a way as to make a significant and original contribution to a field of inquiry or practice. A lower postgraduate level might denote familiarity with complex and specialized areas of knowledge and skills, engagement with research issues or advanced technical or professional activity, the taking of responsibility for related decision-making, and the capacity to work independently.
>
> (QAA, 1998, p. 4)

Principles VII to X deal with 'credit', or the 'measure of learning outcomes as quantified by the notional number of study hours required for achieving the outcomes' (ibid., p. 4). Finally, Principles XI to XVIII deal with the nomenclature of postgraduate qualifications. These principles are configured diagrammatically in three alternative operational models. The models contain data on: proposed nomenclature; minimum volume of credits; typical duration of the course; the intellectual and pedagogical character of the course; a list of the named qualifications the course would furnish.

The Harris Report, like the Green Paper 'Teachers Meeting the Challenge of Change' (DfEE, 1998), is part of the 'family' of scripts changing and redefining the culture of the education industry in stated terms of 'ambition', 'achievement', and 'accountability'. In short, the view that public moneys should continue to be used to support part of postgraduate provision, symbolizing a vital national investment, remains a broad aspirational policy. This ought then, so the argument continues, resonate through a national register, or 'typology', of courses conceived to exist in understandable form, a pattern both 'customer-friendly' and institutionally coherent, and which would contribute markedly to the emergence of the 'world-class' education service that the Green Paper (DfEE, 1998) makes the centrepiece of its 'vision' and goal for the UK in the early part of the twenty-first century.

The QAA/ HEFCE 'steer' in these directions is now in full swing. The policy message from the perspective of this 'steer' to the practitioner-researcher is clear: your work must be contemporarily relevant; it must fit into and be expressive of the emerging framework of national qualifications; it must be cost effective within the financial framework of your host institution; it must be efficiently conducted; and it must be capable of recognition and take-up by specialized market sectors, educational consumers and wider society.

The Post-16 Sector and Vocational and Educational Training

Education and training for 16–19 year olds and beyond has become something of a public football in recent years. National debates, sometimes strident and contradictory, have been accompanied by a changing and complex pattern of institutional provision in the school, college and industrial sectors. These debates have at their core: concerns over the future and utility value of General Certificate of Education Advanced Level subjects (popularly referred to in the UK as 'A levels'); the desirability of a broader curriculum in schools that extends from the General Certificate of Secondary Education (GCSE) at 16 to embrace sixth-form colleges, technical colleges, training providers associated with industry; and the establishment of a framework of national qualifications jointly recognized and endorsed by industry and long-established award bodies such as the Royal Society of Arts (RSA), the Business and Technical Education Council (BTEC) and the City and Guilds Institute. The variety and diverging interests of stakeholders in the post-16 sector has contributed to a proliferation of official reports, commentary and analysis. Prominent among these has been:

Dearing, R. (1996) *Review of Qualifications for 16–19 Year Olds*, SCAA, London. (Not to be confused with the Dearing Report on higher education discussed in the final substantive part of this chapter.)

Royal Society (1991) *Beyond GCSE*, Royal Society, London.

Department for Education and Employment (1997) *Qualifying for Success*, DfEE, London.

Organization for Economic Cooperation and Development (1994) *Vocational Education and Training: Towards Coherent Policy and Practice*, OECD, Paris and US Department of Education, Washington DC.

Beaumont, S. (1996) *Review of 100 NVQs/SVQs: A Report on Findings*, National Council for Vocational Qualifications/SCOTVEC, Broadwater Press.

What do these reports signify? Primarily, the reports signify the current of socio-economic change running deep and fast in all Western industrialized societies. In the case of the UK especially, they reflect a growing realization that a narrow focus on a presumed 'Gold Standard' of 'A levels' for only a relative small number of young people in the relevant age cohort is inadequate to meet educational and training demands of the twenty-first century. The reports also reflect a desire to fill gaps left by the decline in traditional craft apprenticeships, and to offer training opportunities to a large population of young people for whom conventional provisions in higher education are deemed unsuitable. In sum, the reports broadly indicate that a historically neglected and under-researched sector of the educational system in the UK is increasingly recognized as vital in response to society's demand for a technologically literate and instrumentally skilled workforce to compete in the labour markets of the twenty-first century.

A defining moment occurred in the UK with the proclamation of the 1993 Further and Higher Education Act. Flowing from this legislation, the corporate status of training institutes, particularly the established 'further education colleges' and how they are funded, was reformulated; new imperatives for the content of technical education curricula were signposted, and innovations in teaching and learning strategies were promoted, including the modularization of A level syllabuses. Parallel to these primarily institutional developments was the stimulation of demand in the post-16 sector by the establishment of target figures for the achievement of National Vocational Qualifications (NVQs). The visibility of NVQs, in turn, contributed to a more general profile-raising of education and training.

Colleges of further education, tertiary colleges, sixth form colleges, adult education institutes, major industrial companies, the armed services and other training organizations are all involved in delivering education and training to an estimated (Further Education Development Agency, 1996) 85 per cent of the post-16 sector, especially the 16–19 age group. Indeed, all these organizations are in responsive mode in respect of the wider pattern of socio-economic and political change. The increasingly technocratic character of the economy suggests there will be a continuing high demand for professionally qualified lecturers, trainers and instructors in a broad range of occupations. Such people will now need to be doubly adept at facilitating and expanding the educated attributes of their trainees. The twin goals of improved employability based on technical competence and improved social adjustment based on attitude development are emerging as norms and somewhat redefining the role of the technical instructor and post-16 tutor. This role, and the supply–demand equation surrounding it, will be regulated by the specific training requirements of industry, by the national endorsement of progress through incentive schemes such as NVQ for trainees and Investors in People for companies, by the articulation of standard productivity indicators as in British Standard B5750, and through a generalized process of accountability expressed in Quality Assurance (QA), Total Quality Management (TQM) and similar performance- and output-describing concepts written into institutional mission statements.

Given the above scenario it is important to identify the measurable shifts that have occurred in post-16 education since 1990. These shifts are characterized by 'uneasy' innovation, as in the development of General National Vocational Qualifications (GNVQs) and their gradual appropriation under the 'umbrella' of the Qualifications and Curriculum Authority (QCA). Other shifts are part of a discernible long-term trend such as the decline in participation in science education. What are some of these shifts? First, there has been a significant increase in provision of, and participation in, the post-16 sector. Under the Thatcher and Major Conservative governments, youth policy could be conceived of as having three strands. Young people aged 16-plus were to be in full-time work, in further education or enrolled on an approved training scheme. This somewhat non-codified policy was partly the product of free-market ideology, but was more indicative of the collapse of the youth labour market in the 1980s. The extension of this policy by the Labour government elected in May 1997 has witnessed a considerable rise in the proportion of young people entering further education after school. More students are progressing towards advanced levels of education including A levels and GNVQs. Fewer students are dropping out, but the student population in further and higher education is diversifying and displaying a wide range of needs and capabilities.

Second, the number of eligible students opting for specialist programmes in A-level mathematics and science has shown a marked decline over a 15–20 year period. This has massive implications for recruitment to professions based on these disciplines, such as civil engineering and industrial chemistry. At the same time, the percentage of students mixing their subject choice across the arts/science boundary has expanded.

Third, the national downward trend in participation in mathematics and science at advanced level is paralleled by the gradual introduction of General National Vocational Qualifications in science at both intermediate and advanced levels. These qualifications are designed to respond to the national downturn. They are intended to provide a broad scientific foundation for students intending to take up employment or advanced science courses in HE. The aforementioned 'key skills' are central to thinking and provision in science GNVQs. However, debates about the adequacy of mathematical knowledge among GNVQ students continues. Similarly, the question as to whether GNVQ is a poor substitute for a science A level will not go away.

Fourth, the diversification and modularization of A-level syllabuses has acted as a popularizer of A-level work. Modular schemes in particular seem to be proving an attractive alternative to traditional 2-year A-level courses with the rigorous examination element at the end of the course.

Fifth, the emergence of 'new' universities from the old polytechnic sector in 1992 is related to the marked increase in student numbers in HE. At the end of the 1990s, the percentage of young people entering higher education is about 30 per cent of the age cohort, a post-war high and the most dramatic indicator of shift towards a mass higher education system. There has also been marked growth in the number of part-time mature students, women 'returners' (i.e. mature women, often married with children, training to re-enter the workforce), and overseas students. In subject terms, the growth is uneven. Social sciences, the humanities, business and IT studies are popular. However, many science and engineering departments in universities find it extremely difficult to recruit students. A frequently heard comment is that contemporary students simply do not have the foundation mathematics necessary to prosper in science-based courses. The year 1997 was a particularly difficult one with some universities closing and/or merging science, mathematics and engineering departments.

Long-term policy encapsulating the above trends is perhaps best expressed in the recommendations of the Dearing *Review of Qualifications for 16–19 Year Olds* (1996). This report, like its predecessor directed at the school-based National Curriculum (Dearing, 1993) and its successor (Dearing, 1997), may be interpreted as the heartbeat of policy formation in the UK in the 1990s. In short, its recommendations for post-16 are:

- A nationally recognized and understood framework of qualifications based on three pathways – A levels, GNVQs and NVQs.
- An AS-level qualification to be reformulated as one-half of an A level and to be normally completed within one year.
- Transferable skills to be emphasized and formalized into all courses leading to formal qualifications and to be defined in terms of 'communication', the 'application of number', and the 'use of information technology'. More is said about core, transferable skills in the next section.
- The development of a national certificate, awarded on the basis of completion of two A levels or equivalent, in any subject, with the addition of key skills.

- The establishment of a National Diploma to be awarded for achievement in 'four domains of study' – science, technology, engineering and mathematics; modern languages; arts and humanities; society, community and their patterns of working. The requirement would include at least two full A levels or equivalents, and at least one AS level or equivalent completed in each of the four domains to provide 'breadth', plus the key skills.

To complete the sketch of educational policy indicators for the UK, we now turn to the report that is most likely to influence the character and provision of HE in the early years of the twenty-first century.

The Dearing Report, Higher Education and Beyond

The Dearing Report (1997), or more formally *Higher Education in the Learning Society*, is the most comprehensive enquiry into higher education in the UK since the Robbins Committee of 30 years or more earlier. Inevitably overshadowing other, more circumscribed, enquiries into HE and post-16 provision, the Dearing Report is an extremely fertile data source as well as the baseline against which future policies for HE will be constructed.

Most public interest in the Dearing Report has focused upon the proposals to charge students for at least part of their tuition to meet, as the report puts it, 'the unavoidable additional cost' of a mass higher education system capable of sustaining the nation's economic competitiveness as well as the social and educational aspirations of its people.

However, Dearing has much to suggest by way of a reconfiguration of higher education. Amongst its recommendations related to research and to research students was the early establishment of an Institute for Learning and Teaching in Higher Education. Among the functions of this agency would be the accreditation of programmes of training for higher education tutors and their connection to research and development in learning and teaching practices, and the stimulation of innovation. Clearly, the device of PBE is enabling in this regard. The reciprocity that exists between tutor and student in PBE activity would be institutionally enhanced in this way.

The creation of an arts and humanities research council, a £500 million loan scheme for HE institutions to purchase laboratory and related equipment, and the provision of an extra £110 million to the research councils are among the more debatable research recommendations of Dearing. These proposals, designed to correct strategic imbalances in resource provision for research, were linked with the view that research ought to be more coherently organized. Indeed, it was thought desirable for there to be an 'umbrella' scheme for all national initiatives designed to encourage applied research. The purpose, content and orientation therefore of PBE work would, even by a long process of attenuation, have to fit in some tangible way with these initiatives. This would occur most obviously in discipline areas that linked university work with industry. It is often presumed, but less often stated, that 'industry' should be taken to mean high-value manufacturing industry with an export base. The more general point, however, that people working in service industries, public sector occupations and the training field must increasingly respond to an evidence-led, output-focused environment is inferred if not actually spelt out. The Industrial Partnership Development Fund (IPDF), as the umbrella scheme might come to be called, would be run jointly by the Department of Trade and Industry, the Welsh Office and the Scottish Office. Its remit would echo the symbolism expressed in the title of the recently merged government department, the Department for Education and Employment (DfEE). If the IPDF were to assume responsibility for the practical financial generation of applied research, then its work ought to be guided in the policy domain by a new and 'high level body' to advise the government of the day on the direction of national policies for the public funding of research in higher education.

It is clear that one of the 'national policies' in Dearing's mind is an emphasis on the professionalization of the process of teaching and learning. There is considerable enthusiasm about the skills/enterprise/work experience parts of students' total institutional education. There does not appear to be a specific separation of undergraduate from postgraduate learning experiences in this regard. The identification of four 'key skills' – numeracy, communication, ability to use IT; and learning how to learn – in which all students should be competent prior to graduating from higher education coheres with the concepts and methodological principles of PBE earlier outlined. This seems most true in the sense that PBE is an integrated learning experience, rather than the detached application of standardized empirical models by acknowledged experts in research design. The 'key skills' question in Dearing, though, has rapidly entered institutional discourse in respect of course provision and is one which has important implications for the technocratic and methodological components of research training in award-bearing courses.

It is in the realms of 'vision' and 'ideas' that Dearing attempts to prefigure national policy. In speaking of a new 'compact' with the people of Britain, 'policy' is considered to be a 20-year orientation towards a 'learning society':

> Our title, 'Higher Education in the Learning Society' reflects the vision that informs this report. Over the next 20 years, the United Kingdom must create a society committed to learning throughout life. That commitment will be required by individuals, the state, employers and providers of education and training. Education is life enriching and desirable in its own right. It is fundamental to the achievement of an improved quality of life in the UK.
>
> (Dearing Report: Executive Summary, 1997)

Dearing envisages a national policy which aspires to be world class in learning at all levels and in a range of research fields and specializations. In higher education, this ideal should be expressed through the new 'compact' involving institutions and all stakeholders therein. The 'historic barrier' between vocational education and academic liberal education is, out of necessity, breaking down. There is, and must be, an increasingly active integration between higher education, industry and commerce, and the public sector. Central to the compact will be the heightened sense of reciprocity, obligation and mutuality. For Dearing, as probably for the many, the future for higher education in the UK is one in which:

- Participants are encouraged to achieve beyond their personal expectations.
- Institutional safeguards will protect the rigour of university awards ensuring that UK qualifications not only meet student needs but have visibility and standing throughout the world.
- Leading-edge practices in effective learning and teaching are commonplace.
- Research is world class in character and of demonstrable benefit to the nation.
- The regional dimension is reflected in collaboration between HE and FE, probably through single franchise arrangements, which takes account of the socio-economic status profile of people within the region.
- An intellectual culture is sustained through disciplined thinking, the encouragement of curiosity, persistent challenge to existing ideas, and the generation of new ones.
- Higher education is part of the 'conscience' of a democratic society, founded on respect for the rights of individuals and the responsibilities individuals have towards society as a whole.
- Clarity of purpose and accountability for process and function are routine features of organizational appearance and where a dynamic for continuous improvement to performance is the norm.

We said elsewhere in the book that the privatized, possibly self-indulgent, pursuit of a *magnum opus* by a research student relatively disconnected from institutional 'ends' and 'means' is gone. Dearing makes it clear that such pursuits are outdated and irrelevant. Research degrees, award-bearing courses including PBE and its ilk, taught masters and so on, will inevitably be part of a much more visible and focused *culture of research and scholarship* in higher education. The challenge for the individual, therefore, is how to retain *intellectual autonomy and professional integrity* under these conditions. The device of PBE, as we have construed it in this book, is a useful variant of the research enterprise that can be mobilized to meet the challenge.

Appendix 1
A Lexicon of Terms for the Language of Research.

Concepts Organizing ideas that compress complexities and reduce complex meanings to single or dual terms. Such ideas often enter public parlance after long periods of trial and error and/or continuous use. Chains of concepts may form a theoretical scheme from which broad generalizations may be constructed and expressed.

Constructs Single and dual terms that often have a tentative meaning in research enquiries. Constructs are often framed as abstract labels which are not usually found in public parlance. Constructs may develop substantively in meaning as evidence is gathered to support the notions they propose.

Determinism A belief system in science which postulates that events have causes; and proceeds on the presumption that causal links can be uncovered and understood.

Empiricism An essentially technical posture in science . It tends to assume that reliable knowledge originates in experience, and processes of trial and error have to be adopted to reveal the full dimensions of experience. An established convention for testing experience is the formulation of hypotheses and conjectural statements that depend upon evidence for verification. When such statements are verified they are said to be lawlike in character and capable of application to other domains of experience.

Generalization A broad summarizing statement. Generalizations are warranted by the data gathering processes and conceptual specification that has preceded them. Forming generalizations is the process by which the scientist uses observations of the concrete particular to explain the world at large. A set of generalizations may constitute a formal theory used to make predictive statements about the future.

Hypothesis A conjectural statement of the relationship between two or more variables. Hypotheses are usually directional insofar as the degree of influence or magnitude of cause and effect of one variable on another is specified.

Methodology   Techniques that are an abstraction of reality and which are used in an orderly manner to reveal the dimensions of reality. The term 'methodology' may be taken to be inclusive of research design, theoretical frameworks, the selection and analysis of literature relevant to the nominated topic, and justified preferences for particular types of data gathering activities.

Parameter   Essentially a term with restricted statistical meaning. A quantity constant in the case under consideration but varying in other cases. A parameter may be regarded as a main indicator of measurement in research enquiries.

Practitioner-Based Enquiry   Small-scale applied research into the practitioner's occupational context. Persons conducting this form of enquiry are usually motivated to improve, via research, their own teaching, learning and organizational situation.

Research   Systematically conducted enquiries into phenomena requiring explanation and understanding. Research may be used in the validation of theory; to determine the character of relationships between people, objects and conditions; as a fact-finding exercise prior to the adoption of recommendations; or as a means to determine the causal influence of one variable on another.

Theory   A rational set of principles constructed by scientists to explain phenomena. Theories bring order and pattern to facts, concepts and data. Theory acts a vehicle for testability, comparability and generalizability. Theory is also the means by which complexities are explained in the simplest possible terms.

Variable   An object, quantity, or condition that varies in its magnitude and function according to circumstance. It is the relationship between two or more variables that is at the core of the research enterprise.

Appendix 2
Conventional Features of Research Reports

Typing/Word Processing/Paper Size

PBE reports should always be typewritten or word processed leading to good quality print output. Italic script may be used judiciously for citations and the emphasis of single words. Font size should be adopted to foster readability, for example, Times New Roman 10 pt. Poor quality dot matrix print output should not be used in final reports. The report should be type-written/printed on one side of the paper in not less than one-and-a-half line spacing on international size A4 (297 mm × 210 mm) paper of good quality. Three copies should be produced. The 'top copy' should be bound in a moderately permanent form such as a ring binder or stiff cover. This is the submission copy and the cover should state clearly the title of the work and the name and affiliation of the author. The author should always retain a copy of the work, and the third copy should be available for assessment, independent review, or for use by interested third parties.

Margins

Inside or left-hand margins should be at least 3 cm wide. The top, bottom and outside or right-hand margins should be at least 2 cm wide.

Order of contents

Title page   The title page or imprint page of the PBE should show: the title of the work in full; the full name and degrees of the author/candidate; the name of his or her department in which the work was submitted; the host university or institution; the degree/certificate/diploma for which the PBE is submitted; the date of submission.

Signed declaration   Most public institutions require a signed declaration from the author to guarantee authenticity of the work, to protect copyright and Intellectual Property Rights and to indicate that the work is within the 'gift' of the institution. An example is:

> This work is submitted in accordance with the requirements for the degree of MA in Education at the University of Portsmouth. I declare that the work presented is to the best of my knowledge original, except as acknowledged in the script, and that the material has not been submitted, either in whole or in part, at this or any other educational institution.

Signed: .... Date: ....

Acknowledgements   A separate page acknowledging those people who have contributed to the PBE should appear after the declaration of authenticity. The acknowledgement page may also identify sources of extended citations or extracts from books and journals used in the script.

Associated papers and publications   Any published work that has emerged from the research should be listed in full on a separate page following the acknowledgements.

Abstract   A one page abstract (approximately 250 words) summarizing the purpose, methods and findings of the PBE should be provided. The abstract is an important statement and is usually located after the title page. It should be written in reported speech. As the abstract is the first part of the PBE to be read, particular attention should be paid to sentence structure, simplicity of vocabulary and brevity.

Table of Contents   A full table of contents should be provided. Care should be given to the wording of chapter headings and section subtitles in the table of contents. Page numbers for the first page of each chapter, as well as the chapter title, should be provided. Pagination as used in the script may, at author discretion, feature in the table of contents. That is, pages numbered onwards from the first substantive page of script, either in the top right-hand corner or in the centre of the bottom margin, may be identified as appropriate in the table of contents. Arabic numerals are usually used to number pages. Roman numerals may be reserved for appendices or for numbering subsections within the script.

List of Figures, Diagrams and Tables   Following the table of contents, a list of any figures, diagrams and tables should be presented. These should be numbered sequentially from 'Figure 1' or 'Table 1' onwards and the page numbers identifying where illustrations are located should be provided.

Main text   The main text or body of the script follows the list of diagrams and figures. No precise format for the main text is prescribed. The structure of this will reflect the purposes, subject orientation, theoretical perspectives and methodology as appropriate to the nominated topic. However, as a rule of thumb, main text will normally attend to: purposes and rationale; research questions; literature reviewed to inform the topic; explanations and justifications of methodology adopted, including details of the sample frame adopted or survey populations accessed; presentation of data and substantive findings; conclusions.

List of References Following the last page of main text a full List of References of all published work used to support the PBE should be provided. The format for the reference list should be the one in conventional use by the host institution. At the University of Portsmouth this is the 'Harvard System'. Whatever format is used, it must be used consistently and particular care and attention should be given to the construction of an adequate List of References for PBE reports.

Appendices Any material such as interview transcripts, questionnaires, extracts from documents, etc., considered important but ancillary to the main text should be placed in appendices which form the last part of the PBE report. Such appendices may be identified by letters or roman numerals.

Footnotes and endnotes In recent years the use of Latin nomenclature in footnoting practice in scholarly writing has declined. It is not recommended that either Latin nomenclature or footnotes be used in PBEs. If amplification or commentary additional to the main text is required, this should be placed in separately numbered endnotes at the end of the PBE report. Given the brevity required for PBE reports, the practice of endnoting should be carefully controlled. It is appropriate, however, to cross-reference to appendices or other subsections in the main text, should the need arise.

Figures, diagrams and tables As the typescript is on one side of the page, full-page illustrations should ideally appear on the right hand page at the first opportunity after references to them in text. Titles should appear in bold print above the illustration, which should not generally take up more than one full A4 page. All figures and tables should carry the legend 'Figure 1' or 'Table 3' prior to the title of the table or figure. Tables and figures should be numbered sequentially in arabic numerals and fully titled in the table of contents at the front of the PBE report. Smaller diagrams should be incorporated into main text. All diagrams and graphics should be reproduced by an electrostatic process which is known not to fade. Photographs may be used and should be permanently affixed to pages with strong adhesives.

Abbreviations and lexicons of terms As most educational research uses a complex technical vocabulary, it is appropriate to provide a glossary or lexicon of terms immediately after the List of References. Alternatively, these may follow normal book order and appear as a preliminary to the main text. Any abbreviation or acronym used in main text should be formally defined. Complex and abstract terms may be also formally defined, succinctly explained, or given their dictionary definitions.

Bibliographic citation

It is conventional in scholarly work to cite all sources from which information has been derived. Sources of quotations and authority for statements of fact, opinion and assertion must be clearly, concisely and accurately cited.

Style of citations   Most PBEs adhere to the conventions of the 'Harvard System' referred to in the Order of Contents. However, certain PBE topics may be required to be written within the citation conventions of a particular discipline, such as psychology. Bibliographical style should be established early in preparation for the PBE report, otherwise a great deal of time-consuming work is required when writing the final manuscript.

Content of citations   For books the minimum citation includes author, title, edition (if other than the first), publisher, place of publication and date of publication. For periodical or journal articles the citation should list the author(s), title of the article, name of the periodical or journal, volume number, part of volume number, date of publication and relevant page numbers. For electronic sources the citation should include where possible author, title, subfile and World Wide Web (WWW) address where it is available.

Given the variation that occurs in citation practice, writers of PBEs should become familiar with the specifications for writing in their subject areas. The detailed elaboration of the Harvard System is to be found in:

> Turabian, K.L. (1973) *A Manual for the Writers of Term Papers, Theses and Dissertations*, Chicago: University of Chicago Press, 4th edn.

Compiling a list of references or bibliography

A beginning point for compiling a list of references is the writer/researcher's own specialist knowledge of a subject. This knowledge will be added to as the enquiry proceeds and as specialist literature is accessed to inform, develop and critique the substantive matters of the enquiry. Earlier, we incorporated ideas on this process with the account of database usage.

Normally, a comprehensive list of references will have been compiled and be readily available for reference during the writing-up of the PBE, either from a card-index system or from floppy disk files as part of a word-processing approach. Usually, a list of references will reflect a writer's progression from the general to the particular in respect of the objects of the enquiry. Articles in encyclopaedias can often fill in general background information and provide recommended additional works for further, more detailed enquiry. The *Encyclopedia Britannica* may be a useful tool to commence with in this respect. Similarly, the multi-volume *Encyclopedia of the Social Sciences* carries detailed entries on classic topics in education and behavioural science.

A comprehensive and systematic list of recent books can be compiled by consulting the British National Bibliography, a cumulative listing based on book holdings in the British Library. The subject and topic arrangement is via the internationally used Dewey Decimal Classification System. British Books in Print is mainly an author/title list, but some books are indexed under the keywords of a subtitle. It is axiomatic that keyword searching for information is a requirement for the production of a List of References for a PBE report (see Chapter 2). Indexes, usually interrogated via keywords, include:

British Education Index
British Humanities Index
Child Development Abstracts and Bibliography
Psychological Abstracts/Psychlit
PAIS – Public Affairs Information Service
Social Sciences Citation Index
Education Resources Information Centre (ERIC)
Current Index to Journals in Education

Normally, an educational researcher will interrogate a database that is current. It is then usual to work backwards or retrospectively for up to five years through published indexes. Some historical topics may require searches to go further back in time. Similarly, books and journal articles given prominence in a list of references are those usually most recent, and which incorporate earlier research and commentary on the topic.

Procite

Procite is specialized software for the organization and management of personal collections of reference materials. Many academic libraries now have Procite or similar facilities. It offers built in information retrieval and handling functions. Similarly, it incorporates printing arrangements that copy bibliographic presentation standards such as those required by professional societies such as the British Psychological Society (BPS). Practitioner researchers are recommended to seek information from their academic libraries on the availability of bibliographic management software. Electronic Current Awareness Services (ECAS) offered by British universities, when used in conjunction with Procite and similar packages, can greatly streamline and quicken the production of reference lists for PBE.

Appendix 3

Information Retrieval Exercise: British Education Index (BEI)

Supplemented by *The Periodicals Catalogue*, Summer 1996.

NOTE: The exercise is designed on the principle that the print version of the BEI is used first and then the exercise is repeated using the networked CD-ROM version. However, competent students may reverse this process.

BY AUTHOR: Refer to 1993 edition of the BEI.

Part A
1   How many articles are listed for the author 'Lawrence, Brenda'?
2   What is the title of this author's entry in the *British Journal of Educational Psychology*?
3   What is the volume number of this journal?
4   What is the edition number of the journal?
5   How many pages long is the article?
6   What is the name of the co-author?
7   What are two (2) keywords listed for this article?
8   Does the Frewen Library hold this journal?
9   If so, for what period (years)?
10 If the Frewen Library holds the journal, where are copies located?

Part B
1   What is the title of the article listed for the author 'Murray, Louis'?
2   What is the title of the journal in which this article appears?
3   What is the volume number?
4   What is the edition number?
5   How many pages long is the article?
6   What are two (2) keywords listed for the article?
7   Does the Frewen Library hold this journal?
8   If so, for what period (years)?
9   If the Frewen Library holds the journal, where are copies located?
10 List another journal title from *The Periodicals Catalogue* covering subject matter similar to this journal?

Appendix 4
Information Retrieval Exercise: ERIC

ERIC: Educational Resources Information Centre. This is a very extensive and analytically powerful database covering documents in a subfile called 'Resources in Education' (RIE) and journals in a subfile called 'Current Index to Journals in Education' (CIJE).

1   Consult the printed thesaurus of ERIC descriptors located at 370.14 THE. Identify three (3) descriptors from the thesaurus that define your specialist subject field.

   (a) .... (b) .... (c) ....

2   From your previous retrieval exercise list any three of the six authors chosen as part of article and journal selection for your specialist field. List surname first, followed by forename.

   (a) .... (b) .... (c) ....

3   Study the attached ERIC document résumés. Note the ways(s) in which the résumés are constructed. For the two numbered documents choose three descriptors.

   ERIC Number ED394683
   (a) .... (b) .... (c) ....

   ERIC Number ED392143
   (a) .... (b) .... (c) ....

4   Check the printed thesaurus to see if your selected descriptors are present.

   P for present; A for absent
   ERIC Number ED394683
   (a) .... (b) .... (c) ....

ERIC Number ED392143

(a) .... (b) .... (c) ....

5 Commence a 'Simple Search' of the ERIC CD-ROM database. Use author name and any of the selected keywords to bring on screen records for ERIC Number ED394683 and ERIC ED392143.

6 For ED394683:

How many 'hits'? .... How many records returned? .... ERIC number? .... Title? .... Author(s)? .... Language? .... How many descriptors? .... Identifiers? .... Publication date? ....

7 For ED392143:

How many 'hits'? .... How many records returned? .... ERIC number? .... Title? .... Author(s)? .... Language? .... How many descriptors? .... Identifiers? .... Publication date? ....

8 For each document write out the first sentence of the abstract.

ED394683 ....
ED392143 ....

9 Commence an independent search using the author keyword 'Neill, A.S.' and the descriptor 'democracy'.

How many 'hits'? .... How many records returned? .... ERIC number(s)? .... Title(s)? .... Author(s)? .... Language? .... How many descriptors? .... Identifiers? .... Publication date? ....

(NOTE: If there is more than one 'hit', limit your inserts to two entries only.)

10 For up to two documents write out the first sentence in the abstract.

ERIC Number? ....
ERIC Number? ....

11 Compare your completed entries with the circulating master sheet.

12 Repeat the independent search procedure using the descriptors and author names compiled for questions 1 and 2. Identify those entries relevant to your research purposes. Either make a note of these entries, print them out, or (preferably) download to diskette as a contribution to your personal database.*

* This activity should preferably inform the literature review aspects of a structured research proposal.

Results of your query

((lawrence Brenda): Keyword and (author): Keyword) and (expulsions): Keyword)

(1 hits, 1 records returned)

-ERIC_NO-
ED394683
-TITLE-
Primary School Children Excluded from School: Numbers, Characteristics, Reasons and Circumstances.
-AUTHOR-
Hayden, Carol; **Lawrence, Brenda**
-LANGUAGE-
English
-DESCRIPTIONS-
Access_to_Education
Behaviour_Problems
Elementary_Education
Expulsion
Foreign_Countries
Suspension
-IDENTIFIERS-
England
Local Education **Authorities** United Kingdom
-ABSTRACT-
Through a national questionnaire, 3 case studies of Local Education **Authorities** (LEAs), and additional case studies of 38 children, this national study examined primary school exclusion. Findings included that: (1) other metropolitan LEAs had about twice the number of exclusions as London and as County Council LEAs; (2) the total number of primary school exclusions, per 1,000 pupils, was highest in London; (3) fixed term exclusions were the most common type utilized by schools, but in metropolitan areas,

about a third of all exclusions were permanent; (4) the majority of excluded primary children were boys; and (5) failure to comply with school rules and verbally and physically aggressive behaviour were cited by schools as the most common reasons for exclusions. During the 1992–93 academic year, there were about 54,423 reported cases of exclusion; about 8,636 of these exclusions were permanent. In the 1993–94 academic year, there were about 1,253 permanent primary school exclusions. (Contains 35 references.) (JW)
-GEOG_SOURCE-
United Kingdom; England
-CLEARINGHOUSE_NO-
PS024104
-PUBLICATION_TYPE-
150; 143
-PUBLICATION_DATE-
1995
-EDRS_PRICE-
EDRS Price – MF01/PC01 Plus Postage.

Results of your query

((murray louis): Keyword and (author): Keyword) and (demography): Keyword)

(1 hits, 1 records returned)

-ERIC_NO-
ED392143
-TITLE-
Homelessness, Schooling and Attainment: A Preliminary Assessment of 'Disruption Indicators' on Children's Performance in the Early Years of Schooling.
-AUTHOR-
Murray, Louis; And Others
-LANGUAGE-
English
-DESCRIPTORS-
Demography
Economically_Disadvantaged
Family_Characteristics
Family_School_Relationship
Foreign_Countries

Homeless_People
Housing_Needs
One_Parent_Family
Primary_Education
Socioeconomic_Influences
Socioeconomic_Status
Transient_Children
-IDENTIFIERS-
England
-ABSTRACT-
This paper, building on information from Portsmouth, Blackpool, and other coastal England towns with transient populations, summarizes data on four theorized indicators of social and economic deprivation that affect families with school-age children. The four indicators measured disruption, housing, family status, and neighbourhood. Methods included analysis of enrollment and demographic data for Year 1 classes (5-year-olds) in 15 Portsmouth area primary schools and a survey of 200 parents of children attending the 15 schools. Coastal towns with unique leisure, tourist, and transitory accommodation functions are characterized by a significant transient population who make uncommon demands on local services, such as education. Following the economic decline of the coastal towns, local **authorities** secured bed and breakfast hotels to provide shelter for homeless populations. The findings indicate that, in general, children who had been disrupted in their housing and/or schooling were doing less well in terms of vocabulary development than those who were not disrupted. However, children living in temporary accommodations were socially well adjusted in the school situation. Nine tables, two charts, a glossary, and list of indicators are included. (Contains 32 references.) (LMI)
-GEOG_SOURCE-
United Kingdom; England
-CLEARINGHOUSE_NO-
EA027372
-PUBLICATION_TYPE-
143
-PUBLICATION_DATE-
1995
-EDRS_PRICE-
EDRS Price – MF01/PC02 Plus Postage

References

Abell, P. (1996) 'Sociological theory and rational choice theory', B.S.Turner (ed.) *Blackwell Companion to Social Theory*, Oxford: Blackwell.

Advisory Board of the Research Councils (ABRC) (1993) *Nature of the PhD*, London: ABRC.

Alwin, D. (1978) *Survey Design and Analysis*, Beverley Hills CA: Sage.

Andrich, D. (1978) 'Scaling attitude items constructed and scored in the Likert tradition', *Educational and Psychological Measurements*, **38**, 3, pp. 665–80.

Argyris, C. and Schon, D. (1974) *Theory in Practice*, London: Jossey-Bass.

Barzun, J. and Graff, H.F. (1977) *The Modern Researcher*, New York: Harcourt, Brace & World, 3rd edn.

Beaumont, S. (1996) *Review of 100 NVQs/SVQs: A Report on Findings*, National Council for Vocational Qualifications/SCOTVEC, Glasgow: Broadwater Press.

Becker, C.S. (1992) *Living and Relating: An Introduction to Phenomenology*, London: Sage.

Bell, J. (1991) *Doing Your Research Project: A guide for first-time researchers in education and social science*, Milton Keynes: Open University Press.

Berelson, B. (1952) *Content Analysis in Communication Research*, Glencoe IL: Free Press.

Berry, R. (1994) *The Research Project: How to Write it*, London: Routledge, 3rd edn.

Boehm, A.E. and Weinberg, R.A. (1977) *The Classroom Observer*, New York: Columbia University Teachers College.

Boud, D., Keogh, R. and Walker, D. (eds) (1985) *Reflection: Turning Experience into Learning*, London: Kogan Page.

Boulton, D. and Hammersley, M. (1993) *Principles of Social and Educational Research*, Milton Keynes: Open University Press.

Brooks, G., Gorman, T., Harman, J., Hutchison, D. and Wilkin, A. (1996) *Family Literacy Works: The NFER Evaluation of the Basic Skills Agency Demonstration Programmes*, London: Basic Skills Agency.

Bryman, Alan and Burgess, Robert G. (1994) *Analysing Qualitative Data*, London: Routledge.

Buck, N., Gershuny, J., Rose, D. and Scott, J. (1994) *Changing Households: The British Household Panel Survey 1990–1992*, Colchester: University of Essex, ESRC Research Centre on Micro Social Change.

Burgess, R.G. (ed.) (1984) *The Research Process in Educational Settings: Ten Case Studies*, London: Falmer Press.

—— (ed.) (1989) *The Ethics of Educational Research*, London: Falmer Press.

—— (1993) *Educational Research and Evaluation: for Policy and Practice?*, London: Falmer Press.

Butler-Sloss, Lord Justice (1987) *Report of the Inquiry into Child Abuse in Cleveland*, London: DHSS–HMSO.

Butt, G. (1992) 'How relevant is geography software?', *Computer Education*, **70**, 23–7.

Carr, W. and Kemmis, S. (1986) *Becoming Critical: Education, Knowledge and Action Research*, London: Falmer Press.

Central Statistical Office (CSO) (1995) *Social trends 25*, London: CSO/HMSO.

Cicourel, A.V. (1970) 'Basic and normative rules in the negotiation of status and role', in Dreitzel, H. (ed.) *Recent Sociology, No. 2*, New York: Macmillan.

Clark, R. and Ivanic, R. (1997) *The Politics of Writing*, London: Routledge.

Cohen, L. and Manion, L. (1994) *Research Methods in Education*, London: Croom Helm, 4th edn.

Coleman, J.S. (1990) *Foundations of Social Theory*, Cambridge MA: Belknap.

Cross, P.K. (1981) *Adults as Learners: Increasing Participation and Facilitating Learning*, San Francisco: Jossey Bass.

Cuff, E.C. and Payne, G.C.F. (eds) (1979) *Perspective in Sociology*, London: Allen & Unwin.

Cuff, E.C., Sharrock, W. and Francis, D.W. (1990) *Perspectives in Sociology*, London: Unwin Hyman, 3rd edn.

Davis, W. and Moore, W.E. (1945) 'Some principles of stratification', *American Sociological Review*, **10**, 2, 242–9.

Dearing, R. (1993) *The National Curriculum and Its Assessment*, London: School Curriculum and Assessment Authority.

—— (1996) *Review of Qualifications for 16–19 Year Olds*, London: School Curriculum & Assessment Authority.

—— (1997) *Higher Education in the Learning Society: Report of the National Committee of Enquiry into Higher Education (The Dearing Report)*, London: HMSO.

Delamont, S. (1976) *Interaction in the Classroom*, London: Methuen.

—— (ed.) (1984) *Readings on Interaction in the Classroom*, London: Methuen.

Denzin, N.K. (1978) *The Research Act: A Theoretical Introduction to Sociological Methods*, New York: McGraw Hill, 2nd edn.

Department for Education (DfE) (1992) *Initial Teacher Training (Secondary Phase)*, circulars 9/92; 35/92, London: DfE.

Department for Education and Employment (DfEE) (1997) *Qualifying for Success*, London: DfEE.

—— (1998) *Teachers: Meeting the Challenge of Change (Green Paper)*, London: Stationery Office.

Douglas, J. (1973) *Understanding Everyday Life*, London: Routledge & Kegan Paul.

Economic and Social Research Council (1997) *ESRC Thematic Priorities Update*, Swindon: ESRC.

Edwards, A.L. (1957) *Techniques of Attitude Scale Construction*, New York: Appleton-Century Crofts.

Elboim-Dror, R. (1973) 'Organizational characteristics of the education system', *Journal of Educational Administration*, **XI**, I, 3–21.

References

Elliott, J. (1991) *Action Research for Educational Change*, Milton Keynes: Open University Press.

Evertson, C. and Green, J. (1985) 'Observation as enquiry and method', in Wittrock, M.C. (ed.) *Handbook of Research on Teaching*, New York: Macmillan.

Fishbein, M. and Ajzen, I. (1975) *Belief, Attitude, Intention, Behaviour: An Introduction to Theory and Research*, Reading MA: Addison-Wesley.

Fitzpatrick, C. (1990) 'Computers in geography instruction', *Journal of Geography*, **89**, 4, pp. 148–9.

Fitzsimons, D. (1989) 'Creating effective type for the classroom', *Journal of Geography*, **88**, 2, pp. 42–5.

Flanders, N.A. (1970) *Analysing Teaching Behaviour*, Reading MA: Addison-Wesley.

Foster, P. (1996) *Observing Schools: A Methodological Guide*, London: Paul Chapman Publishing.

Further Education Development Agency (FEDA) (1996) *Annual Report 1995/6*, London: FEDA.

Garfinkel, H. (1967) *Studies in Ethnomethodology*, Englewood Cliffs NJ: Prentice Hall.

Gerber, R. and Lidstone, J. (1988) *Developing Skills in Geographical Education*, Brisbane: International Geographical Union/Jacaranda Press.

Giddens, A. (1976) *New Rules for the Sociological Method*, London: Hutchinson.

—— (1990) *The Consequences of Modernity*, Cambridge: Polity Press in association with Blackwell.

—— (1998) *The Third Way: Renewal of Social Democracy*, Malden MA: Polity Press.

Glaser, B. and Strauss, A. (1980) *The Discovery of Grounded Theory*, London: Weidenfeld & Nicholson.

Hammersley, M. (ed.) (1993) *Educational Research: Current Issues*, Vol. I, London: Paul Chapman for Open University.

Hammersley, M. and Atkinson, P. (1983) *Ethnography: Principles in Practice*, London: Tavistock.

Harris, M. (1996) *Higher Education Funding Council for England: Review of Postgraduate Education (The Harris Report)*, Bristol: HEFCE.

Herbert, Martin (1990) *Planning a Research Project: A Guide for Practitioners and Trainees in the Helping Professions*, London: Cassell Educational.

Higher Education Funding Council for England (HEFCE) (1996) *Review of Postgraduate Education* (Harris Report), Bristol: HEFCE.

Hillage, J., Pearson, R., Anderson, A. and Tamkin, P. (1988) *Excellence in Research on Schools*, Research Report 74, London: DfEE/Institute of Employment Studies

Hitchcock, G. and Hughes, D. (1989) *Research and the Teacher: A Qualitative Introduction to School-Based Research*, London: Routledge.

Hoyle, Eric and John, Peter D. (1995) *Professional Knowledge and Professional Practice*, Series: Issues in Education, London: Cassell.

Kaplan, A. (1964) *The Conduct of Enquiry*, San Francisco: Chandler.

Kennedy, H. (1997) *Learning Works: Widening Participation in Further Education (The Kennedy Report)*, Coventry: Further Education Funding Council.

Kent, A. (1992) 'IT and geography in the national curriculum: some initial reactions', *Journal of Computer Assisted Learning*, **8**, 1, 2–15.

Kerlinger, F. (1986) *Foundations of Behavioural Research*, Fort Worth: Harcourt Brace Jovanovich College Publications, 3rd edn.

Kinnear, P.R. and Gray, C.D. (1995) *SPSS for Windows*, Hove: Erlbaum/Taylor and Francis.

Knowles, M.S. (1986) *Using Learning Contracts: Practical Approaches to Individualizing and Structuring Learning*, San Franciso: Jossey-Bass.

—— (1970) *The Modern Practice of Adult Education: Andragogy versus Pedagogy*, New York: Association Press.

Kolb, D. (1984) *Experiential Learning: Experience as the Source of Learning and Development*, Englewood Cliffs: Prentice Hall.

Krippendorff, K. (1980) *Content Analysis: An Introduction to its Methodology*, London: Sage.

Kuhn, T. (1962) *The Structure of Scientific Revolutions*, Chicago: University of Chicago Press.

La Piere, R. (1967) 'Attitude versus actions', in Fishbein, M. (ed.) *Readings in Attitude Theory and Measurement*, New York: Wiley.

Lacoste, Y. (1982) [1976] 'Geographic de sous-developpement', in Graves, N.J. (ed.) *New UNESCO Source Book for Geography Teaching*, Paris: Longman/UNESCO Press.

Lazarsfeld, P.F. (1959) 'Problems in methodology', in Merton, R.K., Broom, L. and Cottrell, L.S. (eds) *Sociology Today*, New York: Basic Books.

Lidstone, J. (1989) 'Using computers in geography teaching', in Fien, J., Gerber, R. and Wilson, P. (eds) *The Geography Teachers Guide to the Classroom*, Melbourne: Macmillan, 2nd edn.

Likert, R. (1967) 'The method of constructing an attitude scale', in M. Fishbein (ed) *Readings in Attitude Theory and Measurement*, New York: Wiley.

Lomax, P. (1986) 'Action researchers' action research', *British Journal of Inservice Education*, **13**, 1, 42–50.

McGill, I. and Beatty, E. (1992) *Action Learning: A Practitioners Guide*, London: Kogan Page.

McKenzie, G., Powell, J. and Usher, R. (1997) *Understanding Social Research: Perspective on Methodology and Practice*, Social Research and Educational Studies Series 16, London: Falmer.

McKernan, J. (1991) *Curriculum Action Research: A Handbook of Methods and Resources for the Reflective Practitioner*, London: Kogan Page.

Marshall, C. and Rossman, G.B. (1989) *Designing Qualitative Research*, Beverley Hills CA: Sage.

Mead, G.H. (1934) *Mind, Self and Society*, Chicago: University of Chicago Press.

Miles, M.B. and Huberman, A.M. (1994) *Qualitative Data Analysis: An Expanded Sourcework*, Thousand Oaks CA: Sage, 2nd edn.

Mishler, E.G. (1986) *Research Interviewing: Context and Narrative*, Cambridge MA: Harvard University Press.

Murray, L. and Lawrence, B. (1995) 'Summerhill dismembered: Using controversy to motivate adult learners', *Adults Learning* **7**, 4, pp. 96–9.

O'Hanlon, C. (ed.) (1996) *Professional Development Through Action Research in Educational Settings*, London: Falmer.

Open University (1993) *Professional Development in Education*, Milton Keynes: Open University.

Oppenheim, A.N. (1972) *Questionnaire Design and Attitude Measurement*, London: Heinemann.

References

Organization for Economic Cooperation and Development (1994) *Vocational Education and Training: Towards Coherent Policy and Practice*, Paris: OECD/Washington DC: US Department of Education.

Oxford University Press (1995) *Concise Oxford Dictionary of Current English*, Oxford: OUP, 9th edn.

Parkin, F. (1982) *Max Weber*, London: Tavistock (Key Sociologists Series).

Quality Assurance Agency (QAA) (1998) *A Consultation Paper on Qualification Frameworks: Postgraduate Qualifications*, Gloucester: QAA.

Ralls, C. and Murray, L. (1997) 'Twelve children's perceptions of reading', *New Era in Education*, **78**, 3, 70–9.

Ranson, S. (1994) *Towards the Learning Society*, London: Cassell.

Reed, J. and Proctor, S. (1993) *Nurse Education: A Reflective Approach*, London: Edward Arnold.

Reid, I. and Parker, F (1995) 'Whatever happened to the sociology of education in teacher education?', *Educational Studies*, **21**, 3, pp. 395–414.

Rex, J. (1968) *Key Problems in Sociological Theory*, London: Routledge & Kegan Paul.

Rice, E. (1992) 'Towards a broader conception of scholarship', in Whiston, T.G. and Geiger, R.L. (eds) *Research and Higher Education: UK and USA*, Buckingham: Open University Press/SRHE.

Rice, G.H. (1990) 'Teaching students to become discriminating map users', *Social Education*, **54**, 6, pp. 393–7.

Ritzer, G. (1997) *Postmodern Social Theory*, New York: McGraw-Hill.

Robertson, R. (1974) 'Towards indentification of the major axes of sociological theory', in Rex, J. (ed.) *Approaches to Sociology*, London: Routledge & Kegan Paul.

—— (1992) *Globalization: Social Theory and Global Culture*, London: Sage.

Robinson, R. (1986) 'Geography teachers reflections on their teaching about development', *Journal of Curriculum Studies*, **18**, 4, 409–27.

Robson, C. (1995) *Real World Research*, Oxford: Blackwell.

Roget's Thesaurus, New Edition (1998) London: Penguin.

Rose, D. and Sullivan, O. (1996) *Introducing Data Analysis for Social Scientists*, Buckingham: Open University Press, 2nd edn.

Royal Society (1991) *Beyond GCSE*, London: Royal Society.

Rudestam, K.E. and Newton, R.R. (1992) *Surviving Your Dissertation: A Comprehensive Guide to Content and Process*, London: Sage.

Rudnicki, R. (1990) 'Using spreadsheets in population geography classes', *Journal of Geography*, **89**, 3, pp. 118–22.

Schatzman, L. and Strauss, A.L. (1973) *Field Research: Strategies for a Natural Sociology*, Englewood Cliffs NJ: Prentice Hall.

Schön, D. A. (1983) *The Reflective Practitioner*, New York: Basil Books/London: Temple Smith.

—— (1987) *Educating the Reflective Practitioner*, San Francisco: Jossey Bass.

Schratz, M. and Walker, R. (1995) *Research as Social Change: New Opportunities for Qualitative Research*, London: Routledge.

Segall, E. (ed.) (1987) *World Development Database: A Handbook for Grass and Quest Users*, London: Longman Software/Centre for World Development Education.

Seidman, S. (1995) *The Postmodern Turn: New Perspectives on Social Theory*, Cambridge: Cambridge University Press.

Selbourne, D. (1999) 'Tony, you're talking globaloney', *The Times*, 28 April 1999.

Sheehy, P. (1993) *Inquiry into Police Responsibility and Rewards: Volumes I and II (The Sheehy Report)*, London: HMSO.

Shilling, C. (1992) 'Reconceptualizing structure and agency in the sociology of education: structuration theory and schooling', *British Journal of Sociology of Education*, **13**, 1, 69–87.

Silverman, D. (1993) *Interpreting Qualitative Data: Methods for Analysing Talk, Text and Interaction*, London: Sage.

Skeggs, B. (1991) 'Postmodernism: What is all the fuss about?', *British Journal of Sociology of Education*, **12**, 2, pp. 255–67.

Smart, B. (1996) 'Postmodern social theory', in Turner, B.S. (ed.) *The Blackwell Companion to Social Theory*, Oxford: Blackwell.

Spradley. J.P. and McCurdy, D.W. (1972) *The Cultural Experience: Ethnography in Complex Society*, Chicago: Science Research Associates.

Strauss, A. and Corbin, J. (1990) *Basics of Qualitative Research*, London: Sage.

Tesch, R. (1990) *Qualitative Research: Analysis, Types and Software Tools*, London: Falmer.

Tooley, J. (1999) *The Global Education Industry: Lessons from Private Education in Developing Countries*, London: Institute of Economic Affairs (Education and Training Unit) in association with IFC.

Turabian, K. (1973) *A Manual for Writers of Term Papers, Theses and Dissertations*, Chicago: University of Chicago Press, 4th edn.

Turner, B.S. (1990) *Theories of Modernity and Postmodernism*, London: Sage.

—— (ed.) (1996) *The Blackwell Companion to Social Theory*, Oxford: Blackwell.

UK Central Council for Nursing, Midwifery and Health Visiting (UKCC) (1986) *Project 2000: A New Preparation for Practice*, London: UKCC.

Unwin, B. and Brown, R. (1998) *School Standards and Framework Act 1998 and The Teaching and Higher Education Act 1998*, Bristol: Central Press/Secondary Heads Association.

Unwin, D.J. and Maguire, D.J. (1990) 'Developing the effective use of information technology in teaching and learning in geography', *Journal of Geography in Higher Education*, **14**, 1, pp. 77–82.

Webb, R. (1990) *Practitioner Research in Primary Schools*, London: Falmer.

Whiston, T.G. (1992) 'Research and higher education: The UK scene', in Whiston, T.G. and Geiger, R.L. (eds) *Research and Higher Education: UK and USA*, Buckingham: Open University Press/SRHE.

Woodiwiss, A. (1990) *Social Theory after Postmodernism*, London: Pluto.

Woods, P. (1979) *The Divided School*, London: Routledge & Kegan Paul.

World Bank (1984) *The Development Data Book*, World Bank/Longman.

Writers & Artists Yearbook (1999), London: Black.

Yin, R. (1984) *Case Study Research: Design and Methods*, Beverley Hills CA: Sage.

Youngman, M.B. (1979) *Analysing Social and Educational Research Data*, London: McGraw-Hill.

Index